SHARED LEADERSHIP IN HIGHER EDUCATION

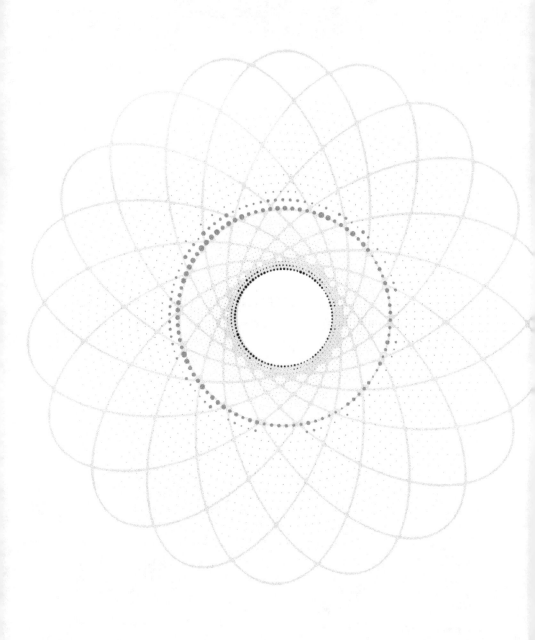

SHARED LEADERSHIP IN HIGHER EDUCATION

A Framework and Models for Responding to a Changing World

Edited by Elizabeth M. Holcombe, Adrianna J. Kezar, Susan Elrod, and Judith A. Ramaley

Foreword by Nancy Cantor

STERLING, VIRGINIA

Published by Stylus Publishing, LLC.
22883 Quicksilver Drive
Sterling, Virginia 20166-2019

Library of Congress Cataloging-in-Publication Data
Names: Holcombe, Elizabeth, editor. | Kezar, Adrianna J., editor. | Elrod, Susan L., editor. | Ramaley, Judith A., 1941- editor.
Title: Shared leadership in higher education : a framework and models for responding to a changing world / edited by Elizabeth M. Holcombe, Adrianna J. Kezar, Susan Elrod, and Judith A. Ramaley ; foreword by Nancy Cantor.
Description: First Edition. | Sterling, Virginia : Stylus Publishing, LLC, [2021] | Includes bibliographical references and index. | Summary: "A volatile financial environment and the need for new business models and partnerships to address the impact of new technologies, changing demographics, and emerging societal needs, demand more effective and innovative forms of leadership. This book focuses on a leadership approach that has emerged as particularly effective for organizations facing complex challenges: shared leadership"-- Provided by publisher.
Identifiers: LCCN 2021040079 (print) | LCCN 2021040080 (ebook) | ISBN 9781642672244 (Cloth : acid-free paper) | ISBN 9781642672251 (Paperback : acid-free paper) | ISBN 9781642672268 (PDF) | ISBN 9781642672275 (eBook)
Subjects: LCSH: Educational leadership--United States. | Education, Higher--Administration. | Teacher participation in administration-- United States. | Educational change--United States.
Classification: LCC LB2805 .S548 2021 (print) | LCC LB2805 (ebook) | DDC 378.1/01--dc23/eng/20211012
LC record available at https://lccn.loc.gov/2021040079
LC ebook record available at https://lccn.loc.gov/2021040080

13-digit ISBN: 978-1-64267-224-4 (cloth)
13-digit ISBN: 978-1-64267-225-1 (paperback)
13-digit ISBN: 978-1-64267-226-8 (library networkable e-edition)
13-digit ISBN: 978-1-64267-227-5 (consumer e-edition)

Printed in the United States of America

All first editions printed on acid-free paper
that meets the American National Standards Institute
Z39-48 Standard.

Bulk Purchases

Quantity discounts are available for use in workshops and for staff development.

Call 1-800-232-0223

First Edition, 2021

CONTENTS

FOREWORD

As I sit in front of my computer screen writing this foreword to the theoretically rich and pragmatically relevant discourse on *Shared Leadership in Higher Education: A Framework and Models for Responding to a Changing World*, it is hard not to be struck by the unexpected irony of the lesson we all have learned in our newly configured 24/7 Zoom world. Just think about the number of faces now showing up on the Hollywood Squares of our routine virtual meetings, often replacing those one-on-one office conversations, and challenging us to learn how to deliberate together across our silos. Yes, it is ironic, if not arresting, that the very remoteness wrought by this pandemic has actually in some ways laid the groundwork for coming more closely together as collective teams when we reunite in person.

Think also of the urgency we feel as we reckon with the failures of our traditional routines and practices to realize our aspirations of racial and economic equity and social justice, very much on our minds now, even as we have worked on overturning systemic barriers for ever so long. This has been a time of reckoning and challenge, and so, as the title suggests, there are few more timely topics for colleges and universities, and for that matter for many sectors in our society, than this one, in an era when old habits and the status quo clearly no longer suffice. While many, including the seasoned editors of this volume, have argued for some time about the power and relevance of more collaborative decision-making in higher education, and indeed all of the case examples here attest to commitments begun some time ago, there is certainly no time to waste now in learning how to benefit from the collective intelligence of diverse teams. Indeed, we need to make the shared leadership that guides us to new and better decisions more normal. Just when we are feeling more remote, we are also waking up to the power and utility of the collective, of collaboration, of interdependence.

So, as we think about searching for a new normal, and ponder what we need to learn in the process, higher education, like every other sector of society, now must reckon more fully and more genuinely than before with what it means to reset the faces in those squares, at its leadership table and throughout its institutions—up and down the so-called hierarchy, across its ranks and roles, spanning its disciplines, and moving more seamlessly and collaboratively back and forth from campus to community, from local to global. By necessity, resetting the table demands and benefits from embracing a less hierarchical, more collaborative, and less individualistic model of decision-making and power distribution—in other words, it calls for shared leadership with an eye toward more equitable and effective practices.

The harder the challenges get for higher education, the more we must learn the lessons of shared leadership. This is ever so true now as we strive to address the persistent and distressingly widening racial and economic gaps in who is getting educated. We must bring as broad a scholarly perspective to bear as possible on pressing, taxing societal threats from climate change to divided politics to the social determinants of health and the future of work. We must reestablish a firm and wide-ranging base of public trust and support, and a good first step is to learn how to listen to and depend on multiple, diverse voices sitting together, crossing the typical silos of our traditional structures, hashing it out in a more collective process. We need to embrace precisely the kinds of coleadership, of teams, of distributed decision-making that the 10 case studies in this volume illustrate so freshly, including of course the challenges that these new modes of leading and learning entail along the way.

Refreshingly, in a time when we all feel pressed for answers, the wisdom in this volume is wide-ranging, crossing lessons learned at very different institutions, touching on topics as varied as maximizing student success, managing budget constraints, fostering high-impact practices and pedagogy in STEM, strategically distributing DEI ownership, collaborating on community-engaged problem-solving, coleadership in a deanship, and more. Nonetheless, a signature of all of these exemplary shared leadership adventures is both the emphasis on trust-building at the core of the effort, and the humility it takes to genuinely learn how to create and nurture shared goals—to move beyond our individualistic ambitions of leadership success to a territory where multiple players play on the same field, even as they each bring a novel perspective to bear in reaching for "victory." And as hard as it is to imagine victories, even small ones, in these challenging times, this trenchant volume sparkles with both honesty and hope—and has lessons from which we can all surely draw.

—Nancy Cantor

INTRODUCTION

Today's higher education challenges necessitate new forms of leadership. A volatile financial environment, the rise of international partnerships, greater accountability pressures, the need for new business models, new technologies, and changing demographics are just some of the challenges that had leaders looking for new strategies and approaches over the past decade. The emergence of a global pandemic and long-overdue reckonings with systemic racism in 2020 brought the need for more effective and innovative forms of leadership into even sharper relief. One leadership approach that has emerged as particularly effective for organizations facing complex challenges is *shared leadership*. Rather than concentrating power and authority in an individual leader at the top of an organization, shared leadership involves multiple people influencing one another across varying levels and at different times. It is a flexible, collective, and nonhierarchical approach to leadership. Organizations that have implemented shared leadership have been better able to learn, innovate, perform, and adapt to the types of external challenges that campuses now face and that will continue to shape higher education moving forward.

However, institutions of higher education have traditionally been organized in a hierarchical manner, which favors a top-down leadership approach. Development of a more horizontal or shared approach takes deliberate strategy and collaboration in ways that may work against the established structures and present many challenges along the way. Why would leaders want to dedicate the time and effort to dramatically change their organization's status quo and invite more people to participate in leadership? Why would they want to give up influence and share their power and authority with others? We wanted to start the book by describing our own journeys to engaging in shared leadership and offer a handful of personal glimpses into why shared leadership might be interesting or appealing, beyond the data and the research. After this look into our own experiences with shared leadership, we will describe the rest of the book's organization and structure.

Elizabeth M. Holcombe

I have long been interested in leadership, both learning about it and practicing it. From a very early age I also carried a genuine curiosity about other people's lives and experiences, especially those that are really different from mine. That curiosity always reminded me how much I still don't know and how much there is left to learn, which influenced my approach to leadership and my inclination toward more shared approaches to leadership.

I had some pretty significant leadership opportunities fairly early on in my career. In 2012, I was tapped to take over a student affairs program that included advising, mentoring, student activities, and 1st-year experience programming. This program was responsible for advising over 2,000 students and managing student affairs functions for the entire college. I would oversee a staff of approximately 25. I knew that I didn't have the knowledge or the credibility to succeed if I tried to go it alone. The program had so many different components and moving pieces, and the staff who had been working with students and organizing events had a lot of expertise that I needed to harness in order to determine the best ways to make improvements.

I organized several different teams within the division, in addition to the formal teams that already existed. Associate directors, assistant directors, and counselors each had their own meetings weekly or twice per month to discuss issues that were coming up with their students or in their roles as leaders or practitioners. I provided tools and resources to help the staff members facilitate the meetings. At first, I modeled how to create an agenda, manage discussions, and plan for and implement action steps. Gradually, the staff started to rotate leadership of these meetings among themselves. Sometimes one staffer would lead the meetings for a month at a time, other times they rotated leadership at each meeting. And as issues were raised, different people would volunteer to lead different projects based on their interests and expertise. My role was to remove barriers to implementation, work to change policies that prevented us from accomplishing our goals, advocate for the team with senior staff, and help team members build capacity and relationships with one another and with key people across campus who could help us make changes. This process was incredibly rewarding for me, as I saw my team members develop the confidence to speak up about problems they saw and the capacity to take action to solve those problems. Because I was putting systems and processes in place and empowering leaders throughout the division, I felt confident that the changes we put in place would endure beyond my tenure as leader. And many of them have.

When I went back to school to get my PhD, I had the opportunity to work with Adrianna to research shared leadership. I realized that there

was a whole theory and language to describe this approach I had instinctually taken. As I have worked on several other projects in the years since,
I have seen both in practice and through research how powerful it is when
people across an organization can bring their unique talents to bear and
lead together, undermining traditional hierarchies and creatively attacking
challenging problems.

Adrianna J. Kezar

My interest in shared leadership emerged from my studies of change on
college campuses. I've always had an aversion to hierarchies and been person-
ally committed to egalitarian approaches and structures that connect rather
than differentiate people, as long as I can remember. In my first administrative role, I shocked the staff by having all staff included in meetings,
and having our first meeting be focused on everyone commenting about
things they wanted changed. I created transparency around the budget by
passing out a copy of the actual budget (which no one had ever seen) and
asked everyone for their input about how we should be spending resources
to best fulfill our mission. No one could believe this was for real! I then
moved into a faculty position where I began research. For one of my first
projects, I studied how 26 campuses engaged in transformational change
ranging from assessment to community engagement to internationalization
to diversity and inclusion. One of the main findings from the study was
that transformational change involved leadership coming together from the
grassroots (faculty, staff, and students), from the middle (centers for teaching
and learning, department chairs and deans, institutional research, librarians,
and deans of students), as well as from senior leaders that were part of the
presidential cabinet or presidents and board members themselves. The institutions that were successful at transformational change included and worked
across all these different layers of leadership. And in fact they tried to find
ways to organize and structure leadership across these levels. They created
new teams and task forces, new types of meetings, and innovative communication strategies to break down silos and to work across the various units of
campus. It was clear to me that shared leadership was essential for the type of
transformational change so needed in higher education. The importance of
shared leadership kept emerging across studies I conducted over time. When
I studied grassroots leadership, I learned that the changes that faculty, staff,
and students made were often fragile if they did not have the support of other
layers of leadership as well.

Similarly, as I studied student success I found that one of the main
solutions for helping to create institutional changes that better support

students was shared leadership, which provided the innovative ideas as well as the implementation support to ensure that these ideas became a reality. My current project on equity-minded leadership teams continues this articulation and further development of concepts around shared leadership. Really, no matter what challenge I explored for improving higher education, shared leadership was central and core to that work. And for many years I hoped to write a book on shared leadership, but I found it challenging because while it's important for higher education to engage in shared leadership, I knew that most campuses do not engage in this work, which made empirical examples challenging to find. I knew that we needed to move beyond the conceptual literature about how campuses might engage and share leadership to actual examples. That is what was so exciting about this opportunity to participate with this group on a book that would identify and capture such examples. And on a personal note, each of the other editors are inspiring scholars I have worked with in one fashion or another related to work on leadership for change.

Susan Elrod

I have always had a problem-solving orientation. Maybe that is why I became a scientist. One of the things I love most about working in a lab or on a project with others is the synergistic discoveries that are made when different ideas and interpretations come together. I cannot see all the aspects of a problem or a data set, but others with different orientations can bring their perspectives to contribute to the whole. So, it is on this foundation of collaborative scientific work that I became an administrator in higher education. There are two threads to how I came to shared leadership as an approach for both my own leadership practice and also one of my scholarly focus areas.

The first thread is my own administrative experience. My first real administrative experience was as the director of a STEM center at Cal Poly, San Luis Obispo in 2007. The center was housed in the College of Science and Mathematics but was charged to make improvements in STEM teacher education, for example, increasing the numbers, improving preparation, and fostering teacher job and career satisfaction. I worked with several departments in the college as well as with colleagues in the School of Education and leaders in K–12 schools. It was a situation that drew me to the rudiments (unknown to me at the time) of shared leadership. Because I was not in any formal position of authority over any of the departments I needed to bring together, I had to assemble a distributed leadership team across these units, bring diverse perspectives to the table and get them to focus on shared goals, build the infrastructure to support cross-campus initiatives, and continue to work at engagement and empowerment to ensure we were making progress. The fruits of this kind of collaborative work were exciting because we created programs that were successful. When I became a dean in 2013 at Fresno State, I used this approach to bring faculty leaders together in a National Science Foundation-funded project to improve freshmen STEM student persistence. The project was co-led by a team of faculty in four departments with support from myself and the associate dean. Again, it had the hallmarks of shared leadership, without intention, and again, I watched these leaders thrive and succeed in meeting their goals. Then, as a provost at the University of Wisconsin-Whitewater, I was involved in a project that was carried out using a shared leadership approach (see chapter 6). By this time, I had read Kezar and Holcombe (2017) and had started to take what might be viewed as a more scholarly approach to developing the structures and processes of the model.

The second thread is my work on national STEM higher education projects. Since 2010, I had been working with Adrianna on national, multicampus projects that were focused on systemic change and leadership in STEM, starting with how to effectively build interdisciplinary programs (Kezar & Elrod, 2012). These projects involved shepherding dozens of diverse campus teams to reach the goals of the project. Through this work, we observed leadership in all its forms, from awesome to mediocre and amazing to completely dysfunctional. Where leadership was awesome and amazing, success followed; where it was mediocre or dysfunctional, teams struggled and not much was accomplished. This led us to projects that focused more deliberately on the development of resources and tools that would help leaders be more effective in these complex institutional initiatives. We published a model (Elrod & Kezar, 2016, 2017) that outlined the steps leaders could use to plan and implement systemic institutional change processes. We are now immersed in a National Science Foundation-funded project that is taking this model one step further to define the specific actions leaders can take during the phases of systemic change initiatives to achieve deep and lasting results. Through the years working on these projects, I began to see that more collaborative approaches, where shared understanding and engagement of all kinds of leaders was central, were more successful and satisfying to the campus leaders. In our work on this book, we have now made connections between the achievement of significant change outcomes and the use of a shared leadership approach.

Along the way, I met and started working with Judith, with whom I share a background as a biologist, a national leader in STEM education, and a career as a higher education administrator. As we interacted in various other national projects and programs, we discussed our own approaches to leadership and also what we were observing in the leadership of project teams we were mentoring. It was through these conversations that we solidified our enthusiasm for shared leadership and conceptualized a conference presentation that we gave with Elizabeth at the Association of American Colleges & Universities (AAC&U) Annual Meeting in January 2018. So, things came full circle for both authors (Adrianna Kezar and Elizabeth Holcombe) of the 2017 publication on shared leadership! Our presentation was met with enthusiasm and after another conference presentation or two, Judith had the idea that we should write a book.

Judith A. Ramaley

Thirty years ago, I began my tenure as president of Portland State University (PSU) as the Governor's Commission on Higher Education in Portland was drawing to a close. The Commission had been set up to address the fact that (a) there wasn't a "real university" in Portland and every major metropolitan region ought to have one, and (b) the two well-established research universities in Oregon were far down the Willamette Valley from Portland.

As soon as I took office in August 1990, I discovered that the commission was heading toward reducing PSU to a regional college and handing off responsibility for most of its graduate and professional programs to the University of Oregon or Oregon State. There was still time to offer a different concept of what an urban university could be, how that model would benefit the region, and how PSU already *was* a robust urban university. However, we had to act quickly.

Making the case for a distinctive mission and direction for PSU required working closely with a broad range of people, both to articulate that vision and to make the case for it. The only way to build that strength was through *shared leadership*. At the time, I had not heard that term but, in retrospect, we practiced all of the defining qualities of that mode of leadership. In those early days, I worked with members of the faculty senate, the student association, the alumni association, members of the Portland City Council, and a network of local employers to create a shared vision of PSU as an urban-serving institution that could bring energy and opportunity to the Portland metropolitan region.

As you will learn in the first four chapters of this book, shared leadership is an important art that is best applied to manage challenges where any response will mean working together in new ways and learning as the challenge unfolds. In 1990, my institution and I were caught up in just that sort of complex problem. In this kind of situation, the participants must have complementary knowledge and skills, enjoy trustworthy connections with each other, and have a stake in the process of developing a solution for the complex problem that challenges them. These kinds of problems require new ways of sharing power and influence. We had to find a way to engage the members of the governor's commission in imagining what an urban research university was and why it would benefit the metropolitan region. To do that we had to make a powerful case showing how PSU had been developing the characteristics of an urban-serving institution ever since its early years after World War II. We showed that we already were responding to the desires of the urban region to have "its own university" and that investing in us would serve the community and its people well.

I have been committed to the practice of shared leadership ever since those challenging days when the fate of the institution I had just come to serve was in the balance. Although I didn't know that we were practicing shared leadership, in fact, that is exactly what we were doing. I have been dedicated to this approach to governance and problem-solving ever since.

Contributions of This Book

This book provides several new insights. First, there are very few existing descriptions of how shared leadership operates within the higher education context. While there is a lot of research in the business and management literature on shared leadership, Kezar and Holcombe's (2017) report on shared leadership issued by the American Council on Education is one of the few resources that exists on the topic in higher education. This report has garnered much attention, and leaders have expressed interest in learning more about shared leadership and in resources that could help them implement it on their own campuses. Second, there are almost no detailed examples of shared leadership in practice in higher education—practical examples of ways that leadership is shared and organized within the unique context of college and university campuses. This book brings together a constellation of important case examples that will be the first of their kind in higher education. Third, we carefully selected case examples that demonstrate different types or models of shared leadership across institutions that also differ by mission, size, sector, and other characteristics. The case studies in this book also tackle a wide assortment of challenges within different parts of the institution, ranging from student academic support to diversity work, from a dean's office to the president's senior team to a grassroots multi-institutional shared leadership effort. Finally, this book connects research about shared leadership with the experience of leaders who have actually executed this approach and learned important lessons along the way. We blend some of the best insights from research with the experience and lessons learned from college leaders in practice. We also present a synthesis of shared leadership approaches and outcomes, based on both the existing research and the case study chapters in this book.

Audience

We anticipate that college and university leaders across both academic and administrative units could benefit from reading this book. This resource is useful for leaders at the highest levels such as presidents and provosts as well as midlevel leaders such as deans, directors, and department chairs. We also believe a secondary audience will be faculty and staff who are interested in collaborating with academic and administrative leaders on campus to become more involved in institutional decision-making or creating new change initiatives. The book contains strategies and resources for those in grassroots (faculty, staff) and midlevel positions to build a shared leadership approach in their units but also for them to "lead up" to influence broader university outcomes. It also contains strategies and resources for those in top-level positions to build capacity for shared leadership across their institutions.

While this book will be a resource for campus leaders, it can also be used as a textbook in leadership courses in higher education administration and leadership. It can be excerpted and assigned in leadership development activities and opportunities. At present there are hundreds of different leadership development programs where this would likely be a needed and helpful resource. Overall, the potential audiences for the book range from individual leaders on campuses to staff running leadership development programs to faculty teaching courses on leadership development and students in such courses.

Organization of the Book

The book's first section contains four chapters that outline the need for and features of shared leadership. These background chapters will be used to help introduce and contextualize the second section of nine chapters that describe case studies of shared leadership in practice at various colleges and universities across the United States. The first section of the book outlines some of the foundational concepts necessary for leaders to implement shared leadership on college campuses, ranging from the most basic descriptions of what shared leadership is and the types of challenges it can help solve; to its benefits and uses; to the issues and obstacles that leaders face when working to share leadership; to ways leaders can build capacity on campus for implementing shared leadership. We have also included reflection questions at the end of each chapter that can help readers make sense of the more conceptual parts of the book and reflect on how the lessons from the case study chapters might translate to their own environments.

In the first chapter we describe how the world is changing and the kinds of complex problems that we now face that necessitate shared forms of leadership. The effects of these changes have altered the role that higher education can play in educating students, conducting research, and entering into partnerships and longer-term collaborations with colleagues in other sectors of society. The rationale for shared leadership on today's college campuses is articulated within this introductory chapter.

In the second chapter we delineate the nature of the characteristics of shared leadership. In brief, shared leadership exhibits the following characteristics: (a) greater number of people involved in leadership; (b) leader and follower roles are interchangeable; (c) multiple perspectives and expertise are included; (d) leadership is not necessarily based on position; and (e) collaboration across the organization is emphasized. Further, it involves: a focus on identification of specific problems that need complex solutions; a reflective study of the problem and identification and marshalling of the expertise needed to address it; a willingness to explore creative, unfamiliar options, and an openness to new ideas; inclusion of multiple perspectives and new voices; provision of a supportive environment that encourages experimentation and risk-taking; and development of new patterns of interaction and communication that create capacity to solve complex problems.

Chapter 3 describes the uses and benefits of shared leadership. In this chapter we articulate situations in which shared leadership is particularly helpful. We review the kinds of problems that shared leadership can address and when shared leadership is most effective, as well as challenges that an institution may face as it seeks to adopt shared leadership for the management and solution of complex problems.

Chapter 4 is focused on creating the capacity to work in a shared leadership mode. This chapter reviews how leaders can reorganize to support shared leadership. Given that higher education institutions were formed in order to support top-down and bureaucratic forms of leadership, instituting shared leadership without making any organizational changes can be difficult.

The introductory section will be followed by nine case studies of shared leadership, each written by an author or set of authors who were involved in the shared leadership effort on their campus. These chapters represent a diverse array of institutional types, problems or issues targeted, and structures or models of shared leadership. We hope that this diversity and range will help readers see the potential for shared leadership within their own contexts, different as those might be.

Chapter 5 focuses on a faculty-led project to revamp STEM education for 1st-year students at Humboldt State University that grew to include leaders all across the institution. Chapter 6 highlights an institutional transformation effort at the University of Wisconsin–Whitewater fostered by the provost and other leaders in academic affairs. Chapter 7 offers an example of shared leadership from the middle of an organization, with a description of the "dean team" that co-led Portland State University's College of Liberal Arts and Sciences. In chapter 8, a team from the University of Richmond describes their efforts to implement a broadly distributed leadership model to thread diversity, equity, and inclusion (DEI) more deeply throughout the institution. Chapter 9 recounts the experiences of faculty and staff at the State University of New York at Geneseo who formed a leadership team to enhance tutor training and academic support services across campus. In chapter 10, a group of faculty leaders at Portland State University discuss their collective experiences leading the Homelessness Research and Action Collaborative, which leverages faculty research expertise and cultivates community partnerships to support the homeless population in Portland. Chapter 11 describes an effort at Winona State University to support and cultivate groups of leaders across the university in collective problem-solving through a leadership academy. Chapter 12 offers the perspective of leaders at Cuyahoga Community College on their efforts at institutional transformation by broadly sharing leadership across multiple divisions and even campuses. And Chapter 13 provides a perspective on sharing leadership across multiple organizations with a description of the work of the Center for the Integration of Research on Teaching and Learning (CIRTL).

We asked the authors of each chapter to reference a common set of questions and prompts when writing their case study. These questions may also benefit readers as they read the case studies and reflect on their own institutional context:

1. What problem are you/were you trying to solve and why did you decide to implement or experiment with a shared leadership approach at your college or university:
   a. How did you get started?

    b. How has your approach developed as you have gained more experience?

    c. How would you describe your "model" of shared leadership?

2. How does your shared leadership approach demonstrate the following characteristics usually associated with shared leadership:

    a. Engage a greater number of people.

    b. Create interchangeable leader and follower roles.

    c. Incorporate multiple perspectives and expertise.

    d. Provide leadership roles for those who do not hold a formal leadership position.

    e. Emphasize collaboration across the organization.

3. How did your campus go about building the capacity to work in this way?

4. How did this approach allow your campus to address the challenge or solve the problem you identified earlier, perhaps in a way that would not have been possible using a different leadership approach? Other benefits and outcomes?

5. What challenges did your campus face in using a shared leadership approach? How did you address or overcome these challenges, or how would you (in hindsight) address them?

6. What lessons did your campus learn about using a shared leadership approach and what advice would you offer to anyone considering this approach to leadership?

The final chapter in the book provides a synthesis of lessons from these case studies and contextualizes them within the broader landscape of shared leadership research. We compare and contrast the models and approaches in the different case studies and provide several questions and tools for leaders who are interested in implementing these approaches on their own campuses to reflect and assess their existing capacity for shared leadership.

At the conclusion of the book, you will find two tools that can help you on your own journey to shared leadership. The first is a set of reflective questions that can be used in concert with or separately from the reflective questions at the end of each chapter. This reflective tool is designed to help you put the lessons from this book into context on your campus and identify ways to get started with or enhance your shared leadership process. The second is a self-assessment tool for building capacity around shared leadership; this tool will help you hone in on particular areas of capacity-building—organizational, team-based, or individual—and identify existing resources as well as reflect on how to create new capacity in any of these areas.

References

Elrod, S. L., & Kezar, A. (2016). *Increasing student success in STEM: A guide to systemic institutional change.* AAC&U.

Elrod, S. L., & Kezar, A. (2017). Increasing student success in STEM: Summary of a guide to systemic institutional change. *Change: The Magazine of Higher Learning 49*(4), 26–34. https://pullias.usc.edu/wp-content/uploads/2017/11/11-15-2017_Increasing.pdf

Kezar, A., & Elrod, S. L. (2012). Facilitating interdisciplinary learning: Lessons from Project Kaleidoscope. *Change: The Magazine of Higher Education 44*(1), 16–25. https://doi.org/10.1080/00091383.2012.635999

Kezar, A. J., & Holcombe, E. M. (2017). *Shared leadership in higher education: Important lessons from research and practice.* American Council on Education.

A CHANGING ACADEMY AND A CHANGING WORLD

Why Shared Leadership Is Important

Judith A. Ramaley, Elizabeth M. Holcombe, Adrianna J. Kezar, and Susan Elrod

The role of higher education is changing in today's world because the world itself is changing (Ramaley, 2014). Our nation's colleges and universities have always sought to prepare their graduates for life and work in their own era. Rudolph (1990) in his classic reflection on the history of higher education in this country wrote about the way that:

> dynamic social and economic changes—these and a multitude of other developments have often thrown the American college back upon itself and forced upon it a moment, perhaps an era of critical self-assessment and redefinition. (p. 110)

We are entering another era of "critical self-assessment and redefinition" (Rudolph, 1990, p. 110). We know that our institutions must continue to adapt if we are to prepare our graduates to live and work in a changing world and contribute to the understanding and management of the complex problems facing our society today. What has changed is the complexities and challenges are emerging faster than ever, driven by worldwide conditions that affect us all, ranging from climate change to deeply interconnected national economies to pandemics. To enhance our capacity to address these complexities, we need to embrace different forms of leadership that can draw on the experiences and expertise of our entire campus community as well as the insights of the people we work with in the larger society we serve. In this book, you will learn about the nature of shared leadership, the contexts in which this form of leadership is most needed, and how to build the capacity to work together in ways that can better help our institutions to address the remarkable changes that are taking place both in our own communities and throughout the world.

We were already working on this book when everything shifted to working and learning remotely as the COVID-19 pandemic grew. In response to the sudden disruption of our campuses, many institutions have found it necessary to work across traditional organizational and hierarchical lines. The phrase "all hands on deck" has often been used to describe how campuses responded to this sudden disruption. The challenge was captured nicely by *The Atlantic*'s Derek Thompson (2020) when he wrote: "Because the pandemic pauses the present, it forces us to live in the future" (para. 2). The disruptions caused by the pandemic have exposed new ways of working together and generated lessons that can help us not only respond to the social and economic and environmental realities we now face but also help us address the issues that we already were facing before this monumental disruption hit us. The lessons that these experiences offer resonate well with the core concepts of shared leadership that we will explore in this book. The idea of working together differently and beyond the boundaries of our usual patterns of work has become not simply an intriguing idea but a necessity.

It is becoming clear that shared forms of leadership have the potential to better support solving the kinds of complex challenges that we are facing today in higher education. But what, exactly, is shared leadership? What are its characteristics? How does it play out in practice? How does shared leadership contrast with traditional forms of leadership and what are its characteristics, models, and assumptions? We will talk about the characteristics and practice of shared leadership throughout this book. For the purposes of this introductory chapter, however, let us simply examine what shared leadership looks like and why it is important when addressing complex problems. These kinds of problems require the expertise, experiences, and insights of a broader range of people in order to understand what is causing them and to design ways to address them.

What Is Shared Leadership?

As Kezar and Holcombe (2017) have described it, shared leadership generally involves more people with different expertise and responsibilities working together in the activities and processes of leadership. Individual members of a leadership team may lead the effort at one point and serve simply as team members at a different time. The person who is spearheading an effort at any particular time may do so because they are the best person for the job rather than because of the formal position they hold. Generally, shared leadership draws upon a much broader range of people who work together across the traditional lines created by the structure of an institution such as between academic and student affairs or across departments and colleges.

The core premise of this book is that we must move from "me-based leadership" to "we-based leadership" when we address problems that can take different forms and express themselves in a variety of ways. These kinds of complex problems, whether addressed across a network of institutions or within a single institution, require new approaches to leadership and ways to learn from our experience as we respond to a difficult problem. Both in our role as educators and as scholars, we will be asking new kinds of questions. We will work in new ways with our students, our colleagues, and members of the broader community to frame those questions and to answer them. We must also learn together as we undertake the work and adapt our approach as we gain more experience. It is in these kinds of situations when shared leadership will be essential. Shared leadership can be thought of as a form of collaboration in decision-making when the issues are complex, hard to interpret, and changing as we seek to understand them. Shared leadership changes the pattern of who asks questions, who contributes to understanding the problem or opportunity, who thinks about how best to address it, and, finally, who has the authority to act. In the sections that follow, we explore some of the challenges and changes that higher education is facing and suggest some ways in which shared leadership might help steward those changes more effectively.

Emerging Challenges: Adapting to a COVID and Post-COVID Reality

No single issue facing higher education in recent years has provoked more uncertainty and unfamiliarity than the COVID-19 pandemic. The complexity of the challenge, ever-changing conditions and knowledge of the disease, and constantly shifting directives and regulations have required different approaches to leadership and operations within colleges and universities. Presidents or top executives could not possibly understand and navigate all the demands of the pandemic response alone and convened coalitions of internal and external leaders to work together to craft effective action plans. New approaches to problem-solving emerged as campuses and their communities sought to work together on complex and often rapidly changing problems. We have learned new ways of working together and have acquired new concerns about the well-being of ourselves and others. These experiences open up (a) new ways of reaching beyond our usual roles and responsibilities to solve problems together across our traditional reporting lines; (b) new ways to help people get the support they need by combining in-person interactions and online connections; (c) new ways for people to participate in the many programs we offer on campus either by participating in person or through online media; (d) opportunities to learn from and work with community partners as we collaborate to create a more equitable social and economic recovery from the experiences of the pandemic; and (e) new approaches to leadership.

During this time of remote learning and work, leaders have also been learning a lot. Many faculty had already begun to shift their approach to teaching from acting as the sage on the stage to becoming the guide on the side. In many ways, the shift from hierarchical to shared leadership is similar—from a single leader walking the path alone to a coach supporting a team of leaders working together. Some campuses discovered that they already had the beginning of a shared leadership culture and a capacity for adaptive thinking. Those underlying networks of people and working relationships became the connective tissue that made a new kind of problem-solving possible. There already were some bridges that connected parts of the institution that were not joined by the organizational chart. New bridges for collaboration and communication were built or repaired. These informal pieces of infrastructure proved to be invaluable and will be critical to a thriving future. People also interpreted their roles more generously. Faculty began helping each other with technology and advice on how to work with students remotely and staff began playing new roles to provide additional support within their department, college, or the university.

Connections to other local and national institutions were leveraged and the lines between organizations blurred as we all worked together to figure out how to respond to this challenge. We have built new and important relationships that we didn't consider forging before. These new connections could be critical to our future. The hierarchy relaxed during this period. This led to the growth of creativity and problem-solving capacity, as well as the inclusion of more people in leadership and decision-making activities. More of us worked together across the usual lines of our formal roles and responsibilities and drew in additional people when we needed their expertise and experience to help with a particular problem or question. This shift toward shared responsibility and consultation opens the way to create a more effective form of shared governance and problem-solving in the future. It also reflects the components of shared leadership. While laying out the various pitfalls that lie along the path to new ways of working together, Heifetz and

Linsky (2002) point out simply that "leadership addresses emotional as well as conceptual work" (p. 116). If there is one key thing that we have learned during our experience with the pandemic, it is that our own vulnerability and the realities of our lives have been revealed to each other as we watched children climb up onto the laps of both faculty members and students, as we noticed the environments in which people were sitting as they interacted with each other online. These emotional connections are crucial for operating in a shared leadership environment, where relationships and collaboration are foundational to success.

Shared Leadership and Higher Education's "Wicked Problems"

Our experiences during the pandemic have helped us create new capacity to address our own internal problems and many of the important challenges that we were facing before this abrupt change took place. The growing gaps in opportunity and wealth between the upper income brackets and the bottom quartile and the changing demographics of our nation call upon us to focus intensely on issues of equity and inclusion if we are to address the growing needs of the communities we serve. Helping communities to deal with issues such as homelessness, poverty, and lack of meaningful employment will also help us with our softening enrollments and poor graduation rates. Similar connections can be made between the majority of our other most pressing problems that we were addressing before the pandemic overtook us and the realities of life in our communities. These issues are extremely complex in their origins and in their impact—the kind of complex problems that require shared leadership. The challenges ahead of us are daunting and, at the same time, exhilarating. This nest of problems is both complex and "wicked" (Rittel & Webber, 1973). Wicked problems share a set of common characteristics that require new approaches to how we educate, the questions we ask and how we seek to answer them, and how we interact with each other both on our own campuses and with people in the broader communities in which our institutions are embedded. According to Camillus (2008):

> A wicked problem has innumerable causes, is tough to describe, and doesn't have a right answer. Environmental degradation, terrorism, and poverty—these are classic examples of wicked problems. They're the opposite of hard but ordinary problems, which people can solve in a finite time period by applying standard techniques. Not only do conventional processes fail to tackle wicked problems, but they may exacerbate situations by generating undesirable consequences. (p. 100)

In addition to institution-specific challenges, some wicked problems facing colleges and universities include waning public support for higher education, declining enrollments, reductions in governmental investment in higher education in the face of other demands on federal and state funds, unacceptably low completion rates, growing costs of a college education, an increasingly divisive political environment, and public criticisms of higher education. One of the most common challenges facing higher education is the problem of student success, or the inequitable rates at which institutions enroll, progress, and graduate students from different racial, ethnic, and socioeconomic backgrounds. According to the Social Progress Index (2019), the United States now ranks 75th among the 149 nations surveyed on the scale of access to a quality education. Furthermore, access is not enough. Three-quarters of the students in the United States whose family incomes are in the top quartile graduate from college, while only 9% of people whose family or personal incomes are in the bottom quartile are likely to do so (U.S. Department of Education, 2017). These are systemic, structural problems that require creative and innovative approaches from leaders.

The complexity of the factors affecting student outcomes and the realities of the many ways that students engage in the educational system require solutions that draw upon principles of shared leadership, both within each institution and across a network of institutions that share responsibilities for those students. These efforts take many different forms, ranging from efforts at a single institution to improve outcomes for students to partnerships that connect Pre-K–12 schools to community colleges and 4-year colleges and universities through collective action networks or other complex partnerships (Ramaley, 2016). Anyone reading a book about shared leadership is probably either involved in one of these cross-disciplinary and cross-institutional efforts or is likely to be drawn into one soon.

To illustrate the challenges of today's student success efforts and how shared leadership becomes a key component in managing a complex portfolio of responses to a problem, let us consider one recent example of such a collaboration and the role of shared leadership. In 2018, the National Association of System Heads (NASH) began a 2-year project with support from the Lumina Foundation to test the hypothesis that working at a system level and on a larger collaborative scale is an effective way to promote student success by bringing together diverse experiences and expertise. Although each system and each participating campus had its own working definition of student success, those definitions had in common three components—deeper learning, successful completion of an undergraduate degree, and career readiness. The focus of the work was based on the approach that NASH calls TS3, which uses three forms of intervention that have been shown to improve student outcomes. These three approaches are as follows:

1. redesigned developmental math
2. guided pathways through the curriculum
3. experiences with high-impact practices for all students (Martin, 2017)

The complexity of this approach—the variety of interventions, each requiring different types of expertise to design and implement—offers a clear example of why shared leadership is becoming essential as a means to guide and support responses to issues facing our campuses today. An individual leader could not effectively create and manage such a program; indeed, leadership of the program is shared beyond a single campus. The shared leadership component works at the level of each campus, but also between the campus and the system office and across the system offices and campuses in the four systems that participated. It is like a three-dimensional tic-tac-toe game in which participants share ideas and observations and offer peer advice to colleagues on their own campus, within their own system, and across the systems. As they do so, they are also working on longer-term strategies that will result in large-scale system changes that address key challenges facing higher education itself while also responding to the needs of their state. Together these efforts can address Michael Porter's argument that we must "deliver meaningful social progress for the average citizen" (quoted in Kristof & WuDunn, 2020, p. 14).

The approach taken by NASH depends upon the fact that state systems are undertaking the challenge of creating a long-term public agenda to link higher education and its educational and research capacities to the goal of improving the educational attainment of the people of their state and improving both the economy and the quality of life in the state. Given the fact that this agenda seeks to address a web of interacting and related problems, the goal of this NASH project has been to explore how these systems and their member campuses can draw upon their diverse expertise, experiences, and complementary missions to promote student success and to educate their graduates for what lies ahead. In this example of responding to a difficult and entrenched problem, the task was to bring the two related but distinctive approaches of a system office and the campuses together while recognizing that the locus of effort is better at the campus level than at the system level and that taking local context into account offers a more promising approach to improving student success than a path shaped by central mandates. Accomplishing this difficult task of working together across different parts of a larger system of organizations and patterns of student enrollment and experience requires the development of a capacity for shared leadership.

Another challenge facing the academy is generational turnover within the ranks of the higher education workforce and the ensuing shift in long-dominant norms and cultures. As older faculty members retire and younger people join the academy and take on leadership roles, the questions that faculty and students ask and the approach to scholarship that they adopt as they seek answers to these questions are changing. A culture of engagement is emerging within many colleges and universities that is changing how we approach scholarship, the design of the curriculum, and our expectations of our graduates. This trend also increases our attention to the nature of the student experience and the importance of creating equitable opportunities for everyone. The generational transitions that we are experiencing are leading to some fundamental changes in our assumptions and our culture. As Trower (2006) has observed, in the 20th century, intellectual merit was seen as an objective concept. Now it is more often thought of as socially constructed. The life of the mind was foremost then. The pursuit of a life of the mind and the heart is embraced now. In the past, faculty sought autonomy and competition was thought to be the way to achieve recognition. Today collaboration is seen increasingly as the best way to achieve meaningful outcomes, and increasingly faculty are embracing shared responsibility for the quality of the curriculum and for student outcomes. In this generational transition, connecting teaching and engagement with the broader community matter more than ever, and scholarship conducted collaboratively with colleagues from other disciplines and with community members is becoming more common. A focus on shared leadership can pave the way for the next generation of leaders to step into leadership roles that are more collaborative and capable of responding to complexity and uncertainty.

Shared Leadership and University–Community Collaborations

Another of the major areas where universities are being pressed to change is with respect to their relevance and connection to wicked problems facing their local communities or society at large. Although this pressure has a heavy focus on engagement with external stakeholders, the response begins with how universities address complex issues internally. In other words, there is a direct connection between the university's capacity to advance external transformations in society and their ability to organize around and advance effective responses to complex issues internally. The same capacities are needed to respond to internal challenges as well as to work with community members to address community challenges. As in the case of the NASH project described earlier, this may require a number of adjustments to our usual allocation of responsibilities and accountabilities and our approaches to decision-making in order to include more people at the leadership table. We will be exploring these issues throughout this book.

Not only is there a connection between internal and external transformations, but there is also a positive feedback cycle. As universities grow their capacity to embrace and address internal complexity, they also increase their capacity to respond to wicked problems in the community. This positive feedback cycle can be strengthened from a few different angles. First, the act of addressing a complex internal issue can remove barriers or open up new opportunities that can directly support the institution's capacity and effectiveness at engaging externally. For example, a major issue facing many universities is how to build diversity, equity, and inclusion into their fabric. Making progress on that complex issue could result in more students, faculty, and staff from diverse backgrounds coming to the institution and thriving there. This greater diversity of background, life experiences, and ways of understanding the context in which problems and opportunities arise can add greatly to the capacity of the institution to recognize, understand, and respond to emerging problems in the community.

The process of creating the capacity to work together in new ways and to introduce shared leadership on campus where it is needed has the added benefit of preparing us to work with other sectors of society and community partners to address issues that campuses and their communities share. While there are many approaches to these more complex and long-term collaborations, lessons can be learned from both collective impact models and other forms of community problem-solving (Ramaley, 2016). These models all require shared leadership in some form that connects the partners together on an equal footing, with hierarchies and power differentials attended to and minimized. Kania and Kramer (2011) described several elements that characterize an effective collective impact model, which may also be useful for leaders who are interested in adopting a shared leadership model to solve complex community problems. These components include: (a) a common agenda arrived at through a thoughtful process of exploration and interaction; (b) shared measurement systems and a willingness to look honestly at the evidence collected; (c) mutually reinforcing activities that draw on the strengths and interests of each participant; (d) continuous communication among the participants; and (e) a mechanism for backbone support that facilitates the building and maintenance of the relationships needed and the capacity of all participants to act knowledgably and in cooperation with the others (Kania & Kramer, 2011). These kinds of collaborative solution-finding efforts will be unlikely to generate equitable and inclusive outcomes so long as "those advantaged by political, economic, or social circumstances exercise undue influence to secure policies and public actions that reinforce their economic or political positions," making it imperative for college and university leaders to recognize their comparatively advantaged role in such collaborative efforts and be mindful of how they can step back and empower community partners (Fung, 2015, p. 519). This fact reinforces the importance of rethinking how we define partnerships, who we choose to partner with, and how we draw these experiences into our curriculum. Building a curriculum around a succession of explorations of increasingly complex problems and the introduction of integrative and applied learning as a culminating or capstone experience offers an especially powerful example of how colleges and universities are adapting to the ways that their graduates will be called upon to use their education in the future (Association of American Colleges and Universities, 2015).

One example of a successful university–community partnership is the Community Engagement Research Academy (CERA) at Portland State University. Through a small-grants program and a series of monthly seminars, CERA is exploring various forms of engaged scholarship and community-based learning and the lessons that these experiences offer about the practice and assessment of community-based learning and university/community partnerships. CERA serves as a home, mostly virtual, for the intellectual core of shared leadership and community engagement work across the university. Its focus is to support and share research about engagement practice and impact and build a collaborative culture within the institution and, in time, the kind of resilience that we will need to address the many wicked problems that we and our community face.

Holcombe and Kezar (2017) have explored the kind of shared leadership that institutions now need if we are to address our volatile financial environment, pressures for accountability, the need for new business models, and changing demographics. This new approach also is needed to create our own capacity to work with other organizations and communities to address wicked problems in the community. As they explain it, "Shared leadership is more flexible than traditional shared governance and identifies various individuals on campus with relevant expertise" (Kezar & Holcombe, 2017, p. v). The conditions that they have found that support this collaborative model include "team empowerment, supportive vertical or hierarchical leaders, shared purpose or goals, accountability structures, interdependence, fairness of rewards and shared cognition" (p. v). We would include the concept of engagement itself, which calls for new approaches to learning and scholarship. In engaged work, new questions are considered in designing and evaluating scholarship (adapted from Glassick et al., 1997):

1. Who names the problem or asks the questions?
2. Who identifies and evaluates the options?

3. Who shares resources to advance the work?
4. Who cares about what choices are made?
5. Who bears the risk and who enjoys the benefits of the work itself and the outcomes?
6. Who interprets the results and decides what success will mean?
7. Who will use the knowledge and insights that are generated?

The CERA seminars at Portland State are exploring the implications of these questions as participants seek to adapt campus infrastructure to support these new kinds of collaboration.

This larger network of efforts to create long-term partnerships between colleges and universities and the communities or regions that host them has produced some initial lessons about the conditions that must be created in order to build these kinds of collaborations. Several conditions seem to support new ways of working together both on campus and with community partners (Allen et al., 2017):

- willingness to experiment with new approaches to problem-solving
- flexible resources that are not tied to specific projects and that support the development and maintenance of the collaboration itself
- a careful process of building mutual understanding of the challenges, conditions, and culture of each of the participating organizations or units, including different degrees of urgency and different timeframes required for action
- a structure that resists the impact of key personnel changes by connecting people across layers of responsibility within each participating organization or unit
- a shared commitment to experiment with this new model and to learn together in order to expand its reach and impact
- willingness to move beyond consulting arrangements or short-term projects to actual co-development of both the model and the measurement and assessment of the impact of this approach

Conclusion

How can institutions develop the capacity to respond to both anticipated challenges and unexpected ones as well? How can we adapt our current institutional models and cultures to create resilience and understand and manage the kinds of complex issues that we face today? As Everly (2011) has pointed out, the elements are simple. The process starts with providing support for each member of an organization to achieve success, to learn from others, and to participate in increasingly complex and difficult solution-finding in an environment that allows for a reasonable amount of risk. These elements help an organization become innovative in times of adversity. Our argument in this book is that the ability to respond to increasingly complex challenges will depend upon the use of shared leadership. Any effort to create a culture of shared leadership will clearly be a work in progress as an institution learns from its own experiences, expands the network of participants, and tackles both acute and chronic problems in new ways. The way forward requires a great deal from each of the participants. First, the people who launch such an ambitious project must consistently model the behaviors and ways of exploring questions that anyone involved in shared leadership will need. These include the capacity to be honest and transparent and to build trust. Second, leaders must find ways to support collaboration and to introduce genuine boundary-spanning across academic and support units by drawing together people who would not normally sit at the same table to work on a mutually important problem. Finally, it is important to make a commitment to the long haul and invest in the relationships that underlie the fabric of this form of partnership. This means honest conversations about what is working and what is not, as well as about who is benefiting and who is not.

In this book, we explore these issues and more in much greater depth and provide many examples from both research and practice to help leaders understand and implement shared leadership on their own campuses. We describe the characteristics of shared leadership, when shared leadership is most useful, ways to create an environment in which shared leadership can be effective, and how to create the capacity to work in a shared leadership model. The case studies in the second section of the book (chapters 5–13) each offer compelling examples of how shared leadership has been used in real-world situations to tackle complex challenges and adapt to changing circumstances. Join us as we explore this rewarding and effective approach to leadership.

Chapter 1 Reflection Questions

1. What challenges is your institution facing now, and how many of them are the types of complex problems described in chapter 1?
2. To what extent has your institution established a problem-solving culture and a capacity for change? How do you know?

3. Do you have a mandate for change? If so, from whom? What level of influence does that individual or group exert at your institution? How is that influence exercised?

4. What changes may be needed in order to create support for using a shared leadership approach, when appropriate, to deal with the issues you are addressing, for example, organizational structure, policies and practices, how decisions are made and who makes them, assumptions about what is possible. Are there others?

References

Allen, J. H., Beaudoin, F., & Gilden, B. (2017). Building powerful partnerships: Lessons from Portland's climate action collaborative. *Sustainability 10*(5), 276–281. https://doi.org/10.1089/sus.2017.0010

Association of American Colleges and Universities. (2015). *The LEAP challenge.* http://www.aacu.org/leap-challenge

Camillus, J. C. (2008, May). Strategy as a wicked problem. *Harvard Business Review, 86*(5), 98. https://hbr.org/2008/05/strategy-as-a-wicked-problem

Everly, G. S. (2011, June 24). Building a resilient organizational culture. *Harvard Business Review.* https://hbr.org/2011/06/building-a-resilient-organizat

Fung, A. (2015). Putting the public back into governance: The challenges of citizen participation and its future. *Public Administration Review 75*(4), 513–522. https://doi.org/10.1111/puar.12361

Glassick, C., Huber, M. T., & Maeroff, G. I. (1997). *Scholarship assessed: Evaluation of the professoriate.* Jossey-Bass.

Heifetz, R. A., & Linsky, M. (2002). *Leadership on the line: Staying alive through the dangers of leading.* Harvard Business School Press.

Holcombe, E., & Kezar, A. (2017, May 10). The whys and hows of shared leadership in higher education. *Higher Education Today.* https://www.higheredtoday.org/2017/05/10/whys-hows-shared-leadership-higher-education/

Kania, J., & Kramer, M. (2011, Winter). Collective impact. *Stanford Social Innovation Review*, 36–41. https://ssir.org/articles/entry/collective_impact

Kezar, A., & Holcombe, E. (2017). *Shared leadership in higher education: Important lessons from research and practice.* American Council on Education.

Kristof, N. D., & WuDunn, S. (2020). *Tightrope: Americans reaching for hope.* Alfred A. Knopf.

Martin, R. R. (2017). Taking student success to scale. *Change: The Magazine of Higher Learning, 49*(1), 38–47. https://doi.org/ 10.1080/00091383.2017.1265391

Ramaley, J. A. (2014). The changing roles of higher education: Learning to deal with wicked problems. *Journal of Higher Education Outreach and Engagement, 18*(3), 7–20. https://files.eric.ed.gov/fulltext/EJ1043282.pdf

Ramaley, J. A. (2016). Collaboration in an era of change: New forms of community problem-solving. *Metropolitan Universities Journal, 27*(1), 10–24. https://journals.iupui.edu/index.php/muj/issue/view/1223/326

Rittel, H. W., & Webber, M. M. (1973). Dilemmas in a general theory of planning. *Policy Sciences, 4*(2), 155–169. https://urbanpolicy.net/wp-content/uploads/2012/11/Rittel+Webber_1973_PolicySciences4-2.pdf

Rudolph, F. (1990). *The American college and university: A history.* The University of Georgia Press.

Social Progress Index. (2019). *The social progress imperative.* https://www.social-progress.org/assets/downloads/resources/2019/2019-Social-Progress-Index-executive-summary-v2.0.pdf

Thompson, D. (2020, May 8). The pandemic will change American retail forever. *The Atlantic.* https://www.theatlantic.com/ideas/archive/2020/04/how-pandemic-will-change-face-retail/610738/

Trower, C. (2006). Gen X meets Theory X: What new scholars want. *Journal of Collective Bargaining in the Academy, 0*(11), 1–6. https://thekeep.eiu.edu/cgi/viewcontent.cgi?article=1030&context=jcba

U.S. Department of Education. (2017). *College affordability and completion: Ensuring a pathway to opportunity.* https://www.ed.gov/college

2

THE NATURE OF SHARED LEADERSHIP

Elizabeth M. Holcombe, Susan Elrod, Judith A. Ramaley, and Adrianna J. Kezar

As described in chapter 1, shared forms of leadership have the potential to better support solving the kinds of complex challenges that we are facing today in higher education. But what, exactly, is shared leadership? What are its characteristics? How does it play out in practice? This chapter discusses the nature of shared leadership, contrasting it with traditional forms of leadership and describing its characteristics, models, and assumptions. There are also a few ways of collaborating or working together that are sometimes confused with shared leadership—namely delegation, committee work, and shared governance. While these ways of working can have some overlap with shared leadership, they do not necessarily operate in a shared leadership manner. Thus, we also review how shared leadership is distinct from these approaches and highlight differences.

Overview of Shared Leadership

One of the most widely used definitions of shared leadership is that of Craig Pearce and Jay Conger (2003), organization and management scholars who pioneered much of the research agenda on shared leadership and authored a key book on the topic. Pearce and Conger define shared leadership as "the dynamic, interactive influence process among individuals in groups for which the objective is to lead one another to the achievement of group or organizational goals or both" (p. 1). This process can involve "peer, or lateral, influence and at other times . . . upward or downward hierarchical influence" (Pearce & Conger, 2003, p. 1). The key is that rather than one individual wielding power and influence over followers, shared leadership involves multiple people influencing one another at varying levels and at different times.

Contrasting shared leadership with more traditional forms of leadership can help clarify its characteristics. Traditional models of leadership tend to be vertically oriented and hierarchical. Influence is directed downward to followers by a single individual—the formal or positional leader, in whom authority and power is concentrated (Bass & Bass, 2008; Bolden, 2011; Pearce & Conger, 2003; Zhu et al., 2018). By contrast, shared leadership involves more horizontal, lateral influence among peers or members of a team or group (Zhu et al., 2018). While traditional models of leadership focus on an individual leader's behaviors, attributes, or actions, shared leadership focuses on the process of leadership and the collective nature of that process (Carson et al., 2007; Chiu et al., 2016; Pearce & Conger, 2003; Zhu et al., 2018). Leadership, in this view, is heavily influenced by context (both within and outside an organization), shaped by participants' interpretations of their environment, and takes place over time—"a motion picture" of events, actions and reactions, and relational dynamics, rather than "snapshots of leadership" behaviors at one point in time (Kezar et al., 2006, p. 59).

Although shared leadership is perhaps most easily understood in contrast to vertical or hierarchical forms of leadership, it is important to note that the two types of leadership are not mutually exclusive. In fact, a supportive vertical or positional leader is often necessary for the successful enactment of shared leadership (Barnes et al., 2013; Fausing et al., 2015; Fletcher & Kaufer, 2003; Sveiby, 2011). Rather, shared leadership and vertical leadership can complement one another, and shared leadership is best utilized in a particular set of situations and contexts that call for a larger set of viewpoints and skills to solve a complex problem (Denis et al., 2012; Ensley et al., 2006; Van Knippenberg, 2017).[1]

Shared leadership is sometimes defined and conceptualized slightly differently across disciplines or industries. It also goes by a number of different names in the literature, including *distributed leadership* (Gronn, 2000; Spillane et al., 2006), *collective leadership* (Contractor et al., 2012), *team leadership* (Day et al., 2004; Northouse, 2004), and *collaborative leadership* (Rosenthal, 1998), among other terms. These different terms are sometimes (though not always) associated with slightly different models or processes of sharing leadership across multiple individuals, which we describe in more detail in the next sections. Despite these differences in terminology, there are some common elements of shared leadership that cut across the various conceptualizations. Kezar and Holcombe's (2017) review of literature on shared leadership found five key elements that characterize shared leadership.

First, a greater number of individuals take on leadership roles than in traditional models. Second, leaders and followers are seen as interchangeable. In some cases, this may mean that leadership occurs on a flexible and emergent basis, while in others it rotates more formally. Third, leadership is not based on position or authority. Rather, individuals with the expertise and skills needed for solving the problem at hand are those that lead. To that end, multiple perspectives and expertise are capitalized on for problem-solving, innovation, and change. And finally, collaboration and interactions across the organization are typically emphasized (Kezar & Holcombe, 2017).

Most definitions of shared leadership in the organization and management literature (where most of the research on shared leadership is located) describe it as an informal and emergent process rather than something that can be "deliberately planned and implemented" (Zhu et al., 2018, p. 838). Such definitions and studies identify shared leadership as emerging in particular contexts or situations that call for more diverse viewpoints or expertise than that of the positional leader alone (Morgeson et al., 2010). In these situations, as groups and their formal leader discover the complexity of the challenge they are facing, they begin to share leadership to leverage the most appropriate and diverse skills and talents to solve a problem. However, there is also some evidence that shared leadership can be formally designed and implemented (D'Innocenzo et al., 2016). Researchers have identified numerous examples of how individuals and organizations can build skills and capacity to formally design and implement shared leadership processes, which we describe in more detail in chapter 4. Briefly, we provide a few examples of how leadership can be formally shared. First, several leadership roles could be designated and appointed within a group and/or team rather than one singular leader. For example, Klein et al.'s (2006) study of trauma resuscitation units found that these units had three formal leadership positions, each with different roles and responsibilities. Another way that leadership can be formally shared is through rotated leadership—when teams formally select different leaders to rotate leadership at different times (Erez et al., 2002; Pearce et al., 2014). Whether emergent or intentionally planned, shared leadership involves multiple people in a process of mutual, often shifting influence.

The Non-Western Roots of Shared Leadership

While shared leadership is a newer concept in higher education and even in the business world, its principles are aligned with long-existing non-White, non-Western, and nonmale approaches to leadership. Collaborative, collective forms of leadership have been traditionally practiced in Black, Native, and Latinx cultures, and women also tend to practice these more collaborative forms of leadership (Astin & Leland, 1991; Bordas, 2012; Eddy et al., 2019; Kezar, 2000, 2002a, 2002b; Kezar & Moriarty, 2000). In their review of shared leadership research, Kezar and Holcombe (2017) note that "the adoption of shared leadership may be an essential step toward cultivating inclusive organizational environments that tap into the unique perspectives and experiences of historically marginalized social groups" (p. 14). Indeed "research has shown that leadership processes capable of empowering historically marginalized individuals and transforming organizations are collaborative in nature" (Kezar & Carducci, 2009, p. 7). Changes from traditional hierarchical leadership structures in American higher education to more shared approaches should be made with the knowledge that these approaches are not new—they are merely new to male- and White-dominated institutions of higher education in this country.

Models of Shared Leadership

Leadership can be shared in different ways through different structures or models (Denis et al., 2012). Three models encompass the major approaches to sharing leadership: coleadership, team leadership, and distributed leadership (see Table 2.1).[2] We describe the structure of each model, as well as several examples of what each model looks like in the higher education context. We also briefly review some of the existing research on each model in higher education, though it is important to note that the literature on shared leadership in higher education is nascent and thus quite limited. Many of our examples are drawn from descriptions of practice. It is also important to note that the three models we describe are not perfect and discrete "types" and that there may be some overlap in practice. For example, an institution may have coleaders at the dean level in their law school, as well as a team leadership approach involving the deans of all the colleges and schools. Despite such potential overlap, it is still helpful to distinguish and delineate among these models in order to understand the different ways that shared leadership has been conceptualized and practiced.

Coleadership or Pooled Leadership

The first and most narrowly conceived model is coleadership or pooled leadership, "in which small groups of people share leadership in the formal top executive function" (Kezar & Holcombe, 2017, p. 6). Coleaders' roles are typically formally delineated and involve specialized and distinct

TABLE 2.1
Three Models of Shared Leadership

	Coleadership	*Team Leadership*	*Distributed Leadership*
Description	Pairs or small groups of people share leadership	Leadership functions shared among team members	Leadership dispersed across multiple organizational levels or even organizational boundaries
Structure	Often built into formal structure of top executive role	Flexible configurations that change based on the problem—although it can also be formally planned and structured	Flexible configurations that arise during particular projects or times of change—although it can also be formally planned and structured
Roles	Roles of coleaders are specialized, differentiated, and complementary	Leadership shared vertically and horizontally across team based on relevant expertise	People across different organizational levels or boundaries assume leadership as problems arise

Source: Adapted from Kezar and Holcombe (2017).

responsibilities designed to complement one another (Hodgson et al., 1965). This type of shared leadership is more common in nonprofit *organizations* and other organizations that have several different purposes or deal with complex challenges, such as health care, arts, or K–12 education organizations (Greenwood et al., 2011). These types of organizations often have competing professional and managerial demands that a single leader can struggle to manage alone (Gibeau et al., 2020). Higher education institutions, too, could fit into this typology, with professional or academic demands often competing with managerial/business/financial demands. Indeed, there are several instances of colleges installing copresidents, coprovosts, or codeans, though these arrangements seem to be more common on an interim basis. We will briefly describe a few examples of more permanent coleadership arrangements in higher education.

First, in the mid-1990s, Birmingham Southern College installed codeans or "dean partners" in the division of business and graduate education (Kelly, 2009). These codeans took a uniquely collaborative approach, working together on every decision and even participating together in every meeting (Kelly, 2009). The law school at Case Western Reserve University takes a similar approach with their current codeans. The two deans have a shared email account, draft statements jointly, and communicate constantly through a variety of different methods. They do, however, make decisions independently as well (Wexler, 2016). This division of labor approach, in which responsibilities are delineated based on expertise or task, is more common for coleadership arrangements than a completely shared approach. For example, the Rutgers University School of Law has two campuses, and the school's codeans each have responsibility for one campus's operations. The codeans work together on strategy and decision-making, but they each have their own sphere of responsibility as well (Elfman, 2019).

There are also a couple of current examples of copresidencies. For example, the College of Idaho announced in 2018 that two of its presidential search finalists would take on the job together as copresidents. Jim Everett and Doug Brigham have a long-standing relationship and felt they were uniquely positioned to share various aspects of the job. An article from *Inside Higher Education* highlighted the proposed split of responsibilities and tasks:

> Generally, Brigham will focus more on finance, academic affairs and student affairs, and the directors in those areas are expected to report to him. Enrollment will be shared. Everett will have athletics and college relations reporting to him and is expected to be heavily involved in fundraising. At the same time, ultimate responsibility for the institution will lie with both presidents. (Seltzer, 2018, para. 13)

While this arrangement of copresidents remains quite rare in higher education, there have been growing concerns that the job of a university president is becoming too complex for one person to undertake successfully. One former college president, Karen Gross, advocated for the copresident model in a piece for the Aspen Institute's blog, claiming that it would not only enhance efficacy in the presidential role but also model such behaviors as collaboration and teamwork, mutual respect, and humility (Gross, 2018).

It is important to note that the few reports of coleadership models in higher education come primarily from trade publications and reports. There is little to no empirical research on how exactly these coleadership arrangements are implemented, challenges to operating in this fashion, benefits or outcomes, or the prevalence of such arrangements in higher education. Fortunately, one of the case studies in this volume features a detailed description of an experiment with coleadership at the dean level—the Portland State University "Dean Team" (chapter 7).[3] However, the majority of research on shared leadership, both in higher education and in the broader management literature, does not highlight coleadership arrangements and instead focuses on models that typically involve more people in leadership and decision-making—the team leadership and distributed leadership approaches that we describe in the next sections.

Team Leadership

The second model of shared leadership is team leadership. This model is perhaps the most commonly studied in the organization and management literature and involves sharing of responsibility and influence within a team (Pearce & Conger, 2003). It is often less formal or planned and instead is more emergent or flexible, with different configurations of leadership emerging in different situations based on the needs and challenges at hand and the expertise of the individuals involved (Yammarino et al., 2012). However, team leadership can also be formally structured and planned, with roles and processes clearly articulated and defined. Team leadership involves a focus on team functions or outcomes rather than on individual leader behaviors or inputs, as well as attention to relationships and interpersonal dynamics (Bensimon & Neumann, 1993; Day et al., 2004; Kezar et al., 2006; Komives et al., 1998; Morgeson et al., 2010). In terms of team functions or outcomes, Morgeson et al. (2010) created a taxonomy of team leadership functions that include composing the team, defining the mission or purpose, training and developing the team, sensemaking, providing feedback, monitoring the team, solving problems, and supporting social climate or relationships, among others. These authors note that different functions may be performed more effectively by either formal/positional leaders or informal leaders on the team. For example, positional leaders are needed to help compose the team and might be especially helpful in solving problems, while informal leaders are instrumental in supporting relationships. A focus on the relationships and interpersonal dynamics of teams centers dialogue, cognition, learning, and the connections that develop among members of the team as central to team effectiveness (Kezar et al., 2006).

In higher education, a prime site for understanding team leadership is the presidential cabinet. Scholars Estela Bensimon and Anna Neumann published a seminal study on presidential cabinets in 1993, laying out the concept of teams as cultural processes and identifying major functions of presidential teams (utilitarian, expressive, and cognitive) as well as their differing purposes and activities. Bensimon and Neumann (1993) also defined eight major "thinking roles" of a team: definer, analyst, interpreter, critic, synthesizer, disparity monitor, task monitor, and emotional monitor (p. 59). These different roles may not all be present on every team, and one person may hold dual roles. These roles are different from operational roles on the cabinet like provost or vice president of student affairs and represent the various processes of team thinking, interpretation, problem-framing, and meaning-making that comprise team leadership (Bensimon & Neumann, 1993). Despite the prominence of this study and the nearly ubiquitous prevalence of presidential cabinets in colleges and universities, there are very few other studies of senior leadership teams in a higher education setting (Kezar et al., 2019). A recent edited volume on team leadership in community colleges presents a few additional examples of presidents and their senior leadership teams (Boggs & McPhail, 2019). One case study of the development of the presidential cabinet at Amarillo College notes that initially "cabinet members did not see the cabinet as leading the entire college as a team; instead, the cabinet members saw themselves as individual leaders of specific divisions" (Lowery-Hart, 2019, p. 109). In order to develop a more collective or team approach among the cabinet, the president worked with external consultants to build relationships and trust, and find and emphasize a sense of collective purpose for the senior team, while also celebrating the unique and diverse backgrounds and skills of each team member.

Boggs and McPhail's (2019) book also provides several additional examples of different types of teams working to lead various redesign or reform efforts in community colleges. One example featured is Macomb Community College, where several teams led the process of redesigning the college's workforce development programs. The teams were comprised of administrators, faculty, and staff and "were responsible for the completion of specific projects and then were disbanded when tasks were completed" (Jacobs, 2019, p. 83). Within each team, team members had responsibility for solving specific problems and building necessary connections across the college and with industry partners. Another example of team-based leadership in the community college setting explored the role of various leadership teams managing the transition of the Community College of Baltimore County from a multicampus system to a single campus (McPhail, 2019). The president/board team, the cabinet team, and a newly formed cross-functional team composed of faculty, staff, and administrators each had specific leadership roles to play in the campus consolidation process. Boggs and McPhail's (2019) book also explores many other aspects of team leadership in the community college setting, including the importance of setting team expectations, gender differences in team leadership, assessing the effectiveness of leadership teams, developing leadership teams, team-building, and succession planning. It is one of the few newer, higher-education-specific resources on shared forms of leadership. Our case study authors from SUNY Geneseo (chapter 9) and the Portland State Homelessness Research Action Collaborative (chapter 10) also provide examples of team leadership approaches.

Distributed Leadership

A third model of shared leadership is known as distributed leadership. While this form of leadership is similar to team leadership in that it also involves "flexible configurations that arise during particular projects or times of change," leadership is shared more broadly across multiple levels of an entire organization or even across organizational boundaries rather than just within a single team (Kezar & Holcombe, 2017, p. 6; see also Denis et al., 2012; Spillane et al., 2001). Scholars of distributed leadership often focus on leadership as embedded in relationships, situations, and practices rather than in individuals (Huxham & Vangen, 2000; Spillane, 2005). The activities, practices, and processes of leadership—such as influencing, agenda-setting, people development—are the focus rather than leaders themselves (Gronn, 2002, 2009; Spillane et al., 2001). When the focus shifts to activities, practices, and processes, the idea of who can lead broadens significantly. In this conceptualization, leadership activities can be formally designated or assigned by positional leaders (e.g., through building formal structures or decision-making processes) or informally and fluidly as issues emerge (Lumby, 2003; MacBeath et al., 2004). Leadership can come from any place within the organizational hierarchy. This form of shared leadership represents the most complexity of all three forms and has been widely studied in K–12 education (including Spillane et al., 2006), as well as in public administration and other nonprofit or community settings (Denis et al., 2012).

In higher education, an example of a more distributed approach comes from Kingsborough Community College in Brooklyn where their Achieving the Dream Equity Wheel features a leadership team and four cross-functional subteams to lead in the areas of teaching and learning, student success, data and technology, and engagement and communications (Kingsborough Community College, n.d.). Teams are made up of people from different departments and units at different levels of seniority, each bringing their unique set of skills, experiences, and expertise to bear on the problem or task at hand while maintaining their formal roles within the organization. Each team has a chair or cochair, an equity liaison, and several at-large committee members from across functional areas, while the steering committee is comprised of senior administrators (Kingsborough Community College, n.d.).

The teams work together and separately to implement the work of Achieving the Dream—specifically a focus on equity of outcomes, not just equality of opportunity.

Another example of a distributed approach to leadership in higher education that encompasses a whole institution is described in a recent book by Freeman Hrabowski, president of the University of Maryland, Baltimore County (UMBC), and his colleagues Philip Rous and Peter Henderson. Hrabowski et al.'s (2019) book provides essentially an extended case study of the development and practice of a distributed approach to shared leadership at UMBC. The authors provide many examples of people leading from various positions and roles within the institution, from students advocating for changes to the campus racial climate and response to sexual assault, to faculty leading course redesign or faculty diversification efforts, to staff "infusing entrepreneurship into the academic core and the student experience" and innovating within the spaces of information technology and data analytics (p. 52).

Distributed approaches to leadership are also found internationally, with several studies in the United Kingdom (UK) and Australian higher education contexts. In the UK, distributed leadership has been strongly promoted in the higher education sector, with examples of both formally planned, more top-down approaches and informally emergent, bottom-up approaches noted (Bolden, 2011; Bolden et al., 2009). A large case study of 12 diverse types of institutions in the UK cited many examples of distributed leadership from interviews with positional leaders on campus, ranging from shared management of budget and finances between schools and central administrators to collaborative research projects spanning multiple departments and community organizations (Bolden et al., 2009). In Australia, distributed leadership approaches have been encouraged (and funded) by the national Office for Learning and Teaching as key tools for improved teaching and learning. Specifically, between 2005 and 2012 the Australian government funded research into 24 projects that were framed by a distributed leadership approach (a selection of research includes: Barber et al., 2009; Chesterton et al., 2008; Lefoe & Parrish, 2008, 2013). Jones and Harvey (2015) presented examples of distributed leadership with a variety of purposes, ranging from curriculum redesign to leadership development to the creation of mentoring programs and university–industry partnerships. The scholars leading the projects created several tools to help promote adoption of distributed leadership more broadly across the higher education sector in Australia (Jones et al., 2012). These tools are helpful reflective guides for practitioners interested in adopting distributed approaches, thought they lack specifics about what distributed models actually look like in practice. Our case study authors from

University of Richmond (chapter 8) and Cuyahoga Community College (chapter 12) provide precisely these types of practical descriptions of distributed leadership approaches. These examples are helpful, as the distributed model is complex and involves lateral and horizontal influence both within and across team, unit, and organizational boundaries, and as few concrete, practical examples exist within higher education.

What Shared Leadership Is NOT

Because shared leadership represents a departure from traditional ways of thinking about leadership, and because several different models reflect a shared approach to leadership, there is often confusion about what "counts" as shared leadership. Several similar concepts or practices are often mistaken for shared leadership, yet they lack key elements of truly shared leadership. Shared leadership is not just creating a new committee to accomplish a defined task. Committees are a common vehicle for problem-solving and task accomplishment in higher education; while they are often collaborative, they typically exist within traditional hierarchical leadership structures and do not necessarily represent true shared leadership. Committees often have narrowly defined tasks and limited authority and accountability. They often have a single leader or report out to a single leader, and there are typically tightly proscribed ways of operating within committees that do not allow for the flexibility and creativity that are important features of shared leadership. Committees are also part of a larger shared governance effort that often requires specific representational membership (i.e., one member from each school, college, or department) and specific service or term requirements (i.e., faculty members must serve on specific committees for specific lengths of time) rather than membership based on expertise or skill. Committees are important structures for shared governance and problem-solving, and while they can operate in a shared leadership manner if specifically set up and supported in doing so, committees are not inherently representative of shared leadership.

Shared leadership is also not establishing new task forces that involve lots of people without clear definition of the problem or development of shared goals. Shared leadership is not simply sending a team to a workshop or conference on a particular topic of interest to the institution with no preparation, discussion, framing, or follow-up. It is also not the top-down announcement of decisions or processes without listening to and engaging employees and stakeholders in discussions that define the problem and scope of solutions. These examples may be tempting for hierarchical leaders to deploy in pursuit of more shared approaches to leadership because they take less time; however, if other leaders are not empowered to make decisions, then leadership is not authentically shared. These surface approaches may result in resentment from participants who were expecting to have more authority and responsibility, as well as shallow solutions or incomplete resolution of problems and issues.

Perhaps the concept most commonly confused with shared leadership, especially in the higher education context, is shared governance. Shared leadership and shared governance have interrelated but different outcomes. Shared governance is the system and process by which institutions of higher education make collective decisions (Eckel, 2000). In a shared governance system, authority regarding different institutional responsibilities is often delegated to different groups (e.g., faculty have authority over the curriculum, the administration is accountable for fiscal outcomes). Many in higher education confuse shared governance with shared leadership and believe that, because colleges and universities operate under a system of shared governance, that leadership is also shared. This is not necessarily true. There are some key differences related to how shared governance "actually" operates in practice that preclude it from being automatically characterized as shared leadership. First, shared governance is focused on making decisions related to institutional policy, whereas shared leadership is intended to focus on larger, more complex, strategic issues and changes to traditional ways of operating. Second, while shared governance is often lauded as a means of including both faculty and administrators in decision-making, in practice it can be characterized by an atmosphere where either faculty or administrators dominate, or where conflict between the two groups is the norm (Pearce et al., 2018). As Pearce et al. (2018) note, shared governance

> is focused on populating committees with proportional representation of faculty to address such things as curriculum, human resource issues, and even a committee on committees. They are primarily concerned with forming committees with representatives of the various scholarly units rather than with experts for the stated purpose of each committee. (p. 641)

In addition, many campus stakeholders are left out of shared governance processes, such as staff and nontenure-track faculty. By contrast, shared leadership is characterized by "multiple leaders [who are] focused on enabling key talent to emerge, relative to the task requirements at hand, to facilitate the accomplishment of overarching common goals" (Pearce et al., 2018, p. 641). Leaders can reside anywhere within the organizational hierarchy—not just the president/senior administration or faculty—and lead based on skills, knowledge, or ability rather than position or representation.

Shared leadership and shared governance can coexist, but again, just because a campus operates under a shared governance structure does *not* mean that they have an effective or authentic shared leadership approach. The two processes serve slightly different goals that can be complementary, if both are implemented properly. Campuses may enjoy healthier campus climates when shared governance and shared leadership are operating in concert with one another. Healthy campus climates are built on the establishment of relationships and trust. Use of a shared leadership approach, by its nature, contributes to the development of relationships and builds trust because of the interactional and relational nature of its components. Shared leadership may also be a way to repair broken shared governance systems. By engaging more faculty, staff, and administrators in collaborative problem-solving outside of the formal context of governance processes, people will get to know one another, have common experiences, and discover common ground that may contribute to the development of new ways of working together to more productively achieve shared outcomes.

Conclusion

While the approaches to shared leadership described in this chapter might seem quite distinct from one another, they all share some common elements—namely a greater number of individuals in leadership than traditional models. They represent new ways of working in higher education that stand in stark contrast to traditional notions of hierarchy and single heroic leaders. In the second half of this book, you will read about many examples and different models of shared leadership in higher education in various case studies from different types of institutions. The next two chapters fill in more details about the benefits of shared leadership, the most appropriate situations for using a shared approach to leadership, challenges to its implementation, as well as ways to build capacity on campus to best support the development of shared leadership.

Chapter 2 Reflection Questions

1. Have you been involved in any sort of shared leadership effort before? How did it align with the three models described in this chapter (coleadership, team leadership, distributed leadership)?

2. Is shared leadership being used anywhere on your campus now? If so, can you identify any of those efforts as coleadership, team leadership, or distributed leadership? How do they align with some of the characteristics described in chapter 2? How do they differ?

3. To what extent do you feel that shared governance at your institution is effective, and how would you explain to your colleagues how shared leadership differs from governance?

Notes

1. In chapter 3, we discuss when it is most effective to utilize a shared leadership approach, and in chapter 4 we describe the role of positional or hierarchical leaders in more detail.

2. As noted in the previous section, there are a variety of ways that people have shared leadership in non-Western or non-White contexts. Because American higher education is structured and organized within the context of dominant, Western ways of thinking and operating, we focus in this section on models and structures drawn primarily from mainstream, Western business and management literature. It is important to remember, however, that even these approaches to shared leadership represent nondominant ways of operating and run counter to traditional, heroic, and hierarchical notions of leadership that are still quite prominent in American higher education contexts. For more information on non-Western or non-White studies of leadership, see for example Bordas (2012); Case & Gosling (2007); Warner & Grint (2006).

3. The Humboldt State University Klamath Connection program (chapter 5) and the University of Wisconsin-Whitewater example (chapter 6) also have some elements of coleadership.

References

Astin, H. S., & Leland, C. (1991). *Women of influence, women of vision: A cross-generational study of leaders and social change.* Jossey-Bass.

Barber, J., Jones, S., & Novak, B. (2009). *Student feedback and leadership.* Australian Learning and Teaching Council.

Barnes, B., Humphreys, J. H., Oyler, J. D., Haden, S. S. P., & Novicevic, M. M. (2013). Transcending the power of hierarchy to facilitate shared leadership. *Leadership & Organization Development Journal, 34*(8), 741–762. https://doi.org/10.1108/LODJ-01-2012-0015

Bass, B. M., & Bass, R. (2008). *The Bass handbook of leadership: Theory, research, and managerial applications* (4th ed.). Free Press.

Bensimon, E. M., & Neumann, A. (1993). *Redesigning collegiate leadership: Teams and teamwork in higher education.* Johns Hopkins University Press.

Boggs, G. R., & McPhail, C. J. (Eds.). (2019). *Team leadership in community colleges.* Stylus.

Bolden, R. (2011). Distributed leadership in organizations: A review of theory and research. *International Journal of Management Reviews, 13*(3), 251–269. https://doi.org/10.1111/j.1468-2370.2011.00306.x

Bolden, R., Petrov, G., & Gosling, J. (2009). Distributed leadership in higher education rhetoric and reality. *Educational Management Administration & Leadership, 37*(2), 257–277. https://doi.org/10.1177/1741143208100301

Bordas, J. (2012). *Salsa, soul, and spirit: Leadership for a multicultural age.* Berrett-Koehler Publishers.

Carson, J. B., Tesluk, P. E., & Marrone, J. A. (2007). Shared leadership in teams: An investigation of antecedent conditions and performance. *Academy of Management Journal, 50*(5), 1217–1234. https://doi.org/10.2307/20159921

Chesterton, P., Duignan, P., Felton, E., Flowers, K., Gibbons, P., Horne, M., & Thomas, T. (2008). *Development of distributed institutional leadership capacity in online learning and teaching project: Final project report.* The Carrick Institute for Learning and Teaching in Higher Education.

Chesterton, P., & Gosling, J. (2007). Wisdom of the moment: Pre modern perspectives on organizational action. *Social Epistemology, 21*(2), 87–111. https://doi.org/10.1080/02691720701393426

Chiu, C. Y. C., Owens, B. P., & Tesluk, P. E. (2016). Initiating and utilizing shared leadership in teams: The role of leader humility, team proactive personality, and team performance capability. *Journal of Applied Psychology, 101*(12), 1705. https://doi.org/10.1037/apl0000159

Contractor, N. S., DeChurch, L. A., Carson, J., Carter, D. R., & Keegan, B. (2012). The topology of collective leadership. *The Leadership Quarterly, 23*(6), 994–1011. https://doi.org/10.1016/j.leaqua.2012.10.010

Day, D. V., Gronn, P., & Salas, E. (2004). Leadership capacity in teams. *The Leadership Quarterly, 15*(6), 857–880. https://doi.org/10.1016/j.leaqua.2004.09.001

Denis, J. L., Langley, A., & Sergi, V. (2012). Leadership in the plural. *Academy of Management Annals, 6*(1), 211–283.

D'Innocenzo, L., Mathieu, J. E., & Kukenberger, M. R. (2016). A meta-analysis of different forms of shared leadership–team performance relations. *Journal of Management, 42*(7), 1964–1991. https://doi.org/10.1177/0149206314525205

Eckel, P. D. (2000). The role of shared governance in institutional hard decisions: Enabler or antagonist? *The Review of Higher Education, 24*(1), 15–39. https://doi.org/10.5465/19416520.2012.667612

Eddy, P. L., Hartman, C., & Lieu, E. (2019). Gender differences in team leadership. In G. R. Boggs & C. J. McPhail (Eds.), *Team leadership in community colleges* (pp. 19–40). Stylus.

Elfman, L. (2019, January 3). Mutcherson marks three major firsts for Rutgers Law School in Camden. *Diverse Issues in Higher Education.* https://diverseeducation.com/article/135285/

Ensley, M. D., Hmieleski, K. M., & Pearce, C. L. (2006). The importance of vertical and shared leadership within new venture top management teams: Implications for the performance of startups. *The Leadership Quarterly, 17*(3), 217–231. https://doi.org/10.1016/j.leaqua.2006.02.002

Erez, A., Lepine, J. A., & Elms, H. (2002). Effects of rotated leadership and peer evaluation on the functioning and effectiveness of self managed teams: A quasi experiment. *Personnel Psychology, 55*(4), 929–948. https://doi.org/10.1111/j.1744-6570.2002.tb00135.x

Fausing, M. S., Joensson, T. S., Lewandowski, J., & Bligh, M. (2015). Antecedents of shared leadership: empowering leadership and interdependence. *Leadership & Organization Development Journal, 36*(3), 271–291. http://doi.org/10.1108/LODJ-06-2013-0075

Fletcher, J. K., & Kaufer, K. (2003). Shared leadership: Paradox and possibility. In C. L. Pearce & J. A. Conger (Eds.), *Shared leadership: Reframing the hows and whys of leadership* (pp. 21–47). SAGE.

Gibeau, É., Langley, A., Denis, J. L., & van Schendel, N. (2020). Bridging competing demands through co-leadership? Potential and limitations. *Human Relations, 73*(4), 464–489.

Greenwood, R., Raynard, M., Kodeih, F., Micelotta, E. R., & Lounsbury, M. (2011). Institutional complexity and organizational responses. *Academy of Management Annals, 5*(1), 317–371. https://doi.org/10.1080/19416520.2011.590299

Gronn, P. (2000). Distributed properties: A new architecture for leadership. *Educational Management & Administration, 28*(3), 317–338. https://doi.org/10.1177%2F0263211X000283006

Gronn, P. (2002). Distributed leadership as a unit of analysis. *The Leadership Quarterly, 13*(4), 423–451. https://doi.org/10.1016/S1048-9843(02)00120-0

Gronn, P. (2009). From distributed to hybrid leadership practice. In A. Harris (Ed.), *Distributed leadership* (pp. 197–217). Springer.

Gross, K. (2018, February 1). *How co-presidents could improve leadership in higher education.* Aspen Institute. https://www.aspeninstitute.org/blog-posts/co-presidents-improve-leadership-higher-education/

Hodgson, R. C., Levinson, D. J., & Zaleznik, A. (1965). *The executive role constellation: An analysis of personality and role relations in management.* Harvard University, Graduate School of Business Administration.

Hrabowski, F. A., Rous, P. J., & Henderson, P. H. (2019). *The empowered university: shared leadership, culture change, and academic success.* Johns Hopkins University Press.

Huxham, C., & Vangen, S. (2000). Leadership in the shaping and implementation of collaboration agendas: How things happen in a (not quite) joined-up world. *Academy of Management Journal, 43*(6), 1159–1175. https://doi.org/10.2307/1556343

Jacobs, J. (2019). Team leadership in workforce development practice. In G. R. Boggs & C. J. McPhail (Eds.), *Team leadership in community colleges* (pp. 75–94). Stylus.

Jones, S., & Harvey, M. (2015). *Developing a cross-institutional network of experts in the use of benchmarks for distributed leadership to improve learning and teaching: Extension grant final report.* Australian Learning and Teaching Council.

Jones, S., Harvey, M., Lefoe, G., & Ryland, K. (2012). *Lessons learnt: Identifying the synergies in distributed leadership projects: Final report.* Australian Learning and Teaching Council.

Kelly, R. (2009, October 13). Proof a shared leadership model can work. *Faculty Focus.* https://www.facultyfocus.com/articles/academic-leadership/proof-a-shared-leadership-model-can-work/

Kezar, A. (2000). Pluralistic leadership: Incorporating diverse voices. *Journal of Higher Education, 71*(6), 722–743.

Kezar, A. J. (2002a). Expanding notions of leadership to capture pluralistic voices: Positionality theory in practice. *Journal of College Student Development, 43*(4), 558–578.

Kezar, A. J. (2002b). Overcoming the obstacles to change within urban institutions: The mobile framework and engaging institutional culture. *Metropolitan Universities: An International Forum, 13*(2), 95–103.

Kezar, A. J., & Carducci, R. (2009). Revolutionizing leadership development: Lessons from research and theory. In A. J. Kezar (Ed.), *Rethinking Leadership in a Complex, Multicultural, and Global Environment: New Concepts and Models for Higher Education* (pp. 1–38). Stylus.

Kezar, A. J., Carducci, R., & Contreras-McGavin, M. (2006). Rethinking the "L" word in higher education: The revolution of research on leadership. *ASHE Higher Education Report, 31*(6), 1–218.

Kezar, A., Dizon, J. P. M., & Scott, D. (2019). Senior leadership teams in higher education: What we know and what we need to know. *Innovative Higher Education*, 1–18. https://doi.org/10.1007/s10755-019-09491-9

Kezar, A., & Holcombe, E. (2017). *Shared leadership in higher education: Important lessons from research and practice.* American Council on Education.

Kezar, A. J., & Moriarty, D. (2000). Expanding our understanding of student leadership development: A study exploring gender and ethnic identity. *Journal of College Student Development, 41*(1), 55–69.

Kingsborough Community College. (n.d.). *ATD campus sub-committees.* Achieving the Dream. kbcc.cuny.edu/atd/committees.html

Klein, K. J., Ziegert, J. C., Knight, A. P., & Xiao, Y. (2006). Dynamic delegation: Shared, hierarchical, and deindividualized leadership in extreme action teams. *Administrative Science Quarterly, 51*(4), 590–621. http://dx.doi.org/10.2189/asqu.51.4.590

Komives, S. R., Lucas, N., & McMahon, T. R. (Eds.). (1998). A new way of understanding leadership. In *Exploring leadership: For college students who want to make a difference* (pp. 67–106). Jossey-Bass.

Lefoe, G., & Parrish, D. (2008). *The GREEN report: Growing, reflecting, enabling, engaging, networking.* Australian Learning and Teaching Council. https://www.researchgate.net/publication/230746138_The_GREEN_report_Growing_Reflecting_Enabling_Engaging_Networking_A_Report_on_the_Development_of_Leadership_Capacity_in_Higher_Education

Lefoe, G., & Parrish, D. (2013). Changing culture: Developing a framework for leadership capacity development. In D. J. Salter (Ed.), *Cases on quality teaching practices in higher education* (pp. 239–260). Information Science Reference.

Lowery-Hart, R. (2019). Leadership team development and succession planning in times of crisis. In G. R. Boggs & C .J. McPhail (Eds.), *Team leadership in community colleges* (pp. 108–123). Stylus.

Lumby, J. (2003). Distributed leadership in colleges: Leading or misleading? *Educational Management & Administration, 31*(3), 283–293. https://doi.org/10.1177/0263211X03031003005

MacBeath, J., Oduro, G. K. T., and Waterhouse, J. (2004). *Distributed leadership in action: A study of current practice in schools.* National College for School Leadership.

McPhail, I. P. (2019). Team building through collaborative leadership and strategic planning. In G. R. Boggs & C. J. McPhail (Eds.), *Team Leadership in Community Colleges* (pp. 95–107). Stylus.

Morgeson, F. P., DeRue, D. S., & Karam, E. P. (2010). Leadership in teams: A functional approach to understanding leadership structures and processes. *Journal of Management, 36,* 5–39. https://doi.org/10.1177/0149206309347376

Northouse, P. (2004). *Leadership: Theory and practice* (3rd ed.). SAGE.

Pearce, C. L., & Conger J. A. (Eds.). (2003). *Shared leadership: Reframing the hows and whys of leadership.* SAGE.

Pearce, C. L., Manz, C. C., & Sims, H. P. (2014). *Share, don't take the lead: Leadership lessons from 21 vanguard organizations.* Information Age.

Pearce, C. L., Wood, B. G., & Wassenaar, C. L. (2018). The future of leadership in public universities: Is shared leadership the answer? *Public Administration Review, 78*(4), 640–644.

Rosenthal, C. S. (1998). Determinants of collaborative leadership: Civic engagement, gender or organizational norms? *Political Research Quarterly, 51*(4), 847–868. https://doi.org/10.1177/106591299805100401

Seltzer, R. (2018, March 5). Are two presidents better than one? *Inside Higher Ed.* https://www.insidehighered.com/news/2018/03/05/college-idaho-hires-co-presidents-breaking-higher-ed-tradition

Spillane, J. P., Halverson, R., & Diamond, J. B. (2001). Investigating school leadership practice: A distributed perspective. *Educational Researcher, 30*(3), 23–28. https://doi.org/10.3102%2F0013189X030003023

Spillane, J. P., Halverson, R., & Diamond, J. B. (2006). Towards a theory of leadership practice: A distributed perspective. In I. Westbury & G. Milburn (Eds.), *Rethinking schooling* (pp. 196–230). Routledge.

Sveiby, K. E. (2011). Collective leadership with power symmetry: Lessons from Aboriginal prehistory. *Leadership, 7*(4), 385–414. https://doi.org/10.1177/1742715011416892

van Knippenberg, D. (2017). Team innovation. *Annual Review of Organizational Psychology and Organizational Behavior, 4*(4), 211–233. https://doi.org/10.1146/annurev-orgpsych-032516-113240

Warner, L. S., & Grint, K. (2006). American Indian ways of leading and knowing. *Leadership, 2*(2), 225–244. https://doi.org/10.1177/1742715006062936

Wexler, E. (2016, April 6). Law school co-deans: "Like a marriage." *Inside Higher Ed.* https://www.insidehighered.com/news/2016/04/06/why-universities-hire-two-deans-lead-their-law-schools

Yammarino, F. J., Salas, E., Serban, A., Shirreffs, K., & Shuffler, M. L. (2012). Collectivistic leadership approaches: Putting the "we" in leadership science and practice. *Industrial and Organizational Psychology, 5*(4), 382-402. https://doi.org/10.1111/j.1754-9434.2012.01467.x

Zhu, J., Liao, Z., Yam, K. C., & Johnson, R. E. (2018). Shared leadership: A state of the art review and future research agenda. *Journal of Organizational Behavior, 39*(7), 834–852. https://doi.org/10.1002/job.2296

3

UNDERSTANDING THE
OUTCOMES AND USES OF
SHARED LEADERSHIP

Susan Elrod, Adrianna J. Kezar, Elizabeth M. Holcombe, and Judith A. Ramaley

I n chapter 2, we discussed several different ways that leadership can be
shared, all of which represent very different ways of structuring operating and decision-making processes in higher education. Why would
a leader or an institution want to make such significant changes to their
leadership process? How would it benefit the institution or the individuals
involved? What sorts of obstacles do those operating in shared leadership
arrangements typically face? And are there certain situations when shared
leadership works better than others? In this chapter, we answer all these
questions, providing examples of the benefits of shared leadership from
both research and practice, factors that moderate its impact, challenges to
its implementation, and an overview of the circumstances that are most
conducive to effective shared leadership.

Outcomes and Moderators of Shared Leadership

What are the outcomes when leadership is shared more broadly across an
organization—whether among coleaders or on a team or distributed more
broadly throughout? Research in the management and organization literature shows generally positive outcomes for organizations using shared
approaches to leadership. As we noted in the previous chapter, research
on shared leadership in higher education is quite limited, but we bring it
in where it exists. Studies in the K–12 education sector also show notable
benefits of shared leadership approaches. In this section, we discuss these

outcomes or benefits of using shared leadership, which can be separated into two major categories—outcomes for participants who are part of the shared leadership process and outcomes for the organization as a whole.

Outcomes for Participants

Researchers have identified many beneficial outcomes for participants in the shared leadership process (D'Innocenzo et al., 2016; Nicolaides et al., 2014; Wang et al., 2014; Wu et al., 2020; Zhu et al., 2018). Shared leadership influences how participants *think* and *feel*, as well as how they *act* or *behave*. In terms of how people think and feel (cognition and attitudes), shared leadership produces greater cognitive complexity, or the type of complex thinking needed to evaluate problems from multiple frames and create solutions (Bensimon & Neumann, 1993). It leads to increased satisfaction among team members, both with their own jobs and with their colleagues (Avolio et al., 1996; Robert, 2013; Serban & Roberts, 2016; Shamir & Lapidot, 2003). Other attitudinal benefits are increased feelings of cohesion or belonging among team members (Balthazard et al., 2004; Bergman et al., 2012; Mathieu et al., 2015) and increased confidence in their abilities for both individuals and teams (Guzzo et al., 1993; Hooker & Csikszentmihalyi, 2003; Nicolaides et al., 2014). Finally, shared leadership builds increased trust among team members, as they get used to working together and depending on one another to lead and accomplish important tasks (Bergman et al., 2012; Drescher et al., 2014).

When examining the behavior of participants in shared leadership processes, researchers have also found a number of positive outcomes or changes to both individual and team behaviors. First, shared leadership leads to improved problem-solving quality, or the speed and accuracy with which team members can solve problems (Pearce et al., 2004). As noted previously, having more perspectives at the table brings additional cognitive complexity to bear when teams or groups are considering how to solve problems. Additionally, the trust and goodwill that participants in shared leadership arrangements build can help them entertain more creative ideas and more quickly discard potentially ill-fitting solutions. Second, shared leadership promotes increased organizational citizenship behavior, or people's willingness to proactively seek out and solve organizational challenges that may not be within their direct scope of responsibilities (Pearce & Herbik, 2004). When people are used to working together on projects that are complex and multifaceted, they may feel more broadly responsible for an organization's overall mission and goals rather than just the tasks and responsibilities in their job descriptions. Third, shared leadership fosters more constructive interaction styles and better conflict management among its participants, as they learn to work together, communicate well, and successfully navigate challenges and disagreements (Balthazard et al., 2004). Fourth, higher levels of information-sharing among participants result when people work more closely together in shared leadership arrangements (Khourey-Bowers et al., 2005). As participants interact more constructively and share information, team learning increases as well (Liu et al., 2014).

While there is not much research on the outcomes of shared leadership in a higher education setting, our experiences suggest that similar outcomes will result in practice when shared leadership is used in colleges and universities. As people begin to work together across the institution in the structure of a shared leadership system, additional cross-departmental collaborations may emerge spontaneously and become easier. For example, too often departments in academic and student affairs operate in silos, sometimes focused on the same problem. If brought together deliberately to address a complex institutional issue, such as 1st-year student success, they may learn about one another, see the value in what each department brings to the problem, and gain trust in the intentions and abilities of the other. When a new problem arises, they may be more likely to reach out and consult or engage across these divisional lines. They may also begin to see that there are many that can contribute to managing a complicated problem or situation and that they are not alone in laboring to fix it. Participating in a successful shared leadership effort may lead to increased feelings of organizational connection and citizenship. In turn, when people are encouraged to step up and work in new ways, faculty and staff across the university may emerge who can be cultivated for additional leadership roles. Many people have the potential for leadership but may not realize it themselves until given an opportunity to lead, or they may not be recognized as potential leaders by others who have the opportunity to mentor and help new leaders develop their talents. When organizations outside the institution are involved, the shared leadership approach may also have these impacts on them, increasing their stake in institutional programs and outcomes for the achievement of shared goals and collective impact. Most universities do not exist in a vacuum but in a community that they serve in one way or another, from a regional public institution that enrolls a majority of its students from the area to a private research institution that provides services, tax revenue, or business startup resources.

There are numerous potential benefits for individuals and teams participating in shared leadership processes. In many cases, these beneficial outcomes for participants are also mediators that lead to additional positive outcomes for the organization. In the next section, we discuss some of these positive organizational outcomes in more detail.

Outcomes for Organizations

As previously noted, the people-focused outcomes of shared leadership may also lead to improvements in how the organization functions (Figure 3.1). One of the most consistent findings in the research on shared leadership

Figure 3.1. Benefits of shared leadership for participants and organizations.

How people THINK and FEEL

- Cognitive complexity (feel challenged)

- Increased satisfaction (feel valued)

- Stronger group cohesion (feel like they belong)

- Increased confidence and trust (feel positive)

How people ACT

- Increased social integration, brings new voices to the table

- Improved problem-solving

- Organizational citizenship behavior

- More constructive interaction styles

- Engagement across departments and levels of an organization

- Cultivates development of leadership capacity and team creativity and innovation

How Organizations PERFORM

- Improved performance on specific work tasks

- Overall improved financial and strategic performance

- Improved creativity and innovation

is that it fosters improved performance of both teams and organizations (Drescher et al., 2014; Ensley et al., 2006; Hmieleski et al., 2012; Hoch et al., 2010; O'Toole et al., 2003; Small & Rentsch, 2010; Wu et al., 2020; Zhu et al., 2018). *Improved performance* has been defined in a number of different ways by researchers, from performance on specific tasks (Drescher et al., 2014; Small & Rentsch, 2011) to financial and strategic performance (Ensley et al., 2006; Hmieleski et al., 2012; Karriker et al., 2017; O'Toole et al., 2003) to customer satisfaction (Galli et al., 2017) to improved student learning in the K–12 literature (Heck & Hallinger, 2010). In addition, shared leadership is associated with greater creativity and innovation among teams and organizations (Zhu et al., 2018). Again, research on shared leadership in the higher education setting is very limited, especially on the outcomes of shared leadership, but one study from the UK indicated that on campuses where shared leadership was practiced most authentically, it promoted greater teamwork and communication, improved responsiveness to student concerns, and offered more incentives for innovation—similar to studies of shared leadership in other contexts (Bolden et al., 2009).

Moderators of Shared Leadership

The effects of shared leadership are also contingent on various moderators that act as thermostats to "turn up" or "turn down" the effectiveness of the interactions, such as the nature of the team's task and characteristics of the team. There is an extensive body of research on moderators of shared leadership in the business and management literature (see D'Innocenzo et al., 2016; Mathieu et al., 2015; Wang et al., 2014; and Wu et al., 2020 for recent meta-analyses and Zhu et al., 2018 for a thorough review of literature). In this section, we briefly describe a few examples of moderators that can influence the process of shared leadership, and in chapter 4 we review in more detail how campuses can build capacity around these moderators and enhance effectiveness.

First, the degree of complexity and creativity of the task tackled by shared leadership teams or groups influences the team's performance; shared leadership is more strongly linked to positive performance for tasks that are more complex and require more creativity to solve versus simpler tasks (Zhu et al., 2018). Additionally, various team characteristics can influence the degree to which shared leadership promotes positive outcomes. Some of these characteristics seem fairly straightforward, such as team member competence and supportive culture—shared leadership is more strongly linked to positive outcomes when participants are good at what they do and when the culture is supportive of shared leadership (Zhu et al., 2018). However, other moderating team characteristics are potentially more complicated. For example, team diversity moderates the relationship between shared leadership and performance (Drescher & Garbers, 2016; Kukenberger & D'Innocenzo, 2019). Evidence is mixed, however, on precisely how this moderator operates (positively or negatively) and how it varies depending on type of diversity (e.g., diversity of task or functional expertise, personality, or social/identity characteristics; Drescher & Garbers, 2016; Kukenberger & D'Innocenzo, 2019; Wu et al., 2020; Zhu et al., 2018).

These studies and others highlight emerging research that is identifying the complexities inherent in effectively forming and enacting a shared leadership model that is effective in achieving the desired goals. While this is not a comprehensive review, it points to the importance of considering issues that can shape effectiveness. Again, chapter 4 discusses these issues in much more detail. In the next section we further explore the complexities of when to use shared leadership and review some of the potential challenges that emerge when pursuing shared leadership approaches.

When to Use Shared Leadership

Shared leadership is most effective when used for addressing specific kinds of problems or when faced with specific kinds of change. Being smart in our approach to change in higher education requires an understanding of the best approach to leadership for each of three types or approaches to change: routine change, strategic change, and transformative change (Baer et al., 2008). Each of these approaches may be in use simultaneously at different levels of an organization and in response to different needs, and each may require a different approach to leadership.

Some challenges can be addressed by using well-practiced approaches to familiar problems. *Routine change* applies existing expertise to well-defined problems for which clear answers exist (Baer et al., 2008). Generally, the problem is solved within an administrative or academic unit. The problem is identified by the leader of that unit and the solution is put in place when that person approves it. Examples of these kinds of problems are updating a policy or adapting operating procedures. Other issues require more planned-out approaches. *Strategic change* generally is focused on redesigning or reengineering a more complicated process to speed it up or reduce errors or cost (Baer et al., 2008). Redesigns of this kind have been very popular as campuses try to operate more efficiently and effectively with fewer resources or fewer people or both. The results may affect a number of areas and leaders from different parts of the campus may coordinate their efforts to solve this kind of problem. The leaders share a common interest in improving the way that things are done and may appoint a task force to study the process and recommend improvements. *Transformative change*, in contrast, works on emerging challenges where there are no clear answers, where an effective response will mean working together in new ways and learning as the challenge unfolds (Baer et al., 2008). These kinds of problems do not fit readily into a standard organization chart. Transformative change is particularly well-suited to a shared leadership approach, especially one that is facilitated and encouraged from the top of the organizational hierarchy (i.e., by a president or provost). In this kind of situation, shared leadership participants must have complementary knowledge, skills, and experiences to effectively shepherd transformation. Table 3.1 shows these three categories of change that institutional leaders may be faced with in addressing problems or issues.

Shared leadership can also be effectively used in other situations or for more general operational functions. Shared leadership that is more bottom-up or driven from the middle of an organization might not involve significant, transformative change, yet it can still be beneficial for the participants and the organization as a whole. Characteristics of certain situations or tasks are particularly well-suited to a shared leadership approach. These characteristics include interdependence, creativity, complexity, and criticality (Cox et al., 2003). First, initiatives that require individuals to work interdependently to accomplish goals are good candidates for a shared leadership approach. Several of the case studies in this book demonstrate how problems or tasks requiring interdependence were helped by a shared leadership approach. For example, Portland State University's Homelessness Research and Action Collaborative (HRAC), featured in chapter 10, provides an excellent description of how their task required different parts of the university and different people working interdependently in order to effectively run their center. Additionally, Humboldt State University's Klamath Connection project (chapter 5), which redesigned the college transition and 1st-year experience for students in science, technology, engineering, and math (STEM), required people from academic disciplines, student affairs, advising, assessment, the registrar's office, and more to work together in order to make the types of changes that aligned with the project's goals. Second, tasks or problems that require creative solutions (i.e., not problems with well-tested solutions or routine challenges) lend themselves well to a shared leadership approach, as one noted outcome of shared leadership is increased creativity and cognitive complexity (Bensimon et al., 1989; Zhu et al., 2018). Relatedly, throughout this book and particularly in chapter 1 we note how so many challenges facing higher education are increasingly complex and require insights and expertise from multiple areas and people in order to find effective solutions.

TABLE 3.1
Types of Institutional Challenges

Type of Change	Description	Example	SL Usefulness
Routine	Challenges addressed by using well-practiced systems (e.g., committee with a clear charge)	Changes to policies that remedy easily solved or noncontroversial problems (e.g., accommodating a new federal financial aid rule)	Probably not necessary
Strategic	Challenges require planned-out approaches that may or may not cross departmental or unit boundaries	Streamlining processes to remove transactional inefficiencies (e.g., human resources hiring transaction flow)	Might be useful
Transformative	Complex challenges that require the engagement of multiple departments and stakeholders, perhaps some external to the institution, to work together in new ways	Improving student retention and persistence	Definitely useful

Note: Adapted from Baer et al. (2018).

For example, institutions' responses to the COVID-19 pandemic represent incredibly complex challenges which required novel and creative solutions; institutions that approached the transition to hybrid or remote operations, testing and contact tracing, and other pandemic-related challenges with a shared leadership approach were able to bring more perspectives to the table and craft more creative and effective solutions to these problems. In this book, the University of Richmond's use of shared leadership to tackle issues of diversity, equity, and inclusion (DEI) represents an example of a particularly complex challenge requiring creative solutions. And finally, an often overlooked but important characteristic in deciding to use shared leadership is the criticality of the task toward an organization's mission. More peripheral or specific tasks could perhaps be handled by one department or leader, but mission-critical tasks usually require the input of more stakeholders and are strong candidates for shared leadership. Our case study chapters from University of Wisconsin-Whitewater (chapter 6) and Cuyahoga Community College (chapter 12) provide examples of mission-critical efforts (specifically related to student success) that used shared leadership in order to cultivate the insights and expertise of multiple campus leaders across all levels of the organization.

Potential Barriers to Shared Leadership

We have alluded to some challenges in operationalizing shared leadership throughout the first few chapters. In this section, we provide more detail on some of the most common barriers that organizations face when trying to implement shared leadership approaches. We also offer suggestions for managing or overcoming these challenges to help those new to this approach build capacity for effective implementation. Additional details for building the capacity to address effectively creating a shared leadership culture can be found in chapter 4.

First, *power dynamics* may present barriers if not identified and addressed early on. Shared leadership involves people of different levels of power, authority, and expertise, as well as members of both dominant and nondominant groups. As a result, status differentials and power of those in formal leadership positions can stifle the voices or contributions of ground-level leaders if intentional efforts are not taken to diminish these concerns (Bensimon & Neumann, 1993; Denis et al., 2012; Jones et al., 2014). Relatedly, shared leadership may be used by formal leaders as a rhetorical or political device to promote support and a veneer of collegiality rather than an authentic approach to sharing power and influence (Bolden et al., 2009).

Second, *bureaucracy and existing structures* may present challenges and obstacles to forward progress. As Beaudoin and colleagues note in chapter 7 of this volume, leaders in other parts of the organization who do not necessarily buy in to the shared leadership arrangement may not be willing to work with multiple leaders when they are used to working with just one. Incentives and rewards may not be structured for those who share leadership, as in the case of the Portland State "dean team," where salary structures were not changed to reflect the fact that three people were coleading the dean's office rather than a single dean. Ideally, formal leaders will help manage the streamlining or relieving of bureaucratic or structural barriers, and informal leaders should be prepared to bring bureaucratic challenges or policy barriers to those who can make the changes.

Next, *accountability* must be clearly delineated and defined among members of the shared leadership group so that tasks get accomplished. If accountability is not clear and individuals do not have specifically defined roles and responsibilities, effectiveness will diminish and groups will flounder. Additionally, without clear accountability, free riding or social loafing behaviors may emerge among members of the group, putting additional burdens on a select few members and undermining the shared approach (Locke, 2003; Zhu et al., 2018).

Groupthink may develop among individuals working in tightknit groups, especially if diverse perspectives or skeptics are not included on the teams or in the leadership structure (Janis, 1982; Turner & Pratkanis, 1998). Groupthink could lead to some who do not always align with the group feeling ostracized. It can limit diversity of thought and keep those on the margins, including racially minoritized individuals or others from underrepresented groups, from full engagement. Fortunately, studies suggest that "team cohesion generally does not lead to groupthink and instead usually facilitates groups' relationships, interactions, and performance" (Kezar & Holcombe, 2017, p. 19, citing Ensley & Pearce, 2001). As long as shared leadership groups are mindful of this potential challenge and seek out feedback and criticism, it should be manageable.

Additionally, formal leaders may experience *psychological territory infringement* to their authority or position when team members take on assigned or assumed leadership roles within the shared leadership structure (Zhu et al., 2018). This may, in turn, inhibit the development of formal leaders or cause a loss of confidence and efficacy in their primary roles. Those in charge of enabling the shared leadership culture should be cognizant of these leadership threat issues and provide mechanisms for formal leaders to continue their development and be assured of their roles and responsibilities.

Finally, *time and resources* are required to fully develop the structures and culture of a shared leadership approach (Zhu et al., 2018). Decisions made in a shared leadership environment generally take more time than decisions that are made unilaterally by a single positional leader, a challenge that many of our case study authors note in their chapters. Patience and persistence are therefore required to maintain momentum and also avoid frustration in the face of setbacks or roadblocks. Leaders must be responsive to demands on the time and effort of participants. Leaders working on development of this approach should take stock periodically of the process, listen to feedback from groups on the pace and expectations, and make adjustments to pacing and/or workload to relieve pressures that may bubble up as a result of the intensive collaborations that characterize a shared leadership approach.

Conclusion

Shared leadership is a powerful approach for campus leaders to use in addressing complex challenges that often cross divisional lines and involve multiple stakeholder groups, perhaps even those in the local community, that more traditional approaches may not be effective at satisfactorily resolving. Using this approach has many potential benefits for how employees think, feel, and act; as well as for how the organization performs. There are challenges, though, to successfully building a shared leadership culture. These challenges traverse the entire trajectory of implementation, from getting started and ensuring effective uptake to building trust and avoiding groupthink. More difficult challenges to overcome may be related to issues of prohibitive bureaucracy, equity of team contributions, and delineating lines and responsibility of formal leadership authority. Time and resources are also a challenge because this approach is more complex, involves more people, and requires more attention to team and group functioning than more traditional, top-down approaches.

Chapter 3 Reflection Questions

1. Shared leadership can foster a number of benefits for an institution including better problem-solving, more constructive interaction styles and better conflict management, a stronger sense of shared purpose and community, and better sharing and use of information. Based on your own experience, how would you rate your institution on these characteristics?

2. If you are using some form of shared leadership on your campus now, what kind of problem are you addressing? If you cannot identify any shared leadership efforts on your campus, what problems are you facing at your institution that might lend themselves best to the process of shared leadership?

3. Are there any challenges covered in this chapter that seem particularly relevant for shared leadership efforts at your institution? How might you (or how have you) addressed these challenges? As a reminder, challenges can include power dynamics, the effects of existing bureaucracy, approaches

to accountability, limitations of time and resources, disciplinary conflicts, and the dynamics of the group itself including groupthink.

References

Avolio, B. J., Jung, D. I., Murry, W., & Sivasubramaniam, N. (1996). Building highly developed teams: Focusing on shared leadership processes, efficacy, trust, and performance. *Advances in Interdisciplinary Studies of Work Teams, 3*, 173–209.

Baer, L. L., Duin, A. H., & Ramaley, J. A. (2008). Smart change. *Planning for Higher Education, 36*(2), 5–16. https://www.scup.org/resource/smart-change/

Balthazard, P. D., Waldman D., Howell, J., & Atwater, L. (2004, February). *Shared leadership and group interaction styles in problem-solving virtual teams*. Proceedings of the 37th Hawaii International Conference on System Sciences. https://www.researchgate.net/publication/4055085_Shared_leadership_and_group_interaction_styles_in_problem-solving_virtual_teams

Bensimon, E., & Neumann, A. (1993). *Redesigning collegiate leadership*. Johns Hopkins University Press.

Bensimon, E., Neumann, A., & Birnbaum, R. (1989). *Making sense of administrative leadership: The "L" word in higher education*. George Washington University Press.

Bergman, J. Z., Rentsch, J. R., Small, E. E., Davenport, S. W., & Bergman, S. M. (2012). The shared leadership process in decision-making teams. *The Journal of Social Psychology, 152*(1), 17–42. https://doi.org/ 0.1080/00224545.2010.538763

Bolden, R., Petrov, G., & Gosling, J. (2009). Distributed leadership in higher education: Rhetoric and reality. *Educational Management Administration & Leadership, 37*(2), 257–277. https://doi.org/10.1177%2F1741143208100301

Cox, J. F., Pearce, C. L., & Sims, H. P., Jr. (2003). Toward a broader leadership development agenda: Extending the traditional transactional-transformational duality by developing directive, empowering, and shared leadership skills. In S. E. Murphy & R. E. Riggio (Eds.), *Series in applied psychology. The future of leadership development* (pp. 161–179). Erlbaum.

Denis, J. L., Langley, A., & Sergi, V. (2012). Leadership in the plural. *Academy of Management Annals, 6*(1), 211–283. https://doi.org/10.1080/19416520.2012.667612

D'Innocenzo, L., Mathieu, J. E., & Kukenberger, M. R. (2016). A meta-analysis of different forms of shared leadership–team performance relations. *Journal of Management, 42*(7), 1964–1991. https://doi.org/10.1177%2F0149206314525205

Drescher, G., & Garbers, Y. (2016). Shared leadership and commonality: A policy-capturing study. *The Leadership Quarterly, 27*(2), 200–217. https://doi.org/10.1016/j.leaqua.2016.02.002

Drescher, M. A., Korsgaard, M. A., Welpe, I. M., Picot, A., & Wigand, R. T. (2014). The dynamics of shared leadership: Building trust and enhancing performance. *Journal of Applied Psychology, 99*(5), 771–783. https://www.researchgate.net/publication/261732696_The_Dynamics_of_Shared_Leadership_Building_Trust_and_Enhancing_Performance

Ensley, M. D., & Pearce, C. L. (2001). Shared cognition in top management teams: Implications for new venture performance. *Journal of Organizational Behavior: The International Journal of Industrial, Occupational and Organizational Psychology and Behavior, 22*(2), 145–160. https://doi.org/10.1002/job.83

Ensley, M. D., Hmieleski, K. M., & Pearce, C. L. (2006). The importance of vertical and shared leadership within new venture top management teams: Implications for the performance of startups. *The Leadership Quarterly, 17*(3), 217–231. https://digitalcommons.unl.edu/cgi/viewcontent.cgi?article=1073&context=managementfacpub

Galli, B. J., Kaviani, M. A., Bottani, E., & Murino, T. (2017). Shared leadership and key innovation indicators in six sigma projects. *International Journal of Strategic Decision Sciences, 8*(4), 1–45. https://doi.org/10.4018/IJSDS.2017100101

Guzzo, R. A., Yost, P. R., Campbell, R. J., & Shea, G. P. (1993). Potency in groups: Articulating a construct. *British Journal of Social Psychology, 32*(1), 87–106. https://doi.org/10.1111/j.2044-8309.1993.tb00987.x

Heck, R. H., & Hallinger, P. (2010). Collaborative leadership effects on school improvement: Integrating unidirectional- and reciprocal-effects models. *The Elementary School Journal, 111*(2), 226–252. https://doi.org/10.1086/656299

Hmieleski, K. M., Cole, M. S., & Baron, R. A. (2012). Shared authentic leadership and new venture performance. *Journal of Management, 38*(5), 1476–1499. https://doi.org/10.1177/0149206311415419

Hoch, J. E., Pearce, C. L., & Welzel, L. (2010). Is the most effective team leadership shared? The impact of shared leadership, age diversity, and coordination on team performance. *Journal of Personnel Psychology, 9*(3), 105. https://psycnet.apa.org/doi/10.1027/1866-5888/a000020

Hooker, C., & Csikszentmihalyi, M. (2003). Flow, creativity, and shared leadership. In C. L. Pearce & J. A. Conger (Eds.), *Shared leadership: Reframing the hows and whys of leadership* (pp. 217–234). SAGE.

Janis, I. L. (1982). *Groupthink* (2nd ed.). Houghton Mifflin.

Jones, S., Harvey, M., Lefoe, G., & Ryland, K. (2014). Synthesising theory and practice: Distributed leadership in higher education. *Educational Management Administration & Leadership, 42*(5), 603–619. http://doi.org/10.1177/1741143213510506

Karriker, J. H., Madden, L. T., & Katell, L. A. (2017). Team composition, distributed leadership, and performance: It's good to share. *Journal of Leadership & Organizational Studies, 24*(4), 507–518. https://doi.org/10.1177/1548051817709006

Kezar, A., & Holcombe, E. (2017). *Shared leadership in higher education: Important lessons from research and practice.* Washington DC: American Council on Education.

Khourey-Bowers, C., Dinko, R. L., & Hart, R. G. (2005). Influence of a shared leadership model in creating a school culture of inquiry and collegiality. *Journal of Research in Science Teaching: The Official Journal of the National Association for Research in Science Teaching, 42*(1), 3–24. https://doi.org/10.1002/tea.20038

Kukenberger, M. R., & D'Innocenzo, L. (2019). The building blocks of shared leadership: The interactive effects of diversity types, team climate, and time. *Personnel Psychology, 73*(1), 125–150. https://doi.org/10.1111/peps.12318

Liu, S., Hu, J., Li, Y., Wang, Z., & Lin, X. (2014). Examining the cross-level relationship between shared leadership and learning in teams: Evidence from China. *The Leadership Quarterly, 25*(2), 282–295. https://doi.org/10.1016/j.leaqua.2013.08.006

Locke, E. A. (2003). Foundations for a theory of leadership. In S. E. Murphy & R. E. Riggio (Eds.), *The future of leadership development* (pp. 29–46). Erlbaum.

Mathieu, J. E., Kukenberger, M. R., D'Innocenzo, L., & Reilly, G. (2015). Modeling reciprocal team cohesion–performance relationships, as impacted by shared leadership and members' competence. *Journal of Applied Psychology, 100*(3), 713–734. https://doi.org/10.1037/a0038898

Nicolaides, V. C., LaPort, K. A., Chen, T. R., Tomassetti, A. J., Weis, E. J., Zaccaro, S. J., & Cortina, J. M. (2014). The shared leadership of teams: A meta-analysis of proximal, distal, and moderating relationships. *The Leadership Quarterly, 25*(5), 923–942. https://doi.org/10.1016/j.leaqua.2014.06.006

O'Toole, J., Galbraith, J., & Lawler, E. E., III. (2003). The promise and pitfalls of shared leadership: When two (or more) heads are better than one. In C. L. Pearce & J. A. Conger (Eds.), *Shared leadership: Reframing the hows and whys of leadership* (pp. 250–267). SAGE.

Pearce, C. L., & Herbik, P. A. (2004). Citizenship behavior at the team level of analysis: The effects of team leadership, team commitment, perceived team support, and team size. *The Journal of Social Psychology, 144*(3), 293–310. https://doi.org/10.3200/SOCP.144.3.293-310

Pearce, C. L., Yoo, Y., & Alavi, M. (2004). Leadership, social work, and virtual teams. In R. E. Riggio & S. S. Orr (Eds.), *Improving leadership in nonprofit organizations* (pp. 180–203). Jossey-Bass.

Robert, L. P. (2013, February 23–27). *A multi-level analysis of the impact of shared leadership in diverse virtual teams.* Proceedings of the 2013 Conference on Computer Supported Cooperative Work—CSCW '13. https://www.researchgate.net/publication/262329616_A_multi-level_analysis_of_the_impact_of_shared_leadership_in_diverse_virtual_teams

Serban, A., & Roberts, A. J. (2016). Exploring antecedents and outcomes of shared leadership in a creative context: A mixed-methods approach. *The Leadership Quarterly, 27*(2), 181–199. https://daneshyari.com/article/preview/887678.pdf

Shamir, B., & Lapidot, Y. (2003). Shared leadership in the management of group boundaries. In C. L. Pearce & J. A. Conger (Eds.), *Shared leadership: Reframing the hows and whys of leadership* (pp. 235–249). SAGE.

Small, E. E., & Rentsch, J. R. (2011). Shared leadership in teams. *Journal of Personnel Psychology, 9*(4), 203–211. https://doi.org/10.1027/1866-5888/a000017

Turner, M. E., & Pratkanis, A. R. (1998). Twenty-five years of groupthink theory and research: Lessons from the evaluation of a theory. *Organizational Behavior and Human Decision Processes, 73*(23), 105–115. https://doi.org/10.1006/obhd.1998.2756

Wang, D., Waldman, D. A., & Zhang, Z. (2014). A meta-analysis of shared leadership and team effectiveness. *Journal of Applied Psychology, 99*(2), 181–198. https://doi.org/10.1037/a003453

Wu, Q., Cormican, K., & Chen, G. (2020). A meta-analysis of shared leadership: Antecedents, consequences, and moderators. *Journal of Leadership & Organizational Studies, 27*(1), 49–64. https://doi.org/10.1177%2F1548051818820862

Zhu, J., Liao, Z., Yam, K. C., & Johnson, R. E. (2018). Shared leadership: A state of the art review and future research agenda. *Journal of Organizational Behavior, 39*(7), 834–852. https://doi.org/10.1002/job.2296

4

CREATING AN ENVIRONMENT OF SUPPORT FOR SHARED LEADERSHIP

Building Organizational, Team, and Individual Capacity

Adrianna J. Kezar, Judith A. Ramaley, Susan Elrod, and Elizabeth M. Holcombe

*J*ose is excited to begin his role as a new dean of humanities. Within his first few meetings, he identifies a major missed opportunity to work with local arts organizations to improve the recruitment of local students into programs at his university, as well as to improve K–12 arts education outcomes. Community groups have been wanting to partner with the school for many years but have been turned away. The provost comes to him saying the university is committed to greater community engagement and wants him to make it a priority. With this new knowledge of the school's poor history of community engagement and after a few initial communications that are received very coldly by the community, he realizes there is some work to be done. The dean realizes he does not have all the expertise, relationships, and knowledge needed to accomplish his goals. Jose finds out that some of the other schools and colleges within the university have better relationships with the community. He wonders whether he might learn from these colleagues while also forming a larger cross-university group to leverage existing relationships and build new ones. He decides to bring together a group of key people from other schools and units who have strong community partnerships, community partners, and faculty and staff in his own school *who aspire to partner to lead the process in the hopes that incorporating more people's perspectives and experiences would lead to better outcomes. But within a few meetings, the work is on the verge of falling apart. The faculty from other schools are not showing up to meetings and from what he can find out, they note that this work will not "count" in any way for them in terms of promotion and tenure. Community members were not included in a key communication due to inadequate staffing for the group, and this has reinforced the second-class status they had felt to begin with. Several community members stop attending meetings, and those that come appear defensive and guarded. Staff in the school express that they are unsure why they are there—in the past their recommendations have been overlooked—and they feel their presence on the group is token. The team cochairs have not been trained to navigate this type of conflict and distrust. They do not know how to build trust or reconcile the errors that have occurred. The cochairs come to Jose with this list of challenges—the lack of staffing support for the group, no rewards for faculty involvement, staff members feeling a lack of empowerment, the community members' distrust, and their inability to navigate it. Jose sits back and thinks, I could have done this better . . .*

The goal of this chapter is to help leaders avoid the problems described in this scenario. While many leaders may have the desire to lead in a shared way, there may not always be the knowledge of how to set up such work or the structures and talent in place to support such work. And the lack of support or capacity for shared leadership is not always obvious. Given that institutions were formed with structures that support top-down and bureaucratic forms of leadership, trying to institute shared leadership without making any organizational changes can be difficult. *Organizational changes* refers in particular to structural changes that can provide the support for shared leadership processes. Additionally, as we consider leadership as a process and not a set of individuals, the idea of building capacity and supporting a process becomes much more understandable. If leadership is understood as only people in positions of authority then the focus is on individual development, but if leadership is understood as a process then the need to support processes through the campus organizational structures becomes much more evident. As Bolden et al. (2015) note, "There is greater need to focus on how to support and develop collaboration, relationships and networks rather than simply develop the skills, traits and behaviours of individuals in formal leadership roles and structures" (p. 15).

However, not only the organization needs capacity-building—so does the team and the individuals on the team.[1] As Bolden et al. (2009) highlight, individuals have been trained to work within hierarchical leadership structures, so they also need new skills in order to know how to act in a shared leadership process. Both senior leaders (those in positions of power) as well as informal leaders need skill-building and new leadership mindsets to work within a shared leadership process. The team itself also needs capacity-building so that the group can be as effective as possible.

In this chapter, we outline some of the important changes that are needed to support and create the capacity for shared leadership work at the organizational, team, and individual levels. (See Table 4.1 for a comprehensive breakdown of these different skills.) Organizational capacity-building helps lay the groundwork for the team and individual capacities. Shared leadership teams and the individuals working within them need to exhibit the characteristics of shared leadership and be high-functioning to help create an environment where shared leadership can flourish.

Organizational Capacities or Development

We begin with the organizational capacities that need to be established to create the right conditions for shared leadership. These include structures and resources for shared leadership, incentives and rewards, coconstructed goals and accountability structures, empowerment, relationships, and a culture of trust and experimentation. In the research on shared leadership, scholars note the tendency to focus on skill-building of individuals who will be part of shared leadership, but there is a general disregard for the organizational supports that need to be in place. Organizations that focus on individual skill-building to the exclusion of developing these supportive conditions are likely to find "frustrations and inhibited effectiveness and engagement" among those tasked with sharing leadership (Van Ameijde et al., 2009). Thus, we start this chapter by describing organizational capacities since they are most likely to be overlooked and often less visible or tacit. They may also be the most difficult to construct because they may interact with or depend upon institutional culture, policies, or practices that have been developed to support top-down leadership.

Build Structures and Resources for Shared Leadership

Campuses generally have hierarchical structures that often prevent shared leadership work. Shared leadership involves interactions that typically cross boundaries between or among units and roles and responsibilities and will require new structures to be developed to support their work. These structures could include, for example, a cross-functional team, a learning community, or a new task force. Kezar and Lester (2009) found that collaboration is much more successful on campuses when integrating structures are created such as institutes, initiatives, and cross-functional

TABLE 4.1
Skills or Capacities for Shared Leadership

Organizational Capacities or Skills	Team or Group Capacities or Skills	Individual Skills (Positional or Senior Leaders)	Individual Skills (All Shared Leadership Participants)
Build structures and resources for shared leadership	Compose diverse teams with appropriate expertise	Provide needed organizational support for shared leadership process	Build consensus and generate diverse input
Create rewards for shared leadership	Structure the team with a clear, shared purpose	Practice interchangeable leadership roles (learn how to follow)	Cultivate a collaborative, inclusive, and relational approach
Coconstruct goals and accountability structures for shared leadership	Establish clear and appropriate role definition	Support coordination, collaboration, and consensus-building	Coach peers and give feedback
Empower others for policy- and decision-making	Plan effectively for team process and operations	Develop learning and empowerment mindsets	Navigate difficult conversations and effectively manage conflict and disagreement
Develop relationships and a culture of trust	Encourage collaborative team dynamics		Develop self-awareness, self-reflection, and self-leadership
Foster an environment of organizational learning, risk-taking, and experimentation	Team coaching and development		

teams. Integrating structures allow for information to be shared that typically is not, more complex problem-solving, and creation of networks that cross typical organizational boundaries. Shared leadership can occur within existing structures but is more easily facilitated when new work structures that cross boundaries are established. In addition, these new structures need to have the financial and human resources to be successful. A cross-functional team that lacks data to support its work, administrative staff, or other resources will be unable to operate effectively. Therefore, it is critical that as a positional or formal leader embarks on a shared leadership process, they consider the need for financial, staff, and other resources to get the work done.

The leader in the vignette at the beginning of this chapter, Jose, failed to consider appropriate staff support for his shared leadership group. He also created a structure that did not have individuals who had worked together before and had no built-in process for them to start working together successfully. The structure was not thoughtfully aligned to its purpose. Jose could have met regularly with the team's coleaders to check in, ask what challenges they were encountering, check on progress, monitor pacing, and make adjustments. If Jose had done that, he might have been able to head off the negativity and also help the team leaders learn how to do that themselves.

Create Rewards for Shared Leadership

One often overlooked support is rewards or incentives for shared leadership. Since our current reward structures (annual review, promotion and tenure, and merit systems) generally support individual rather than group contributions, this can make it challenging for those involved in shared leadership to be rewarded for their leadership work. Rewards can include salary, job security, career options, promotion, or even just recognition or appreciation. Research exploring shared leadership has shown that perception of fair reward structures is critical for getting individuals to assume or continue in shared leadership roles (Fausing et al., 2015). Rewards were clearly an issue in this chapter's opening vignette, with faculty deciding not to participate in the initiative because their involvement was not being rewarded in any way. Faculty and staff are much more likely to do the extra work of contributing to the overall organizational goals and objectives such as implementing changes and supporting collective problem-solving when they feel those efforts are rewarded by the organization. Simple kinds of activities such as rethinking annual merit reviews to include shared leadership activities, for example, could help support shared leadership work. Elrod and Whitehead (2018) suggest some additional examples of how institutions can create rewards for institutional service that help support shared leadership on campuses. Leaders should explore both intrinsic and extrinsic motivators, as different stakeholders in higher education are motivated by different types of rewards.

Coconstruct Goals and Accountability Structures for Shared Leadership

A key first task for shared leadership groups is coconstruction of goals with senior leaders. Shared leadership processes work best when there is a back and forth to develop the goals, an iteration until everyone understands and is clear on the goals. If goals are established by hierarchical leaders and decreed to shared leadership teams in a top-down fashion rather than coconstructed together, there is less likely to be authentic buy-in around the shared leadership effort and leaders may be disengaged or mistrustful of the process. Similarly, goals cannot be set without any input from senior leaders; there must be some alignment with institutional mission and priorities. This coconstruction process can take time due to the number of people involved, the differing priorities they may have, and the iterative process required to reach consensus or at least agreement on the team's goals.

While the process of coconstructing goals can be challenging, campuses are often able to enact it effectively, as deliberation and consensus-building are already part of the culture of many institutions of higher education. However, even when shared goals are effectively established, accountability processes are often missing (Kezar & Lester, 2009; Spillane & Diamond, 2007). Accountability structures ensure that progress is made and goals are met. As leadership is distributed, more accountability structures may need to be put in place because as more people are involved there could be miscommunication or lack of consensus over values or strategy (Spillane & Diamond, 2007). When more people are invited to be a part of a leadership process, new structures are necessary to help people understand what is at stake in their decision-making and actions. These structures can range from strict performance measures and regular reporting to mutual performance monitoring, which involves team members taking account of each other's activities and offering feedback, help, or suggestions when needed (Van Ameijde et al., 2009). Without accountability structures, shared leadership efforts can devolve and become mired in process (Spillane & Diamond, 2007).

For Jose to be successful with his community-engaged arts initiative, he will need to task the group with developing a set of goals they will be held accountable for over the 3-year time period of the initiative. The allocation of new resources each year can be dependent on meeting established goals. Furthermore, goals should be approved by senior leaders as well as a group of designated stakeholders who are invested in the arts initiative.

Empower Others for Policy- and Decision-Making

Once accountability structures are in place, shared leadership groups should be empowered to make policy and inform priority-level decisions. In traditional hierarchies on campus, faculty and staff are not allocated the responsibility to make policies. While they may make decisions, their authority is typically limited to a very narrow sphere—typically around curriculum or admissions for faculty and local practices or implementation of existing policy for staff. Empowerment involves those in positions of power delegating authority for decisions and policy-making to the shared leadership groups. When decision-making or policy-making is not delegated, empowerment can also be established through structures that allow for the shared leadership group's recommendations to be considered; if the group's recommendations are not followed, accountability structures can be put in place to communicate why they are not followed. Shared leadership groups often accomplish this through a proposal development process, where a series of recommendations are made outlining options for consideration by other groups or executive leadership. Senior leaders must be prepared to grant the team meaningful input into decision-making so that team members remain motivated and incentivized to continue their engagement with shared leadership processes.

In the opening example, staff had a history of disempowerment. Jose could have met with staff prior to establishing the task force and acknowledged this challenging history, noted that this process would be different, and that their advice or recommendations would be taken seriously. He could outline how they could propose a set of ideas and explain the process for decision-making that would ensue. These steps would help empower the team and promote engagement.

Develop Relationships and a Culture of Trust

Studies of shared leadership identify the importance of building supportive institutional structures that develop relationships and fostering a culture of respect for and trust in the value of shared leadership (Jones et al., 2014a). Shared leadership is more likely to succeed if participants have worked together successfully before, due to the power of existing relationships and trust. Also, shared leadership can be undermined if there are bad relationships among groups that come together in a shared leadership setting. As Jose's example showed, poor relationships can make shared leadership challenging. Therefore, putting structures in place to support the development of positive relationships lays the ground work for shared leadership. Trying to overcome negative group dynamics can overwhelm a shared leadership process, so ways that relationships are built up front is important. Research has shown that leaders can invest in key network-building activities (i.e., hosting symposia, reading groups, social events, campus celebrations, common meeting spaces, and professional development) that create social networks which foster collaborative work on campuses (Kezar & Lester, 2009). Hierarchical leaders can also enhance shared leadership by supporting individuals or existing structures that play a networking role, such as a center for teaching improvement where the director is active in connecting people. Additionally, network-building can be incentivized by asking that applications for internal grants or projects include cross-unit collaboration or by celebrating leaders or teams through awards or other prestigious recognitions (e.g., campus news articles, featured lectures, campus presentations). It is critical once a group is established to spend time up front creating positive dynamics and, if poor histories exist, to restore quality relationships.

Foster an Environment of Organizational Learning, Risk-Taking, and Experimentation

Shared leadership depends on an environment of risk-taking since the work crosses typical boundaries and forges new working relationships and processes (Zhu et al., 2018). Senior leaders need to provide tangible support for risk-taking and experimentation. They can do this by modeling risk-taking and, more importantly, recognizing and rewarding this activity. Solutions to complex problems do not generally come from the first try at solving them; thus, pilot-testing and flexibility to make adjustments must be allowed and supported in order to reach a satisfactory and effective solution. Additional approaches may involve breaking the problem into manageable pieces, as relieving one aspect of the problem may open up other solutions not visible until the initial piece is isolated and managed.

Jose might have started off the shared leadership group by recognizing a few faculty and staff that had partnered with the local community to share their work and help people see across boundaries. Or he might have hosted an event with the community—small in scale—to try out this work. Through learning and role-modeling, faculty, staff, and community members would have been better able to engage in the shared leadership work.

Team or Group Capacity-Building

While campuses regularly establish teams or groups for various functions, shared leadership teams are different because they are connected to solving a complex problem identified on campus. Campuses can best support shared leadership by ensuring that their team not only has the organizational support but also a clear purpose, is initially composed of the appropriate individuals from diverse backgrounds, roles are defined adequately, the team plans their activities together, collaborative team dynamics are developed, and there are opportunities for coaching and skill development (more on this in the last section of the chapter).

Structure the Team With a Clear, Shared Purpose

Shared leadership processes need agreement around purpose and goals—which for shared leadership is typically around a complex problem that requires individuals working across typical boundaries on campus (Pearce, 2004). The team's parameters trace back to the problem being solved and must be aligned with the overarching goals for the larger project or program. Remember, shared leadership is not an approach needed for all types of problems we might encounter on campus (refer back to chapters 1 and 3 for more information on this). A shared sense of purpose exists when team members have similar understandings of their primary objectives and take steps to ensure a focus on collective goals (Carson et al., 2007). However, this shared sense of purpose is certainly not automatic, and studies have identified how the establishment and initial structuring of the team and process is pivotal to its success (Pearce, 2004). Ensuring a shared purpose is both the responsibility of the senior leaders who establish the group as well as the members of the team. In order to create shared purpose, the leader who establishes the team can orient members prior to joining, can attend early meetings to communicate the purpose, and can have processes where the teams communicate progress so that others can monitor the work and ensure they stay guided by the shared purpose and goals. The team members can create initial discussions about the group charge and spend time ensuring that each team member can articulate the team purpose and charge or add to it if they feel that it does not reflect important interests, perspectives, or viewpoints. It is important for teams to stay on track with their vision, check in often on their progress, and close the loop on actions relative to the accountability measures discussed earlier.

It seems clear that if Jose had sat down with his shared leadership group to explain their important and unique purpose, he might have gotten more buy-in and faced fewer challenges. As we noted in the last section, Jose did not work to ensure a shared or clear purpose and thus the team was adrift.

Compose Diverse Team(s) With Appropriate Expertise

Shared leadership is best facilitated when the appropriate team members are recruited and multiple perspectives are included. Studies find that one of the most significant factors that shapes whether a shared leadership process is successful and will meet its goals is its composition, or the careful selection of team members based on the core competencies needed for executing tasks and addressing challenges (Morgeson et al., 2010; Wheelan, 2009). Another characteristic of shared leadership that has been consistently researched is whether the membership of a team is diverse by role, background, and experience. Intragroup diversity is key to success and leads to more complex decisions and thinking (Morgeson et al., 2010; Wiersema & Bantel, 1992). In higher education, Bensimon and Neumann (1993) and Fincher et al. (2010) determined that members of teams with diverse backgrounds (race, gender, socioeconomic status) and experience (employment, role) can play different roles and support more complex decision-making and problem-solving. Research also suggests that the composition of a shared leadership team needs attention throughout its tenure and is not something to be attended to only during team formation. Studies indicate that removing difficult team members or "derailers" right away is also important to maintaining positive outcomes (Wageman et al., 2008; Wheelan, 2009). Team composition and functioning will require time and care to ensure the team's composition continues to be relevant as the project evolves.

In our example, Jose did create a diverse team with the appropriate experience, but diverse teams need careful management and he was not involved enough in their initial meetings to ensure that they got off to a good start.

Establish Clear and Appropriate Role Definition

Research shows that clearly defined roles help team members capitalize on their expertise and more effectively coordinate shared tasks. In studies of project teams in the UK, Van Ameijde et al. (2009) note that clearly defined roles and responsibilities for team members are critical for successful shared leadership. Such specifically designated roles are often missing in higher education settings, where people are used to juggling multiple roles and responsibilities in their formal positions. Bensimon and Neumann (1993) highlight some of the roles that people can play to support shared leadership processes.[2] For example, successful shared leadership processes often have an individual who serves as the task monitor; this person strives to remove obstacles to the team's thinking and keep them on task. Teams may also have an emotional monitor who helps maintain the interpersonal relationships developed through team-building. There is someone who elicits and synthesizes diverse perspectives of the group, working to achieve consensus. Successful teams also have a critic who redefines and analyzes issues so that the shared process does not end up in "groupthink." One major difference that these researchers saw between effective and ineffective teams is that effective teams have members who are sensitive to the fact that different people are likely to see the same reality in varying ways. These teams are not afraid of the conflict that can be inherent in cognitively diverse teams. Thus, individuals who shape shared leadership processes such as senior leaders need to articulate their appreciation for different viewpoints, and they need to model this behavior in their interaction with people during shared leadership processes. What research points to is that as shared leadership processes begin, discussion on roles and the value of different roles is important for the team to be successful in its work.

Plan Effectively for Team Process and Operations

Another important area of team development that emerges repeatedly in studies of shared leadership is the importance of team planning. Team planning includes onboarding (helping team members become familiar with their roles and expectations) and socialization (individual meetings with people as well as group process and retreats); establishing norms for the group; developing trust and relationships critical to functioning and achieving goals; and establishing structures to support the team (e.g., resources, information, people support, appropriate meetings, accountability measures; Morgeson et al., 2010). These aspects of the team process can be planned and help improve its overall functioning. If these preliminary considerations are not given careful thought and the process is not implemented in a systematic manner, it will be very difficult, if not impossible, to achieve a successful shared leadership process (Carpenter et al., 2004; Morgeson et al., 2010; Parker, 2007; Purser & Cabana, 1998). Senior leaders can support the capacity of the team in providing onboarding and socialization support by hosting some of the initial events and helping develop shared purpose and role familiarity, which we alluded to earlier. Facilitators can be offered to shared leadership teams to help them in some of the early training to help establish a plan and support relationship development and ground rules.

Next time, Jose might consider being a part of the initial planning process for his shared leadership effort. He might also offer the help of facilitators to assist the group with developing strong relationships, trust, and norms, which would have helped significantly with the next area of collaborative team dynamics.

Encourage Collaborative Team Dynamics

Research also suggests the importance of the previous group processes (carefully choosing people to participate in shared leadership processes, orientation sessions, group development, and spending time developing relationships) in facilitating shared leadership dynamics. As noted throughout, typical campus hierarchical structures mean that collaboration is not the norm for working groups, so ensuring positive team dynamics will often require intentional work and planning. Teams that are well-structured and planned tend to encounter far fewer negative team dynamics than poorly structured or unstructured ones. Yet even the best-structured and planned teams can experience negative interpersonal dynamics over the course of their time working together. Ignoring team dynamics is one of the most significant challenges of shared leadership (Cranston & Ehrich, 2009; Wageman et al., 2008). Studies suggest that unproductive collaboration is widespread (e.g., Kruyt et al., 2011; Wageman et al., 2008). Team leaders often ignore the role they can play in shaping team dynamics and instead leave dynamics to emerge on their own, risking the emergence of unproductive or negative dynamics (Carpenter et al., 2004; Mangano, 2007).

One of the most important ways for leaders on teams to avoid negative dynamics is to build relationships actively and work to create a positive team culture (Wageman et al., 2008). Building relationships should be both an individual activity, such as when the leader meets with members of the team, as well as a group activity, such as creating social opportunities outside work, retreats, and lengthy times together where team members get to know each other better (Carpenter et al., 2004; Kruyt et al., 2011). Relationship-building helps solidify a team, and good leaders also monitor relationships on an ongoing basis so as to ensure that people continue to get along (Bensimon & Neumann, 1993; Carpenter et al., 2004; Wageman et al., 2008). In addition to promoting relationship-building among members of the team, positional leaders need to nurture their own relationships with team members. One way to build relationships and trust is taking members' input into account, which affects their commitment to decisions, perceptions of fairness, and trust in the leader and overall team relationships (Carpenter et al., 2004; Wageman et al., 2008). Team dynamics relate highly to team planning and processes which help to create strong team relationships. Onboarding, creating expectations and ground rules and norms, building strong interpersonal relationships, leaders role-modeling healthy team relationships, building common purpose up front—all these processes support better relationships and dynamics (Wageman et al., 2008).

Team Coaching and Development

One of the most consistent findings in the research is the role of team development and coaching for effectiveness. There are various development practices that can help improve a shared leadership process, ranging from self-study, to audits, to monitoring, to external consultants, to leaders or members who take on development activities (Bensimon & Neumann, 1993; Carpenter et al., 2004). The literature is clear that teams improve when they put into place a regular mechanism for obtaining feedback and then work on areas that need improvement. By coaching, the literature is usually suggesting a senior leader helping individual team members as well as role-modeling good practices for the team (e.g., conflict management, shared vision, etc.). Coaching may also refer to bringing in consultants or other external people to provide feedback to the team or help them in navigating challenging areas. Research in higher education identifies how campuses tend not to have systems for gathering input and typically lack ongoing development for teams (Woodfield & Kennie, 2007). Studies show that leaders in general, but in higher education in particular, tend to downplay the role of development and coaching. While consistently identified as important to team improvement and organizational outcomes in higher education, team development and coaching are rarely used on campuses today (Carpenter et al., 2004; Wageman et al., 2008).

Individual Capacity or Support

In addition to considering ways the overall campus can develop enabling structures and promote positive team interactions to support shared leadership processes, campus leaders need to be thinking about how they can ensure that individuals can be developed in ways that make them better able to participate in shared leadership. This development likely needs to start with senior leaders themselves, who must rethink their own approaches to decision-making, delegation, and staff development in order to set the stage for a new form of collaboration that ensures shared leadership can flourish. What follows is a summary of what we know about the skills and mindsets that should be fostered among those who participate in shared leadership groups and how best to foster them. We start by outlining skills for senior leaders or those in formal positions of authority, followed by a section on skill sets for individuals who are part of shared leadership groups but are not in positions of authority atop the formal organizational hierarchy. While building organizational support for shared leadership can take significant time, building the capacity of individuals to participate in shared leadership can happen more rapidly and is often a good place for starting the development process.

Skills for Positional or Hierarchical Leaders

While shared forms of leadership advocate for a broader conception of leadership and run counter to more traditional or hierarchical styles, they also require support from positional or senior leadership. Hierarchical leadership and shared leadership are not mutually exclusive. As described in chapter 2, shared leadership is more of a process than a set of relationships defined by organizational charts. Both forms of leadership (shared and hierarchical) can and should be aligned. Senior positional leaders play an important role in fostering shared leadership. Fletcher & Kaufer (2003) refer to this as one of the paradoxes of shared leadership by pointing out that "hierarchical leaders are charged with creating less hierarchical organizations" (p. 24). Researchers have identified several steps that positional leaders can take that promote effective shared leadership. These steps can help senior leaders identify the skills they need to develop in order to support shared leadership on their campuses.

Provide needed organizational support for a shared leadership process. In research on shared leadership in higher education, Van Ameijde et al. (2009) found that support from key senior leaders ensured a flow of information and resources needed by the team, as well as empowerment to make important decisions at the team level. Similarly, Jones et al. (2014a) emphasized the importance of formal leaders' encouragement and support for shared forms of leadership. To promote this type of skill-building for senior leaders, knowledge and education about what shared leadership entails are foundational. If leaders have a strong knowledge of what shared leadership is (and is not) and what things should look like when they are running smoothly, they can better encourage and support their colleagues in working in this way.

Practice interchangeable leadership roles. In a shared leadership culture, leader and follower roles are interchangeable (Kezar & Holcombe, 2017). Senior leaders will need to learn when to lead and when to follow, and those not in formal leadership positions will need to learn how to lead when it is their role. This means letting go of prior assumptions about roles and learning to adapt to different ones, which may be challenging for both kinds of leaders.

Support coordination, collaboration, and consensus-building. Senior leaders will need development in how to coordinate and coach, when to encourage collaboration and consensus-building, or deciding on when to be more directive or controlling (Zhu et al., 2018). Senior leaders are well versed in direction and control but may need to temper that and learn skills in how to instead orchestrate more from behind the scenes. Leaders will benefit from learning how to coach others so that they can direct the work themselves (Jones et al., 2014b). And leaders need to recognize and select the right opportunities for working in shared and collaborative ways (Van Ameijde et al., 2009). As we have noted throughout the book, not all situations are best served through shared leadership; one of the key skills that senior leaders must develop is identifying when shared leadership is needed and when other approaches to problem-solving might be more appropriate. Senior leaders need to be connected more to others across the organization so they can see these opportunities for shared work, as well as the individuals who might be best to serve in shared leadership groups. Relationship-building across all levels of the organization is a critical skill to help foster the collaboration needed for shared leadership (Zhu et al., 2018).

Develop learning and empowerment mindsets. Shared leadership processes are established in order to distill the best thinking of complex groups. Yet, this thinking may not occur if the individuals involved do not feel the group process is set up for them to explore and learn and that they are empowered to contribute to an outcome (Zhu et al., 2018). Leaders in positions of authority need to learn how to empower employees and diffuse authority so that individuals at multiple levels do not feel hindered in acting as leaders (Zhu et al., 2018). Senior leaders also need to learn how to support team learning and encourage teams to take risks. This relates to the earlier described culture of risk-taking. Senior leaders must make it safe to take thoughtful risks, and they need to model this behavior themselves. In order to model it, though, they need to learn to feel free to experiment themselves and set an expectation that so long as there is learning from any project that can be applied to future efforts, work that does not yield the desired results is still valuable.

Skills for All Shared Leadership Participants

As noted in the section on building capacity for shared leadership processes, team members will need to learn skills to be a part of collaborative processes. Groups that provide training for their members on consensus-building, creating shared vision and goals, generating feedback, navigating difficult conversations, and self-awareness are more successful at sharing leadership. This list of skills is not fully exhaustive but does suggest some key areas that campuses may want to emphasize as they consider professional development in support of shared leadership.

Build consensus and generate diverse input. Part of building a shared vision or purpose, creating a team plan, and developing clear and appropriate roles will require consensus-building. And as noted earlier, a diverse team better supports complex thinking, so consensus-building among very diverse individuals can be a challenging task (Zhu et al., 2018). Thus, training on approaches to consensus-building will be required for members of teams who participate in shared leadership. Additionally, coming to appropriate consensus with diverse groups also means being able to help the group brainstorm, draw out multiple ideas, and generate diverse input. Leaders need to create a space where team members feel comfortable sharing their ideas.

In our opening vignette, team members would have been much better able to guide the team if they knew how to help their fellow team members have conversations about a shared vision and assist them in seeing their essential roles on the team. Instead, each member saw themselves as an individual or a constituent not as part of a collective, which is built through consensus processes.

Cultivate a collaborative, inclusive, and relational approach. Studies have identified that leadership skills associated with successful collaboration include frequent interaction with team members, inclusion of individuals in decision-making, fostering healthy relationships, encouraging networking and partnerships, and actively creating alliances (Allan & Cherrey, 2000). Thus, leaders on teams need to learn strategies and approaches for building relationships necessary for the group to work effectively together. This also means developing the skills to monitor the emotions of teams and groups. Leaders need to learn skills of inclusiveness, such as inviting participation, active listening, bidirectional communication, and encouraging feedback (Kezar et al., 2006).

Coach peers and give feedback. For teams to have healthy interactions and problem-solve together, they need to be able to share honestly, give feedback, and help each other as they work in new collaborative ways. As hierarchies are broken down, individuals are not always clear on how to act within teams and may not know their role, communication styles, or interpersonal skills and may need feedback from other team members (Bensimon & Neumann, 1993; Carpenter et al., 2004). Providing nonjudgmental feedback is a skill that team members need to learn. Also, team members must learn how to readily accept feedback and use it to change their behavior. *In our earlier example, if Jose had coached the cochairs on how to give feedback to team members they might have been able to stem some of the early angst.*

Navigate difficult conversations and effectively manage conflict and disagreement. Research repeatedly identifies the role of learning to navigate difficult conservations and conflict management as key skills in shared leadership processes (Zhu et al., 2018). Shared leadership processes will always involve disagreement, as they bring together people with diverse perspectives, empower them, provide them with complex tasks, and encourage them to provide open communication and feedback. There will be differing views, and many times these views can turn into disagreements. This disagreement is a natural part of shared leadership, and groups need to understand both that it is natural and that they can navigate through conflict. Team members need to learn skills around empathetic and active listening that help them hear others, perspective-taking skills that allow individuals to move beyond their own mindsets to see others, and establish ground rules so that disagreements are addressed with respect. There are dozens of techniques and skills that teams can learn related to conflict management. (See, for example, Cranston & Ehrich, 2009; Wageman et al., 2008.)

Develop self-awareness, self-reflection, and self-leadership. Studies also identify meta-skills such as self-awareness and self-reflection as important to learn as part of shared leadership since individuals will be acting in ways counter to many societal and institutional norms. If people who are involved in shared leadership are not self-aware, they can fall back into hierarchical patterns of leading. Pearce & Manz (2005) note how a leader's self-awareness was repeatedly identified in successful shared leadership processes. This includes leaders knowing when they should guide the team or let others step up based on their expertise, as well as knowing when processes are going well or when negative dynamics might be developing.

Conclusion

Jose's shared leadership efforts would have benefited from the advice in this chapter. He could have started by considering his own abilities to support shared leadership—did he have the skill set to cocreate a process, understand how to empower others, coach and role model for the team, and coordinate and collaborate the work? Imagine if he had started by making a compelling case around the shared leadership challenge of improving arts education in the community and on campus and had worked to construct a shared sense of purpose and goals. And what if he had considered the staff and faculty of the shared leadership group and assessed their skill sets to support shared leadership? He could have provided professional development to enhance their skill sets to support shared leadership—not only thinking about individual skill development but also team development and how to manage difficult dynamics, set ground rules, and plan a complex shared leadership process. Jose could also have worked to establish the support the team needed in terms of resources, rewards, accountability, relationship-building, and development of a culture that supports experimentation, either by creating these supports himself in his capacity as dean or advocating for them at higher levels of the organization. This chapter provides the blueprint for leaders such as Jose to establish the capacity organizationally, within the team, and among individuals to have a successful and effective shared leadership process.

Chapter 4 Reflection Questions

1. What are some of the organizational capacities for shared leadership that are already in place at your institution? Are there pockets of these capacities you might be able to identify that you could leverage or build upon? What first steps could you take to begin building capacity at the organizational level in areas where your institution may not be strong?
2. How might you go about building team- or group-level capacity? Are there any highly effective teams at your institution you could learn from?
3. What individual-level skills do you feel strong in already? What skills could you enhance to strengthen your ability to participate in shared leadership?
4. If you are not a senior-level leader, what skills do you feel that your senior leadership needs to develop in order to effectively support shared leadership?

Notes

1. While we mostly use the term "team" in this chapter, we do want to note that we are not necessarily referring to the "team leadership" model of shared leadership, but rather the group of people involved in the shared leadership effort. That may be a team or it may be a larger and more distributed group of people.

2. This work was specifically focused on presidential cabinets, but we included it here because it is one of the few detailed studies of team roles in higher education.

References

Allan, K., & Cherrey, C. (2000). *Systemic leadership: Enriching the meaning of our work.* University Press of America.

Bensimon, E. M., & Neumann, A. (1993). *Redesigning collegiate leadership: Teams and teamwork in higher education.* Johns Hopkins University Press.

Bolden, R., Petrov, G., & Gosling, J. (2009). Distributed leadership in higher education: Rhetoric and reality. *Educational Management Administration & Leadership, 37*(2), 257–277. https://doi.org/10.1177%2F1741143208100301

Carpenter, M. A., Geletkanycz, M. A., & Sanders, W. G. (2004). Upper echelons research revisited: Antecedents, elements, and consequences of top management team composition. *Journal of Management, 30*(6), 749–778. https://doi.org/10.1016/j.jm.2004.06.001

Carson, J. B., Tesluk, P. E., & Marrone, J. A. (2007). Shared leadership in teams: An investigation of antecedent conditions and performance. *Academy of Management Journal, 50*(5), 1217–1234. https://doi.org/10.2307/20159921

Cranston, N., & Ehrich, L. (2009). Senior management teams in schools: Understanding their dynamics, enhancing their effectiveness. *Leading & Managing*, *15*(1), 14–25. https://www.researchgate.net/publication/27483984_Senior_management_teams_in_schools_understanding_their_dynamics_enhancing_their_effectiveness

Elrod, S. L., & Whitehead, L. (2018, March 7). Turning on the thrive channel to accelerate change in higher education. *Accelerating Systemic Change Network*. https://ascnhighered.org/ASCN/posts/201117.html

Fausing, M. S., Joensson, T. S., Lewandowski, J., & Bligh, M. (2015). Antecedents of shared leadership: empowering leadership and interdependence. *Leadership & Organization Development Journal*, *36*(3), 271–291. http://doi.org/10.1108/LODJ-06-2013-0075

Fincher, M., Katsinas, S., & Bush, V. B. (2010). Executive management team demography and minority student retention: Does executive team diversity influence the retention of minority students?. *Journal of College Student Retention: Research, Theory & Practice*, *11*, 459–481. https://doi.org/10.2190/CS.11.4.b

Fletcher, J. K., & Kaufer, K. (2003). Shared leadership: Paradox and possibility. In C. L. Pearce & J. A. Conger (Eds.), *Shared leadership: Reframing the hows and whys of leadership*, (pp. 21–47). SAGE.

Jones, S., Harvey, M., Lefoe, G., & Ryland, K. (2014a). Synthesising theory and practice: Distributed leadership in higher education. *Educational Management Administration & Leadership*, *42*(5), 603–619. http://doi.org/10.1177/1741143213510506

Jones, S., Hadgraft, R., Harvey, M., Lefoe, G., & Ryland, K. (2014b). *Evidence-based benchmarking framework for a distributed leadership approach to capacity building in learning and teaching*. Faculty of Social Sciences, University of Wollongong Australia. http://ro.uow.edu.au/sspapers/592/

Kezar, A. J., Carducci, R., & Contreras-McGavin, M. (2006). Rethinking the "L" word in higher education: The revolution of research on leadership. *ASHE Higher Education Report*. Wiley.

Kezar, A., & Holcombe, E. (2017). *Shared leadership in higher education: Important lessons from research and practice*. American Council on Education.

Kezar, A., & Lester, J. (2009). Supporting faculty grassroots leadership. *Research in Higher Education*, *50*(7), 715–740. https://doi.org/10.1007/s11162-009-9139-6

Kruyt, M., Malan, J., & Tuffield, R. (2011, February). Three steps to building a better top team. *McKinsey Quarterly*, *1*, 113–117. https://www.veruspartners.net/wp-content/uploads/old_articles/thst11.pdf

Mangano, K. J. (2007). *College presidents and administrative team members: An investigation of a team leadership approach to financial decision-making in liberal arts colleges* [Unpublished doctoral dissertation]. University of Massachusetts Amherst.

Morgeson, F. P., DeRue, D. S., & Karam, E. P. (2010). Leadership in teams: A functional approach to understanding leadership structures and processes. *Journal of Management*, *36*, 5–39. https://doi.org/10.1177/0149206309347376

Parker, S. K. (2007, August). *How positive affect can facilitate proactive behavior in the work place* [Paper presentation]. Academy of Management Annual Meeting, Philadelphia, PA.

Pearce, C. L. (2004). The future of leadership: Combining vertical and shared leadership to transform knowledge work. *Academy of Management Perspectives, 18*(1), 47-57. https://doi.org/10.5465/ame.2004.12690298

Pearce, C. L., & Herbik, P. A. (2004). Citizenship behavior at the team level of analysis: The effects of team leadership, team commitment, perceived team support, and team size. *The Journal of Social Psychology, 144*(3), 293–310. https://doi.org/10.3200/SOCP.144.3.293-310

Pearce, C. L., & Manz, C. C. (2005). The new silver bullets of leadership: The importance of self- and shared leadership in knowledge work. *Organizational Dynamics, 34*(2), 130–140. https://doi.org/10.1016/j.orgdyn.2005.03.003

Pearce, C. L., Yoo, Y., & Alavi, M. (2004). Leadership, social work, and virtual teams. In R. E. Riggio & S. Smith Orr (Eds.), *Improving leadership in nonprofit organizations* (pp. 180–199). Jossey-Bass.

Purser, R. E., & Cabana, S. (1998). *The self managing organization: How leading companies are transforming the work of teams for real impact.* Simon & Schuster.

Spillane, J. P., & Diamond, J. B. (2007). A distributed perspective *on* and *in* practice. In J. P. Spillane & J. B. Diamond (Eds.), *Distributed leadership in practice* (pp. 146–166). Teachers College Press.

van Ameijde, J. D. J., Nelson, P. C., Billsberry, J., & van Meurs, N. (2009). Improving leadership in higher education institutions: A distributed perspective. *Higher Education 58,* 763–779. https://doi.org/10.1007/s10734-009-9224-y

Wageman, R., Nunes, D. A., Burruss, J. A., & Hackman, J. R. (2008). *Senior leadership teams: What it takes to make them great.* Harvard Business Review Press.

Wheelan, S. A. (2009). Group size, group development, and group productivity. *Small Group Research, 40,* 247–262. https://doi.org/10.1177/1046496408328703

Wiersema, M. F., & Bantel, K. A. (1992). Top management team demography and corporate strategic change. *Academy of Management Journal, 35,* 91–121. https://doi.org/10.5465/256474

Woodfield, S., & Kennie, T. (2007). Top team structures in UK higher education institutions: Composition, challenges, and changes. *Tertiary Education and Management, 13,* 331–348. https://doi.org/10.1080/13583880701535521

Zhu, J., Liao, Z., Yam, K. C., & Johnson, R. E. (2018). Shared leadership: A state of the art review and future research agenda. *Journal of Organizational Behavior, 39*(7), 834–852. https://doi.org/10.1002/job.2296

5

A FACULTY-LED EFFORT TO BUILD CAMPUS COMMUNITY AROUND INCLUSIVE EXCELLENCE IN STEM

Amy Sprowles and Matthew Johnson

O ver the last 5 years, we have worked with many other faculty, staff, and administrators to grow a university-wide program to transform how we welcome 1st-year STEM students to campus, the region, and their academic disciplines. In this chapter, we first describe our campus context and the development of our programming. Next, we articulate the conditions that we feel gave rise to a shared leadership approach and some of the methods we used to work with a relatively horizontal leadership structure. Finally, we describe challenges and lessons learned, including recognition of missteps along the way that we hope sharing our story may help others avoid.

Campus Context

The conditions of Humboldt State University (HSU) are similar to those of many other institutions, yet the setting is also unique. In line with the national trend in higher education, the number of HSU students who are from a cultural background traditionally underrepresented on college campuses and/or are first in their family to attend college has been steadily increasing. These students, now referred to as the new majority by the American Association of Colleges and Universities, the Howard Hughes Medical Institute, and others (Schneider, 2005), has increased from 19% of the HSU 2009 student body (n = 7954) to 40% of the 2019 student body (n = 6983). Furthermore, many arrive from distant urban centers in Southern California (700–800 miles away) and the San Francisco Bay Area (300–400 miles away), places that are environmentally, economically, and culturally quite different than rural Humboldt County, California, which is both predominantly non-Hispanic White (approximately 75%; U.S. Census Bureau, 2010) and home to nine federally recognized American Indian tribes. The campus itself sits on the ancestral lands of the Wiyot, who have called the Humboldt Bay region of Northern California home since time immemorial. As the only California State University (CSU) campus situated among a large Indigenous population, American Indian scholar Vine Deloria, Jr. recognized HSU as "absolutely unique within the California State University system" (Deloria, 1989, p. 2).

HSU has a long tradition of providing support for new majority students, particularly for Native students. Beginning in 1969 with the founding of the Indian Tribal and Educational Personnel Program (ITEPP), just 3 years later, the Native American Career Education in Natural Resources (NACENR) was established to train Indigenous students for professional resource management positions in American Indian communities, federal and state government agencies, and the private sector. In 1991, the mission and programming of NACENR expanded and evolved into the Indian Natural Resources, Science and Engineering Program (INRSEP), which is still in existence today. With new upper administrative leadership and the shifting student demographic, HSU expanded the model of providing academic support in a cultural context in 2012 with the establishment of several cultural centers for academic excellence, designed to promote the individual and academic advancement of all students in a culturally welcoming environment. Despite these efforts, data from our campus continued to indicate that the campus struggled to help students from diverse backgrounds develop the self-efficacy, academic behaviors, and the sense of belonging necessary for academic achievement, particularly in the disciplines of science, technology, engineering and math (STEM). Even as late as 2015, HSU's 4-year graduation rate for incoming students majoring in STEM was 10% overall, 4% for students from traditionally underrepresented ethnicities, and 8% for first-generation students. The rapidly shifting student demographic demanded new practices and a disruption of the status quo, creating an opportunity for leaders to offer and organize a vision for change that spanned academic and student affairs divisions.

Student learning communities are time-tested high-impact practices (Kuh, 2008) that can bridge academic and student affairs. The term *learning community* is used for many different education strategies, but here we define it as a curricular approach that intentionally links a cluster of two or more courses around an interdisciplinary theme and enrolls a cohort of students (Smith et al., 2009). Although preliminary ideas for a learning community model were hatched in 2011 when HSU's then-provost sent a cross-disciplinary team to the National Summer Institute on Learning Communities at The Evergreen State College, efforts to launch a learning community stalled. In 2014, a competitive funding opportunity by the CSU system created an opportunity to pilot experimental 1st-year reforms specifically for incoming students in STEM, known as the CSU STEM Collaboratives project. We took this opportunity to pilot place-based learning communities (PBLCs) for first-time 1st-year STEM students.

Our PBLC was designed by faculty, staff, and off-campus communities to include five strategies shown to be effective in increasing diversity in STEM: (a) a summer immersion experience, (b) a major-focused 1st-year seminar, (c) peer mentors, (d) block-scheduled courses, and (e) integration of linked programming in the division of Housing and Residence Life. By designing the associated assignments and activities around scientific and social themes of our unique location, students examine how multiple disciplines can be marshaled to solve challenging social, environmental, and cultural issues faced by people from all places ("grand challenges"). Through an interdisciplinary curriculum connected to social and student support programs, we hoped to foster a sense of community and belonging for 1st-year students that enables them to see how their own life experiences relate to new peoples and landscapes, and empower them to quickly self-identify as young scientists in their discipline. We also hoped that if students could recognize the relevance of basic introductory science courses to pressing civic and environmental issues, they would be motivated to excel in their coursework and retain in STEM.

Why a Shared Leadership Approach?

When the CSU launched the STEM Collaboratives program, they did it in a manner that demanded a commitment to institutionalization. This was such a priority that the call for proposals was circulated specifically to CSU campus administrators. It was a casual conversation with the HSU Sponsored Programs Office that alerted us to the opportunity. As two STEM faculty members with shared interests in interdisciplinary education; a passion for empowering students from diverse backgrounds; leadership experience with undergraduate training programs (NSF REU, NSF URM, HHMI, LSAMP, and CIRM Bridges); an eye for external funding opportunities that could be leveraged to advance inclusive student success; and a history of collaboration to advance such efforts, we immediately identified the potential. We presented a proposal to pilot a PBLC for first-time 1st-year students majoring in the natural resource and biological sciences to our dean and vice provost. They gave us the green light to work with the HSU-sponsored programs director to submit a proposal. Along with seven other CSU campuses (Kezar & Holcombe, 2017), HSU received funding, and preparations to launch our first pilot learning community began in earnest in spring 2015.

We worked with faculty, staff, and partners from the Karuk and Yurok Tribes to design a PBLC focused on environmental and social justice issues of the Klamath River Basin, an area strongly associated with our region. Since the initiative was grounded in curricular improvements and emerging best practices in STEM education, it was essential to incorporate new ideas that would engage faculty and propel change in academic affairs. At the same time, the scope of the program required diverse leadership from multiple campus departments and divisions in student support services as well as partnerships with scientists, cultural practitioners, and leaders of our local Tribal nations. We were fortunate to be working in a climate where improving student academic outcomes, especially for students from historically minoritized backgrounds, was a campus priority. This allowed us to quickly assemble a core leadership team composed of faculty from multiple academic departments, leaders of student success initiatives in student affairs, HSU administrators, and Tribal partners interested in improving outcomes for their communities.

Our hope was that if there was sufficient evidence that our pilot PBLC was improving student academic outcomes, retention, and graduation rates, university administration would support the transformation of the 1st-year experience to include a PBLC for all STEM students. As the culture of scientific research promotes collaboratively developed experimental designs tested by multiple laboratories of related disciplines, we instinctually took a horizontal approach to leadership that began with a collective visioning of the project that included rigorous assessment. We then reached out to assessment professionals in student affairs (then called Office of Retention and Inclusive Student Success) and HSU's Office of Institutional Effectiveness (then called Institutional Research) to identify the metrics we should use to assess various dimensions of the program. This resulted in efficient real-time analyses that produced preliminary evidence that the program was helping 1st -year STEM students achieve a sense of belonging and retain in the program into their 2nd year. These data coupled with the overwhelmingly positive experiences reported by the Klamath Connection community of faculty, staff, administrators, and Tribal partners generated the collective will required to not only continue but grow the program.

Our leadership team partnered extensively with the dean of our college and department chairs to refine a vision that was ultimately financed by two external grants (U.S. Department of Education Title III Hispanic-Serving Institution grant and HHMI Inclusive Excellence award). As the programming grew, we established a steering committee composed of key administrators, staff, and a few faculty, and we created subgroups responsible for different dimensions of the project. By employing a distributed leadership model, the design and implementation of the PBLCs benefited from the expertise of individuals who specialized in a wide range of areas including first-time student experiences, housing, tutoring, registration, library resources, Native American studies, and different STEM disciplines relevant to local scientific, environmental, and social justice issues. Five years and literally hundreds of participants later, all first-time 1st-year students in the HSU College of Natural Resources and Sciences have the option to participate in a PBLC.

Building Capacity

Growing from an opt-in pilot program in 2015 for 63 students in specific majors and funded exclusively by an external grant to a program with five opt-out PBLCs for all incoming STEM 1st-year students (approximately 400 students) funded predominantly by the institution by fall 2021 required building support and capacity quickly and across many areas of the institution. Our approach involved incremental growth in the number of people involved, a comparatively horizontal leadership structure, establishing communities of practice, forming a steering committee comprised of key administrators, and a deliberate "hump shape" in staff and financial support.

Our work began with hiring a single staff person whose role spanned design, implementation, communication, and clerical duties. We grew to include additional staff, dividing responsibilities accordingly, peaking with four full-time and one part-time staff members, while shifting most design responsibilities to faculty teams. The first staff person hired has remained with the program through all phases, and their role has been elevated to a PBLC director. The growth trajectory of staff paralleled the increase in learning communities, which were added at the rate of one per year: Stars to Rocks (for chemistry, physics, and geology majors) in 2017, Rising Tides (for marine biology and oceanography majors) in 2018, Among Giants (for biology, botany, and zoology majors) in 2019, and Representing Realities (for math and computing science majors) in 2020.

In order to plan the design and implementation of each new PBLC, a lead faculty member was identified to serve as a faculty coordinator by the project principal investigators (PIs), the PBLC director, PBLC staff, and the deans of the college. The faculty coordinator received approximately a full course release each semester of the academic year prior to the launch of the PBLC so they would have the time to plan the program. The faculty coordinator's first duty was to identify campus and off-campus partners to join the full PBLC planning and development team. In most years, their work began at the National Summer Institute on Learning Communities at The Evergreen State College a full 15 months before welcoming their first cohort of students. Attending these institutes achieved the immediate objective of educating and empowering the PBLC team to build the foundation from which they would design the activities and curriculum associated with their theme. Once a new learning community was launched, the faculty coordinator continued to receive release time. The rest of the team of faculty were able to claim pay for the hours spent running the program.

The regular meetings of the PBLC teams helped bond each group together and establish a commitment to pursuing the lofty goals of cohort-based, academically themed learning communities. As PBLC team members continued to work together in subsequent years, "communities of practice" coalesced around a shared vision of implementing a PBLC and bonding over the triumphs and challenges therein. As cross-PBLC subgroups emerged around specific dimensions of the program (e.g., summer immersion, 1st-year experience, service learning, culturally responsive pedagogical practices), additional communities of practice began to emerge. These were all connected through periodic events that brought everyone involved in the PBLCs together to build community. In the beginning, we hosted "happy hour" social gatherings for faculty, staff, and administrators. These first events were not intended to discuss much content or make decisions; rather, their tone was social and aimed at celebrating the initiation of the project and some its earliest success. As a sense of community grew and the work enlarged, we began to hold periodic retreats to share data, discuss progress, and strengthen the community. Over time, these sessions evolved to also include discussing important themes like Native American Traditional Ecological Knowledge or student inclusivity in field settings. Initially these events were organized mainly by PIs. Once the practice was established, this responsibility shifted to PBLC staff and key faculty. Five years later, the PBLCs are run by seven faculty coordinators working with staff in a largely horizontal and dispersed leadership model. With this expansion in leadership, our role as PIs in designing and implementing the PBLCs has significantly retracted; we are now focused more on institutionalization, staff supervision, and assessment and dissemination.

We invited key administrators to join the PBLC development teams at The Summer Institutes for Learning Communities so they could learn about the potential of learning communities to meet vital institutional goals of retention and inclusive student success and be partners in covisioning the future of the program. This increased understanding of learning communities as a high-impact practice coupled with the perspective of administrative leadership enabled fairly rapid adjustments within university divisions essential for the success of our program (enrollment management, communication, facilities, registrar). These administrators and others were invited to be part of a steering committee that would meet regularly to discuss the progress of the program, review evidence of effectiveness, coach us through difficulties, and guide us toward a model the campus could ultimately sustain.

The incremental growth in work, people, and costs was designed to be *hump shaped*, meaning growth should be rising in early years, peak in middle years, and diminish in the last years of a 5-year grant-funded timeline, owing to both a relaxation of work as the program evolved from a "develop & design phase" to a "sustain phase," and to a gradual shift in the ratio of funding from external grants and institutional support. This design has been partially successful, and with approximately one more year of primary external funding, more work is needed to operationalize sustainable, less costly structures, including a reduction in faculty workload and staff support. Institutional financial backing has indeed risen each year, and staff support is scheduled to diminish as we shift from a broad and robust assessment plan involving research and external dissemination to a smaller assessment plan aimed at internal monitoring of data for a continuous improvement cycle.

Throughout this work, the two of us have held coleadership roles. Many early one-on-one meetings and traveling together to conferences afforded time and discussion to cooperatively arrive at a shared vision and, to some extent, workstyle. As noted earlier, this coleadership model emerged organically for us, and may have arisen partly out of a STEM culture of co-PIs who work on a shared research project as equal partners, with which each of us had prior experience before launching this education reform effort. We cowrote all three grant proposals (CSU STEM Collaboratives, HSU STEM, and HHMI) and technically split the lead directorship of the two larger grants between us, which provided some distinction of responsibilities and division of labor. But generally, most of our collective work has been entirely shared. As every professor who has cotaught a course understands, this design can help improve the product, but it often also means extra labor. Fortunately (or unfortunately, depending perhaps on perspective), we each committed to the tremendous time and effort the initiative has demanded.

Challenges and Lessons Learned

In our experience, it is rare for faculty to lead institutional change at the university level. While we knew this was not common practice, in our situation it seemed appropriate because the PBLCs were developed to foster community around academic discipline. We also believed faculty leadership would result in rich interdisciplinary and cross-cultural programmatic development with the depth and attention required to implement best practices in STEM education: innovative curricular design, culturally responsive pedagogical practices, and increased participation in experiential learning and research. Another goal was for program participants to cultivate a deeper sense of belonging with the greater HSU community that would ultimately lead to increased retention and academic achievement. Finally, we hoped these curricular reforms would result in meaningful personal, academic, and professional cross-cultural engagement that would assist participating students in developing an intercultural knowledge of Indigenous environmental, scientific, and cultural issues.

Achieving these outcomes required robust partnerships within existing academic departments, campus divisions, and our local Tribal communities. Our intention was to work together to covision and implement the Klamath Connection program with these partners. However, because our vision for the PBLC was grounded in building community around shared academic interests, we neglected to fully educate ourselves on the complementary efforts in campus divisions responsible for providing infrastructure that supports student success outside the classroom. These included the Educational Opportunity Program (EOP), freshman orientation, housing and residence life, academic advising, enrollment management, the learning center (tutoring and supplemental instruction), retention through peer mentoring, the cultural centers for academic excellence, the registrar's office, financial aid, and the library, which was undergoing its own transformation to provide more holistic supports to student education. In our enthusiasm to "improve" STEM students' 1st-year experience, there were times we did not acknowledge the expertise that dedicated professionals in each of these divisions had gained through their experiences working with HSU's first-time students. Were it not for their willingness to collaborate and educate us on the best practices in student support they employed, the PBLCs could not have been successful.

We also learned that our professional culture was more unique to academic scientists of our disciplines than we were aware. The manner in which we were accustomed to communicating with other faculty sometimes complicated conversations with staff and university administrators, who have slightly different professional communication styles. The academic method of multitasking between teaching and research could make it challenging for our dedicated staff to navigate our management style and timelines, which could be confusing, unclear and, in the worst cases, disrespectful. We also discovered that differences in disciplinary-specific language could complicate interactions among the PBLC faculty. For example, when educating Klamath Connection students about the role of nitrogen in the toxic algal blooms of *Microcystis aeruginosa* in the reservoirs behind the Klamath dams, it became clear that the term *limit* has a very different meaning for mathematicians and biologists. The biology faculty were using it to describe the concept of a limiting factor (Liebig's law of the minimum), or the component responsible for determining the amount of cell growth/division that could occur in the system. Our math faculty first interpreted it to mean *inhibit,* meaning if you add more nitrogen, the growth would not increase and would possibly diminish.

Perhaps the most important lesson we have learned is to ensure that the goals of all collaborators are considered when developing programmatic objectives. Six months after the launch of the Klamath Connection pilot, we began hearing concerns that the program was not in the best interest of Native American students nor our local Tribal collaborators. Student and administrative leaders in campus HSI initiatives publicly questioned why the program didn't include programming specifically to support our rapidly growing Latinx student population. Some administrators have been critical, identifying examples that demonstrated our insufficient attention to equity and cultural humility. Student testimonials regarding the microaggressions that occur from faculty to student and among students raised additional concerns about the attitudes of STEM faculty. Through continuing conversations with leaders from each of these groups as well as colleagues working to increase equity in higher education at other institutions, we restructured our approach to include stakeholder voices in the development and expansion of the PBLCs and companion professional development programming. Although we are still working to improve these dimensions of the program, our place-based curriculum has evolved so that it gives credence to the epistemological traditions of the Native people of our region, and the activities have broadened to include community service work to benefit our local Tribal communities. We are working more collaboratively with student support staff, students, and the campus

Hispanic-Serving Institution Steering Committee to identify specific needs of Native American, Latinx, and other students historically underrepresented in STEM so we can continue to improve our programming. PBLC faculty now have a better understanding of Indigenous ways of knowing, culturally responsive pedagogies, and some of the barriers faced by students and faculty of color, including the reality of systemic racism and settler colonialism in Western STEM traditions.

If we had taken more time to learn from our partners early on, develop behavior norms for communication, and understand everyone's motivations for participation, we could have avoided many of these issues. Perhaps we would have been more considerate had we not been driven by the timeline imposed by the grants funding our work. We have learned that sometimes the pace required to achieve grant deliverables can be too aggressive for collaborative efforts toward institutional change. Fortunately, we received extensive mentoring in academic leadership and cultural responsiveness through the program directors and mentors associated with two of the funding agencies that supported our work. The CSU STEM Collaboratives was guided by leading experts in higher education innovation, including all four editors of this book. Similarly, the AAC&U Inclusive Excellence Commission was a partner in the development and implementation of the HHMI Inclusive Excellence initiative. Both funders organized participants into learning communities and prescribed regular meetings for grantees that afforded the opportunity for professional development and community building. The relationships we have built among our peers and workshops focused on catalyzing institutional change (Elrod & Kezar, 2016) and Multicultural Organizational Development (MCOD; Jackson, 2006) have helped us develop the self-awareness required to recognize shortcomings in our leadership styles and provided us with some tools to help us address them.

We are now in year 6 of the 7 years the three grants provided to reform the STEM student experience at HSU. As we complete the final years of this project, we find ourselves navigating the transition from externally funded capacity-building to programmatic institutionalization. Since the majority of the grant dollars were dedicated to capacity-building, we are fortunate in that much of the design and implementation of the PBLC components has been completed. However, to date external grant expenses have only modestly declined, and transitioning to a sustained phase with few changes from the previous year's programming has proved elusive even for the longest running PBLCs. Recent efforts to move out of designing and into sustaining programming were complicated by the COVID-19 pandemic. The unexpected pivot to a virtual format required substantive program revision even for the more experienced teams. Our hope is that a no-cost extension on at least one of the 5-year external grants may afford additional time to achieve the sustainable structure and its corresponding reduced workload and costs.

We recognize that the university may have difficulty supporting the totality of our program as they seek to implement orientation programs for other groups of students arriving at HSU for the first time, including non-STEM 1st-years and transfer students. We are hopeful the essential elements of our robust curricular design will be maintained. The final phase of our work will require a new set of collaborations across divisions to identify the aspects of our program most critical to the improved outcomes we have described (Johnson et al., 2017; Johnson et al., 2020) and what will still be required to realize additional gains in student success, especially for historically minoritized groups in STEM. Although not an insignificant challenge, we believe the improved campus collaborative spirit coupled with an increased faculty awareness of the student experience, renewed administrative appreciation of faculty dedication to student success, and deeper relationships with our Tribal collaborators will help us find a way to institutionalize the PBLC model. More importantly, we believe this work has laid the foundation for future campus efforts to improve inclusive excellence not only in STEM education, but throughout multiple dimensions of university life.

Chapter 5 Reflection Questions

1. As you studied this case, did you see any new ways to approach shared leadership in a more equitable and socially responsible way on campus and, where appropriate, within the broader community?
2. What cross-disciplinary and community-based connections do you have now that you could draw upon to support a shared leadership approach?
3. Shared leadership draws differently upon existing institutional capacity. Are there lessons for you in the ways that HSU built the capacity to support their initiative? What resources do you already have that can support this approach to problem-solving and action?
4. This case offers insights into how the experiences of leaders affects how shared leadership unfolds. Who will be working together to lead your own project, and what can you learn from this case that might be useful as you learn how to work together with people who may see issues through a different frame than you do and who may have different goals?

References

Deloria, V., Jr. (1989). *American Indians and Humboldt State.* Humboldt Digital Scholar Center for Indian Community Development Annual 1966–2000 and Other Reports. http://hdl.handle.net/2148/1244

Elrod, S., & Kezar, A. (2016). *Increasing student success in STEM: A guide to systemic institutional change.* Association of American Colleges and Universities.

Jackson, B. W. (2006). Theory and practice of multicultural organization development. In B. B. Jones & M. Brazil (Eds.), *The NTL handbook of organization development and change* (pp. 139–154). Pfeiffer.

Johnson, M., Sprowles, A., Overeem, K., & Rich, A. (2017). A place-based learning community: Klamath Connection at Humboldt State University. *Learning Communities Research and Practice, 5*(2), 4. https://washingtoncenter.evergreen.edu/lcrpjournal/vol5/iss2/4

Johnson, M. D., Sprowles, A. E., Goldenberg, K. R., Margell, S. T., & Castellino, L. (2020). Effect of a place-based learning community on belonging, persistence, and equity gaps for first-year STEM students. *Innovative Higher Education, 45,* 509–531. https://link.springer.com/content/pdf/10.1007/s10755-020-09519-5.pdf

Kezar, A, & Holcombe, E. (2017). *Creating a unified community of support: Increasing success for underrepresented students in STEM, a final report on the CSU STEM Collaboratives project.* University of Southern California Pullias Center for Higher Education. https://files.eric.ed.gov/fulltext/ED591453.pdf

Kuh, G. D. (2008). *High-impact educational Practices: What they are, who has access to them, and why they matter.* Association of American Colleges and Universities.

Schneider, C. G. (2005). Making excellence inclusive. *Liberal Education, 91*(2), 6–17. https://files.eric.ed.gov/fulltext/EJ697349.pdf

Smith, B. L., MacGregor, J., Matthews, R., & Gabelnick, F. (2009). *Learning communities: Reforming undergraduate education.* Jossey-Bass.

U.S. Census Bureau. (2010). *Quickfacts dashboard—Arcata City, California.* https://www.census.gov/quickfacts/fact/dashboard/arcatacitycalifornia/AGE76521 %200)

6

IMPROVING STUDENT SUCCESS AND ENROLLMENT AT THE UNIVERSITY OF WISCONSIN-WHITEWATER

Susan Elrod, Matthew Aschenbrener, and Elizabeth A. John

A shared leadership model was employed to maintain momentum and expand engagement across the campus for successful implementation of the University of Wisconsin-Whitewater's (UW-W) Re-imagining the First Year (RFY) project. UW-W was one of 44 campuses across the country participating in the American Association of State Colleges and Universities' (AASCU) RFY project. The project, which ran from 2016–2018, had the goal to "dramatically improve the quality of learning and student experience in the 1st year, increase retention rates, and improve student success" (American Association of State Colleges and Universities, n.d.). The expectation was that the campus would effect change in 1st-year student success by addressing four areas:

1. curriculum and pedagogy
2. faculty and staff development
3. student-focused programs
4. institutional intentionality

UW-W had been intent on improving retention and graduation rates, particularly for underrepresented minority (URM) students, and had seen much success, reaching record rates (80% retention and 60% 6-year graduation) after 10 years of prior focused effort. However, the campus wanted to continue to improve and joined the RFY project to stimulate additional effort. Campus leaders knew that to be successful, broad engagement and leadership across campus would be required. A new provost joined the campus shortly after they began the RFY project and thought a shared leadership approach would be helpful.

In order to create a shared leadership approach, the provost and the leadership team of the RFY project initially used invitational meetings to bring diverse stakeholders to the table. From these meetings, new participants as well as new leaders were identified. New teams emerged from these interactive, collaborative, cross-campus meetings that resulted in the engagement of a broader and more diverse set of participants as well as in the generation of a novel project framework that evolved from the iterative team-based work. This framework was grounded in growth mindset principles and translated student mindsets into institutional actions that are required to, in turn, support the development of students' own growth mindsets. That framing would not have come about without the broad engagement of different people from across campus. As a result of the RFY project and others that emerged from the collaborative structure that was developed, the campus consistently reached new performance goals of retention rates between 80–82% in the ensuing years and reached an all-time record high 6-year graduation rate of 62.5%.

This chapter will also describe other benefits realized by implementing the shared leadership model, such as increased problem-solving to meet institutional outcomes, stronger group cohesion, and the development of an environment of organizational learning. In addition, the campus gained deeper and more visible engagement of formal campus leaders, empowerment of a broader group of more diverse leaders, realization of unanticipated outcomes, as well as an ability to make swift, collaborative policy decisions and to come together more effectively when faced with new challenges. We will also describe two significant challenges the campus faced in implementing a shared leadership approach: participation fatigue and impatience with the collaborative processes that a shared leadership model requires.

Inviting People to Join and to Lead

A town hall meeting commenced the RFY project and was attended by about 50 people. The provost formed a project leadership team to spearhead each of four committees that aligned with the RFY goals. The original leaders were selected from participants based on several criteria: interest in the project, expertise related to the RFY goals, time commitment, and leadership ability or potential. These leaders also consisted of a range of leader types: faculty, directors, and senior administrators. Others on campus were solicited to join the teams, based on their interest. The RFY initiative was built on a 10-year foundation of campus engagement through UW-Whitewater's LEAP (Liberal Education for America's Promise) workshop initiative.[1] Through the campus LEAP initiative, members of the community would annually form teams that focused on important university goals or themes. These teams were led by student, staff, and faculty leaders who were supported and developed as campus leaders to accomplish their project goals in alignment with campus goals. Over time, dozens of leaders were empowered through the LEAP initiative. While there was a culture of collaboration and engagement based on this long-standing LEAP program, it did not guarantee that this would extend to the newly launched RFY project.

Broadening Understanding and Maintaining Momentum

Over time, momentum and engagement by the RFY teams began to wane with only the primary leaders still focused on the project goal. During this time, there was also a transition in chancellor and provost positions. Progress had begun to slow, participation waned, and as recommendations were being made by the project team, several departments across campus expressed resistance because they were not truly engaged and perhaps did not fully understand the goals and outcomes of the project. The team leaders were frustrated that they could not gain traction on actions they were proposing. It was at this time that the new provost arrived on campus.

In order to re-energize the effort, engage more stakeholder departments across campus, and generate a broader shared set of outputs, the new provost began to put together a shared leadership approach. This started with expanding engagement and perspectives. To begin, a campus-wide meeting was held that 90 faculty and staff attended. This resulted in a significant number of new people gaining a new understanding of the project, but also an understanding of how it connected to their own work or projects. We had people join the effort who would not necessarily have been included previously, which allowed for new voices to be heard. This resulted in new coleaders stepping up organically to the leadership team, by volunteering based on synergistic interests or through selection based on expertise. Upon reflection, the decision to add coleaders was a pivotal moment of the process. This obvious signal of a shared approach cultivated an enhanced commitment and energy into the project which, in turn, deepened or in some cases shifted the course of RFY teamwork. For example, the initial focus on creating a dashboard for monitoring high DFW rate courses[2] led to conversations with newly engaged faculty leaders about gateway course redesign, which led to a new project thread that resulted in new and redesigned introductory courses.

The provost was not directly involved in team direction or support but relied on the associate vice chancellor (AVC) for Enrollment and Retention to coordinate the effort. The provost met regularly with the AVC and also the vice provost, who was only tangentially involved in the RFY project, to learn about team progress, help solve problems, and provide support. The AVC did the same with the team of leaders in each of the four areas in collaborative coordination meetings that were focused on moving project objectives forward. Team leaders, in turn, were supported to create strong project teams that could be more effective in reaching the project goals. There was a lot of communication, sharing, and support among the team leaders, which resulted in refinements of project ideas and output. Leaders of the four teams were also provided professional development opportunities, such as attending AASCU RFY conferences to further enhance their leadership as well as their understanding of the project on a national level.

One key aspect of this shared leadership approach was that different types of people served as leaders, from faculty and staff to administrators. For example, one team was led collaboratively by the vice chancellor (VC) for student affairs and a faculty leader, and other teams were co-led by faculty and staff members or staff and administrators. The team leaders, regardless of their rank or position in the university, were brought together as equals when the leadership team met with the AVC to discuss project progress, share goals or challenges, and work to move the RFY initiative forward. One of the more interesting collaborative leadership pairings was between the faculty leader and the VC for student affairs. The focus on project goals and the situation of both a faculty leader and a VC in equal roles on the team helped to mitigate any power differentials that might have existed. This particular combination of coleaders also enhanced collaboration and relationship building between academic departments and student affairs programs by creating common ground and helping overcome misunderstandings between these two sometimes very disparate units.

Expanding Understanding and Engagement

This new engagement and leadership structure fostered renewed project progress and the expansion of project teams to new people. Renewed progress and expansion led to the important realization that many people and departments across campus shared a common interest in student success but were likely working on solutions in silos and unbeknownst to campus leadership. While it was reassuring to know that so many people were committed to the same goals, there was no established mechanism to bring them together to share what they were learning, to leverage each other's knowledge, or to collaborate on common solutions. Many of these existing projects were started by faculty or staff leaders because of their interest in solving a particular student success challenge they faced in their department, but they were not connected into any broader set of university resources that might help them be more successful. Seeing this, the provost worked closely with the leadership team of the RFY project to organize an even broader convening that explicitly invited other leaders from these newly "discovered" projects to what was called a "birds of a feather" (BoF) meeting. Together, the provost, vice provost, and RFY leaders shaped the BoF meeting invitation, structure, and desired outcomes in collaborative planning meetings where all were on an equal playing field with respect to ideas and contribution. The provost would frequently take notes or synthesize meeting outputs in follow-up emails to the group. Staff in the provost's office provided support so that RFY leaders were free to do the thinking and creating required to host a first-rate convening. When everyone came together for the BoF meeting (60 in attendance), the provost welcomed everyone, but turned it over to the RFY leaders to facilitate the meeting. It was structured as interactive small group discussions with assigned table leaders either from the RFY project or the other newly discovered projects. The RFY leadership team collected the input, synthesized it, and provided a summary to each RFY team. In turn, RFY teams were again expanded to include yet another round of campus participants and additional leaders, who were now connected into this university-wide project. For example, the chair of the psychology department was leading a group of science, technology, engineering, and math (STEM) faculty to analyze reasons for students' change of major into and out of STEM programs. This group had valuable information but could benefit from inclusion in and access to the university-wide RFY effort. The circle of engagement and leadership widened with each round of invitational campus convenings, and the project continued to evolve.

The Fruits of Shared Leadership

The broader inclusion of additional project leaders together in the larger RFY project served to improve problem-solving across units and form stronger cohesion and relationships among people and departments that would not normally interact. This provided a tremendous foundation for action. For example, through our work on the RFY project, it became apparent that many students would benefit from the creation of a new campus emergency fund to assist students with short-term financial crises. This effort required different units across campus to collaborate, including the bursar, registrar, student affairs, and advancement. It grew out of the RFY initiative, in large part, because of the relationships that were built by the team leaders and teams. Once the new campus emergency fund was identified as an important priority, those involved in the RFY project worked together toward action. Tasks were shared across units that were essential for building the processes and supports to create and launch a successful program. An administrative home was found for the fund, grant funding was successfully obtained, and hundreds of students were served annually. The administrative home was one that was not originally included in the RFY project, which served to proliferate the actions and influence of the project across campus and strengthen the infrastructure required to support student success.

Because of the inclusive and evolving nature of the RFY shared leadership structure, a novel framework for focusing on one of the four RFY goals was developed. *Institutional intentionality* was one of the specified goals that the leadership team struggled to define and act upon. AASCU national leaders of the RFY project suggested a focus on using growth mindset to frame student success initiatives on participating campuses. UW-W invited David Yeager, a nationally known expert and researcher on growth mindset, to come to campus for a keynote address and workshop. Over 125 faculty and staff participated, again broadening the circle of understanding of the RFY project. As a result, a new idea for an "institutional growth mindset" framework for institutional actions was created. This framework expanded the student-focused growth mindset principles into institutionally focused ones. For example, the student-focused "persist despite obstacles" was reframed for our institution as "identify and reduce obstacles" for students. Moreover, the institutional growth mindset outlined what we needed to do as an institution to help students achieve a growth mindset. The development of this framework was accomplished in collaborative meetings with RFY leaders, the provost, vice provost, and others who were interested in contributing. Drafts were created, sent out for review, and brought back to the leadership team, and a final institutional growth mindset (IGM) framework was completed.

The completion of the IGM framework led to a campus-wide focus on reducing obstacles that impeded student success. The framework helped us approach institutional infrastructure issues at the root of some of our most persistent student success barriers. In addition, it widened the number of departments participating once again, as well as the actions we took as a university to improve student success. The application of the framework resulted in new insights into the problem. For example, the RFY project required that we regularly review specific institutional data related to 1st-year student success, where we discovered many barriers (and solutions) that cross department lines. For instance, we reduced the number of registration holds placed on a student's account that impacted access to student enrollment in classes. Our marketing department also developed a comprehensive student-focused website redesign. Our advising center and other units revamped student messaging through the growth mindset lens. We revised academic dismissal and withdrawal policies to facilitate, as opposed to impede, student progress. This policy revision was a challenge as it had been in place for years, and there were concerns that changing it would have adverse effects. It required people to come together, agree to makes changes, and assess those changes. These collaborations resulted in policy and practice changes that, in turn, removed barriers for students. In the end, our work in this shared leadership context provided a foundation for enhanced organizational learning and empowerment for people to be creative and take action.

In addition, a mentoring mindset approach was also used to engage faculty and staff in raising the level of their interactions with students. Because the team leading the development of this new mindset was co-led by a faculty member and populated by influential faculty leaders, they had the credibility to gain trust with other faculty colleagues to move this idea forward. And, perhaps more importantly, this was not an idea being advanced by the "administration" but by their faculty colleagues. This new mentoring mindset challenged long-standing views of faculty as advisers whose role it was to help students with every aspect of their academic career to one that focused on their disciplinary expertise and career guidance to help students make choices within the major and beyond into their professional lives. This aspect of the RFY project was the one being co-led by faculty and the VC of student affairs. Power differentials were equalized in this shared leadership team because of the symbiotic focus on student development and success literature and scholarship. They formed a research team to construct their project goals and outcomes. Their research explored how faculty viewed their roles as advisers and mentors. From that IRB-approved research, the mentoring mindset team developed principles and actions that could be used to put new programming in place.

Benefits and Lessons of Shared Leadership

Overall, instituting a shared leadership approach had many benefits for the campus in more effectively reaching goals to improve student success. The approach broadened the scope of people who gained an understanding of the priorities and issues students faced in progressing through our programs. The shared leadership approach provided a foundation of organizational learning that cultivated new insights, such as our IGM framework. This foundation fostered new collaborations and additional organizational learning that was important in a strategic enrollment planning (SEP) process that was launched as the RFY project was ending in 2018. Additional data analysis for SEP revealed a persistent issue with the success of students coming from backgrounds of low socioeconomic status (SES). Because we had built a wide understanding of the RFY initiative and its programs, leaders in the SEP project (some of whom overlapped with RFY) were aware of and able to tap into the newly established campus emergency fund. This new combination of leaders was able to build on RFY successes to create additional programs that further addressed economic disparities among our students, such as a program focused on providing more resources and support to former foster youth. The foster youth project brought advancement staff to the leadership table as partners in program design in order to facilitate fundraising to support the new program.

The senior leadership of campus was already engaged and supportive, starting with the RFY project. However, visible support of senior leaders was critical to maintain momentum and effective engagement of team leaders throughout these intensive projects. The provost, vice provost, associate vice chancellor, director of First Year Experience, and others were consistently and visibly present in every aspect of the effort described previously, making sure the RFY team leaders had the support and resources they needed to do their work. This took the form of promoting as well as attending campus workshops and events, sponsoring conference attendance by those involved, attending conferences with faculty and staff leaders, regular campus communications about the project, and recognition by top leaders of project accomplishments and those leading the effort.

Along the way, the provost and vice provost also served as coaches for team leaders, helping them stay on track, suggesting mechanisms for overcoming barriers, and instilling confidence in their leadership. These formal administrative leaders empowered others to lead, a practice that is not always easy for someone with a title and the corresponding responsibilities to do because it requires letting go and giving the appointed leaders the time and support to do their jobs. It is critical that leaders are self-aware and able to check their egos as they focus on letting others step forward and lead. It also requires patience because new leaders are still learning and perhaps facing additional challenges (e.g., influence, scope, resources, etc.), and thus may take longer to get things done or make mistakes as they encounter new challenges. Having the title of provost means you command more authority (and have more responsibility), so it is tempting to just use that authority to get things done. In a shared leadership model, those with this authority must redirect their efforts to cultivating the leadership skills and talents of others.

In addition, the outcome may differ from what you thought or would have enacted yourself. Leaders working to empower others in a shared leadership approach must come to grips with the fact that different outcomes (many times better ones) may result when you give people the space to lead in their own ways. It is also possible that less than satisfactory outcomes may result. This is when the senior leader needs to work with the team to examine potential setbacks and how to recover. This may require re-articulating project expectations or goals, checking for shared understanding, examining team dynamics, assessing staffing or support levels, or ensuring adequate resource allocation and other aspects of the environment in which the team is operating. Checking in with team leaders regularly is important to provide support and advice. Those who are shepherding the shared leadership system cannot just establish it and then leave it alone, hoping for positive results just because of its establishment. It must be nurtured.

Sharing the leadership responsibilities is another important aspect of shared leadership. This means no one leader plays a solitary leader role, but that a system of leaders works together to address complex, institution-wide goals. At UW-Whitewater, this system of leaders emphasized broad engagement, multiple perspectives, collaboration across the organization, and empowerment of all types of leaders to help them make significant progress on a number of core institutional objectives. As a result, the retention and graduation rates at UW-Whitewater continued to reach new heights, improving the university's performance on these important institutional goals.

We also realized unanticipated outcomes that resulted from engagement and trust-building across campus. The website redesign is a particularly noteworthy effort, as it was conceptualized by the university marketing department as an outcome of attending the growth mindset workshop. They attended the workshop based on the campus-wide invitation and learned important information about the RFY project goals that included the barriers facing students. They reached out to the RFY team to learn more and to join, in essence becoming new leaders in the RFY project. They were empowered to quickly undertake a comprehensive website redesign in collaboration with the admissions department on a fast timeframe to coincide with their recruiting cycle. The departments formed common ground, collaborated on shared outcomes, and co-led the website redesign. Their shared success in this project resulted in stronger cohesion between marketing and admissions that lasted beyond the project. In fact, our marketing staff became leaders in other student success projects, continuing to make significant contributions in new and more constructive interactions across campus. Members of their staff were more regular committee members on other projects that grew out of RFY and were active participants in the campus SEP process. Due to the relationships forged from this approach, more departments consulted their staff for support on marketing and website redesign projects.

During our engagement in this project, we built trust and confidence, making it easier to address critical issues of policy. For example, in our review of policies that may impede students, one of the RFY teams discovered an academic dismissal policy that was not consistent with our new IGM framework and thought it should be revised to improve persistence. The RFY leadership team, with support from the provost, was able to quickly mobilize the Faculty Senate Academic Policy Committee to provide data and support for constructing a revision to the policy. Because many of these faculty, staff, and administrators had spent so much time together in RFY team meetings, getting this task accomplished was not as difficult as it might have been if we had not already built these relationships. It took just a few meetings of the Academic Policy Committee for the RFY team to share information and data, answer questions, and empower the committee to come up with a reasonable solution. In the process of deliberating about this potential policy change, people questioned who had the authority to approve the change if that was the decided direction. A policy like this had not been changed in so long, nobody was sure! Instead of saying, "we cannot make the change," or "we do not have the authority so we will not do it," the group was empowered to figure out the authority and process so they could take the leap on this bold policy change.

In addition, the shared leadership structure we established in the RFY project served as a model for our new SEP effort. Because we had provided a foundation of trust and showed that working together created positive outcomes, people more readily joined this new effort, with team leaders and empowered teams focused on broader enrollment goals. During our RFY and SEP work, the campus was additionally challenged with a new restructuring initiative that was undertaken by the University of Wisconsin (UW) system. In 2019, we were to receive a nearby 2-year campus as a new branch campus in an intensive 18-month merger process. All of the efforts to engage people across campus made it easier to bring people together in this new initiative, although there were still challenges in combining two different campuses to become one. Because a foundation of trust was already in place, we were able to form a collaborative leadership structure with a leadership committee and several task-focused teams to grapple with the myriad of difficult issues required to combine the cultures, policies, and programs of two very different institutions.

Shared leadership began with the LEAP initiative and a stronger foundation for it was established over successive rounds of engagement in the RFY and associated projects described previously. Moving ahead with subsequent initiatives, some by design and others by directive, still took persistence, patience, and positivity by the provost, vice provost, and other senior leaders even with this fortified shared leadership foundation. A shared leadership effort does not always have to be led by senior administrative leaders, but someone has to be mission-focused, set priorities, and read the disposition of the campus environment in order to manage the tempo and pace of the kinds of complex problem-solving processes best suited to using a shared leadership approach.

Challenges

The campus faced two major challenges in implementing this approach. One of the most evident was participation fatigue. We had so many people engaged in RFY, SEP, and other projects that it became difficult to ask people to engage with other new projects or initiatives. So while our efforts developed a new and expanded leadership and engagement structure, they limited the university's ability to address other issues and challenges. Leaders should be careful to implement this kind of intensive shared leadership structure only for more complex, multidepartment, cross-campus initiatives that represent core goals and outcomes. It was also challenging to maintain the comprehensive collaborations required for inclusive and sustainable success in some aspects of the RFY project. The RFY leadership team had to be sensitive to the timeframe under which team members could get work done as well as what they needed to be successful. For example, in the SEP process, we had to revise the timeline to adjust for faculty engagement on the SEP teams. In response to expressed concern with the expedited timeline, we made adjustments that extended the length of the project.

Relatedly, another challenge was for everyone to realize that it takes significant and dedicated time to implement the ideas and plans that were developed by shared leadership teams. It took nearly a year to implement growth mindset principles into our comprehensive communication plan for incoming students; however, other departments such as Admissions, University Housing, and First Year Experience were able to implement the growth mindset framework more rapidly. The latter departments had leaders who were regularly engaged in the RFY project, which may explain their faster uptake. Sustainable implementation of new strategies requires that new leaders are continually being recruited and developed. It is also incumbent on those involved in a shared leadership system to remain committed to the principles of shared leadership as they work with new leaders. A cycle of consistent leadership development, perhaps in a university-wide program, would help to keep building the bench of leaders who are prepared to engage and step up. Further, development of leaders as managers who can effectively implement strategies recommended by project teams is also important. This commitment could help sustain shared leadership processes long term.

Conclusion

Engagement in the RFY project at UW-W enhanced the university's focus on student success and provided an additional opportunity for deepening its culture of shared leadership. Positive project outcomes were achieved, and many new benefits were realized that continue to serve the campus in the current challenging environment.

Chapter 6 Reflection Questions

1. As with many other campuses, the shared leadership journey in this case was full of stops and starts and team formations and re-formations. How did the iterative nature of the process at UW-W help them construct a more effective shared leadership process? What were some of the challenges of this constant tweaking and readjustment?
2. What processes do you have in place at your institution to monitor the effectiveness of a project or leadership process? How might you build in reflective or evaluative time to ensure that shared leadership is working effectively?
3. How did the UW-W team deal with hierarchy and power differentials in their shared leadership efforts? Do you have other ideas for how some of these concerns might be minimized if people from very different places in the formal hierarchy are leading together?

Notes

1. LEAP is an initiative of the Association of American Colleges & Universities (AAC&U).
2. Courses with high rates of students receiving a grade of "D," "F," or withdrawing from the class ("W").

Reference

American Association of State Colleges and Universities. (n.d.). *Re-Imagining the first year of college.* https://www.aascu.org/RFY/

7

CREATING A SHARED LEADERSHIP APPROACH TO MANAGING A COLLEGE OF LIBERAL ARTS AND SCIENCES

Fletcher Beaudoin, Matthew Carlson, DeLys Ostlund, and Todd Rosenstiel

Higher education is rapidly changing, facing increased scrutiny from society, disruptive learning technologies, and changing student demographics. This forced evolution will push many universities to reexamine and potentially transform their organizational structures, including institutional leadership models. This case discusses an example of shared leadership that recently emerged in Portland State University's (PSU) College of Liberal Arts and Sciences. Just prior to fall term 2018, the college's dean left PSU to take another position. Although the provost appointed one of the associate deans to be interim dean, all three associate deans made the decision to implement a shared leadership model for executing the functions of the dean. The associate deans saw challenges with both the single decision-maker model within the college, particularly with respect to capturing diverse views and approaches, as well as fundamental issues of overall workload as a result of the dean leaving. These factors (and others) drove their interest in adopting a different approach to leadership. Spreading the dean leadership functions across three people required the team to embrace a series of changes with regard to how they communicated, made decisions, and engaged with the college and campus communities. This case provides a unique and honest assessment of the experience so far, including both the challenges and successes from implementing shared leadership in a large college of liberal arts and sciences, and offers some aspirations for the future.

The Context for the Shared Leadership Journey

The college of liberal arts and sciences (CLAS) is the largest and most complex of the eight schools and colleges at PSU, accounting for nearly 40% of the budget of the Office of Academic Affairs, which oversees all colleges at the university. CLAS has a budget of $65 million and more than 600 instructional faculty, staff members, and graduate assistants spread across 24 academic units from three major divisions: natural sciences, social sciences, and humanities. The size and complexity of CLAS make it uniquely challenging to manage.

The shared leadership journey began in January of 2016, when the dean of CLAS selected her three associate deans. The group had never met each other prior to their appointment to the dean's office. CLAS had experienced a high turnover in its leadership; this dean was the fifth person to assume the deanship in a 5-year period.

The dean assigned each associate dean separate primary areas of responsibility: research and graduate programs, enrollment management and undergraduate programs, and faculty affairs. This new structure meant that department chairs/program directors would interact with all three associate deans depending on their needs. This structure allowed each associate dean to specialize and introduce improvements to the processes overseen by the dean's office (e.g., curriculum review) as well as to develop new programs, such as promotion and tenure workshops and graduate student training. Through these improvements, the perception of the dean's office changed from being seen as punitive to being seen as a central resource for support, slowly gaining the trust of department chairs and faculty college-wide.

Each of the associate deans came from one of the major divisions of the college. The team recognized that this diversity of disciplinary expertise allowed them to bring different perspectives to their work. For example, the associate dean who comes from a biology background conducted his research and teaching in a lab setting; the associate dean who has a Spanish literature background had a deep understanding of humanities scholarship and teaching; and the associate dean with a sociologist background had been doing research and teaching with the college's social scientists for years. The diversity of perspectives represented by the three associate deans, combined with their different functional areas of responsibility, gave them broad coverage of the college.

The dean collaborated with the associate deans and the assistant dean for finance and administration as a team. The team met regularly to discuss management issues, and each member was empowered to make decisions within each of their areas of specialization. However, the CLAS dean's office remained a traditional, hierarchical leadership model in which major decisions, especially budget decisions, were made solely by the dean. Nonetheless, the unique staffing make up combined with the frequent team meetings set the stage for shared leadership in CLAS.

On the same day in July 2018, the dean and the assistant dean for finance and administration both announced that they would be leaving the university. This happened at the same time that a search had just been completed for both a new provost and a new vice president for research and graduate studies and the new president had been at PSU for only a year. This substantial level of administrative turnover at PSU had created a significant amount of campus chaos. In this context, the three associate deans immediately began meeting together to strategize and develop a plan for moving the leadership of the college forward. The associate deans initially identified and absorbed the dean duties that aligned or overlapped with their existing portfolios. Building on that foundation, the associate deans then discussed and eventually adopted a shared leadership approach as the overarching framework they would use to manage the college. The associate deans already had some of the factors in place that would support a coleadership model: trust from having worked together closely, a common understanding of the core issues and opportunities facing the college, and complimentary (and diverse) skills and perspectives. The shared leadership research document titled *Shared Leadership in Higher Education: Important Lessons from Research and Practice* (Kezar & Holcombe, 2017) was a guiding document that the associate deans used to understand the factors that go into a shared leadership approach. It had not been intentional, but the decision of the outgoing dean to create three associate dean positions with distinct portfolios and to work with them as a team had set the stage perfectly for a shared leadership model to naturally emerge.

Building the College's Shared Leadership Approach

Once the decision was made to use a shared leadership approach for running the college, the associate deans engaged the help of a team coach. The team had familiarity with the coach they chose; he was the associate director in a PSU-based institute. The associate deans and the coach had the first team meeting in August 2018. At this first meeting, the group came up with the title of "dean team" to punctuate the collective effort to lead the college. At that point, the assistant dean for finance and administration had left PSU.

The dean had begun to transition to her new position and was often absent from the dean's office.

The dean team and the coach held 1.5 to 2 hours of space in the calendar each week to grow the new team structure. The approach integrated the following pieces:

- **Grounded in shared leadership.** A variety of resources around shared leadership were brought into the dean team consciousness early in the process and was used heavily throughout the 1st year (Kezar & Holcombe, 2017; Wexler, 2016). Specifically, the shared leadership guide (Kezar & Holcombe, 2017) was critical for thinking about team structure, communication, and overall strategy. The guide also confirmed areas of strength that were already latent in the team, such as the existing trust across the different members.
- **Strengths-based assessment.** At the start of the journey, all of the team members took the Gallup strengths-based leadership assessment (Rath & Conchie, 2008), which provides data on the innate talents that each team member had and also the places where they needed support. Strengths-based leadership is grounded in the idea that there is a multitude of types of leaders and that great teams are constructed by complementary perspectives and assets. This assessment created a foundational understanding of the unique strengths of each dean team member, providing critical data to inform conversations about roles and responsibilities.
- **Individual meetings.** The coach also met periodically with each member of the dean team to ensure there was a space for each person to fully share their individual ideas and concerns, which can sometimes get lost or not fully expressed in team meetings. These individual conversations were also a place for the coach to better understand the individual priorities and areas of growth. The information from the individual conversations provided space for each team member to think deeply about their interests and motivations so they could more fully articulate that in the meetings. It also provided the coach with a depth of information about each team member that would prove useful for breaking down unhealthy team dynamics and creating more space for individual and team growth.

To sum it up, the shared leadership document (Kezar & Holcombe, 2017) provided the road and the guardrails for the journey, strengths-based leadership informed the team's positioning in the car, and the individual meetings ensured that the individual voices from each member could be clearly heard.

The Phases of the Shared Leadership Journey

The CLAS shared leadership journey can be divided into four distinct phases, each of which represents a period marked by unique activities, successes, disruptions, and challenges. Each phase also uniquely exemplifies a number of the distinct advantages associated with implementing shared leadership in higher education.

Phase I: Takeoff (August 2018 Through November 2018)

This period is defined by the design of a shared leadership approach, one of the associate deans being appointed by the provost as the interim dean, wrestling to understand how to manage a $65 million budget, and the search for a new senior fiscal officer.

There were two major challenges that defined this period. First was the college budget. Neither the assistant dean for finance and administration nor the dean met with the associate deans prior to their departure to review the college budget. This created a steep learning curve to overcome. A search for a new senior fiscal officer began immediately; to fill the gap in the near term, the dean team identified a team of existing finance staff in the college that could help take on some of the fiscal management roles. The dean team and the existing finance staff worked closely to get a grasp on the budget, in the process clarifying that, although costs were rising rapidly, the allocation from the university was going to remain the same. This work was happening in the fall of 2018 in preparation for college-wide conversations in winter of 2019 and finalizing the budget by the end of spring 2019.

The second major challenge of this takeoff phase was negotiating the new shared leadership model within the confines of the traditional, hierarchical leadership culture of the university (both the historical structure of CLAS as well as the system that CLAS leadership reported into). The dean team advocated to the provost for a shared leadership approach to running CLAS. She was fine with a team-based approach to management but preferred to have a single direct report that could participate in university academic leadership (dean-level) meetings. She chose one of the associate deans to become the interim dean with no changes to the titles of the associate deans. Although the approach was to share the work of the dean role across the team, the group was unsuccessful in advocating for equal compensation across all three of the associate deans who were participating in shared leadership.

The dean team introduced the shared leadership model at one of the monthly meetings of all of the college's department chairs, and it was met with skepticism. Many of the chairs indicated that they preferred to have one dean that could be accountable. Although that opinion was not uniform, it was clear that there was not strong internal support for a shared leadership model within the college.

Even though the team-based approach was not integrated into the leadership structure of the university or supported by the provost or, as yet, by the culture within the college, the group made a conscious decision to refer to themselves as the "the dean team" when engaging with stakeholders inside and outside of the college. This practice carried into college-wide emails, the future meetings with the chairs, and even the signage outside the door for the CLAS dean's office suite. The team was eventually accepted by the bulk of the faculty/staff within the college, with many of the department chairs using the dean team title in their communications with the team. In addition, the title of "dean team" caught on quickly among the faculty and other administrative units on campus.

Within the first few months, the dean team recognized that running CLAS was too big for the three of them and that additional capacity was needed. The first step was an evaluation of the staffing structure of the dean's office. Although CLAS is the largest college at PSU, its dean's office is lean, with only 11 staff members in addition to the associate deans. During this initial phase, two additional staff positions were added to the dean's office: a communications director and a director of student success. Both director positions were initially hired on a temporary trial basis; the permanent hires were finalized during later phases.

This period demonstrated a number of important principles of shared leadership (Kezar & Holcombe, 2017). First, although the team was not empowered by campus leaders, it was clear that many of the big budget processes and decisions were going to be left up to the discretion of the team. What the team lacked in empowerment, it made up for in its relative autonomy. Second, since accountability was often cited as a major concern for shared leadership, the team worked diligently to develop transparent accountability structures. This played out most prominently in the budget process. The team was intentional and deliberate in communicating budgetary decisions so that campus leaders within and outside of the college would have a deep understanding of how decisions were made and executed. Finally, the team was unable to create complete fairness in rewards, although the new interim dean was able to negotiate a higher salary for the associate deans based on the increased workload resulting from being without a permanent dean.

Phase II: Acceleration (November 2018 Through June 2019)

This period is defined by the dean team (now including the new senior fiscal officer) being in place and starting to make significant progress. It also includes the necessity to cut more than $2.5 million from the budget at a time of significant campus uncertainty. This uncertainty was due to the resignation of PSU's president under a cloud of accusations of unethical behavior and a sudden leadership change as the board of trustees named an interim president. During this period, a shared leadership and higher education expert was also brought in as adviser to the shared leadership team.

The team continued with the day-to-day business of the college, and the budget became an increasingly prominent part of the work. The team was committed to being transparent in budget decisions. A tool for accomplishing this was to develop a dashboard that included financial data (budget and grant productivity), enrollment data (undergraduate and graduate), and academic outcomes (time to degree and graduation rates). The team also developed budget reports that detailed rising costs, declining reserves, and the remaining delta between the two. Department chair meetings were increased from once a month to once a week in order to share in real time the information received from the university budget office and the team's budget calculations. In short, the team created a highly transparent budget process that was used to gather input from and share decisions with department chairs. During this time the team met weekly, and sometimes more often, to review data and make decisions about budget cuts. At the end of this process, the team achieved deep budgetary reductions, including defunding four low-performing graduate programs and not refilling a large number of faculty positions. These reductions were extremely difficult both in terms of the complexity of information and potential impacts to deal with, but also the emotional toll they took on the team. For the first time in recent college history, cuts were not made across the board but rather sought to protect high-performing programs and consider student success outcomes. During this time, the team also made a number of small investments in graduate studies and research in areas of growth.

At the end of this process, the team developed a budget presentation that highlighted all the cuts and described the data and process used to make the cuts. In the spring of 2019, the dean team visited every academic unit in the college—in what they called a budget road show—to talk with the faculty about the realities of the budget. One of the intents of this road show was to emphasize transparency and the team-based approach to every unit in the college. These faculty meetings were incredibly valuable. Not only did they create considerable goodwill across the college, they also provided the team with important insights into the individual units of CLAS. It was an enormously time-consuming and highly emotionally taxing effort. Even departments that disagreed with the decisions and were upset by the suggested changes often thanked the team for the transparency and emphasis on collaboration. The departmental budget road shows were successful precisely because they were implemented as a team. In each presentation, the team modeled the collaborative nature that defined shared leadership, providing an opportunity for faculty across the college to see what a true team-based approach looks like.

This phase demonstrated a number of the advantages of shared leadership. The team agreed on the shared purpose and goals necessary to make the needed cuts while protecting departments that were growing and prioritizing student success. Strong accountability structures were created by agreeing to make all decisions together through consensus and agreeing on shared criteria for decisions. The team worked together to clearly communicate with CLAS departments about the criteria and the rationale behind decisions. Feedback and conversations were welcomed, and the team provided each other with critical support and guidance as they embarked on these reeling and taxing conversations.

Phase III: Turbulence (June 2019 Through March 2020)

Phase III was the period of greatest disruption to the team. It is defined by a national search for a new permanent dean of the college, the medical leave of a member of the dean team, and the suspension of the shared leadership model.

The provost's decision to conduct a national search for a permanent dean required that the team decide how to proceed with the shared leadership model. Some faculty members and department chairs in the college expressed a strong preference to keep the team in place. They wanted the stability and institutional knowledge and commitment the team represented. Between the three members of the dean team, there is over 50 years of experience at PSU. Other faculty, as well as some vocal department chairs, had a preference for an external dean. Those members put some degree of blame on the dean team for faculty lines not being filled and other budgetary challenges that had been faced during the previous year.

The team discussed the possibility of applying for the dean position together but recognized that a team application would probably not be taken seriously. Instead, the conscious decision was made to deconstruct the team and to put the interim dean forward. For the foreseeable future, the team focused on his success as a dean candidate. The team stopped using the term *dean team* and lifted his voice up, particularly at monthly meetings with department chairs. During this period, the team shifted the use of the coach as well. The coach now met with the associate deans individually, supporting them in their individual portfolios but not as a team.

A not surprising by-product of these decisions is that the group functioned less and less as a team, and overall college leadership suffered. By this time, the team had already defined their respective roles, and each person focused more and more on those individual responsibilities.

Midway through the search process, the interim dean made the decision to withdraw from the national search. He did so with the expectation that the college would find a highly qualified external candidate who could bring new perspectives to leading CLAS. The extended medical leave of a second member of the dean team coincided with all of the on-campus portions of the national search for a permanent dean. Although four candidates were brought to campus, none of them was ultimately hired, and the national search for a permanent dean was declared a failure.

The sudden absence of the team's well-established shared leadership structure served to highlight its advantages even more. During this trying and turbulent period, the interim dean took on the day-to-day responsibilities of the college as a traditional hierarchical leader. He quickly missed the perspective and wisdom from shared leadership. Decisions were difficult to make without the team and with accountability weakened. Emotional appeals made by department chairs for resources were more likely to result in classical "deal-making" to support an individual faculty member or provide resources for a favorite program. As a team, the group had held each other accountable through setting shared priorities and using data to inform decisions. The team was more immune to the emotional appeals of individuals and focused on making decisions that benefit the college as a whole. The interim dean felt less and less effective as a decision-maker without the team. He mentioned how the job had become noticeably more difficult and less fulfilling as the same stresses of the role returned, but the emotional and decision-making support of the team was gone.

Phase IV: Oxygen Masks Deployed (March 2020 Through Present)

This period is characterized by the arrival of COVID-19, which led to a campus closure and the need to work remotely. It also is the period of the internal dean search, in which one of the associate deans, the interim dean, and one of the department chairs were all finalists. The resurgence of team-based leadership in this period further highlighted its advantages, as it sharply contrasted with the recent turbulent period.

PSU is on the quarter system, which meant that the move to remote delivery of curriculum was not just a stopgap measure to get the university through the ending of the term but that the entirety of spring term would need to be offered remotely. The dean team immediately gathered together key people in the dean's office to form a larger team. This team included the office manager, the communications specialist, and the senior fiscal officer. The team also brought in a project manager from another part of the university to help manage the increased workflow, as well as their coach to support the team dynamics and design. This larger team met daily for a month until the immediacy of the emergency had been handled successfully. The project manager then moved on to another assignment, and the daily meetings of the bigger team were moved to weekly. The original triumvirate of associate deans returned to the shared leadership model that had been established the prior year.

The experiences of the turbulence phase, as well as the team's success in responding to the campus closure, helped team members to recognize the vital importance of the team-based approach. The realization was clear: During that phase, the team should have invested more deeply in the shared leadership approach and evolved it to meet the challenge it faced with the external search. Reengaging with the coach highlighted the critical role a coach plays in supporting the structure of shared leadership. The coach knows each member individually and as part of the team, and he provides critical course corrections that keep the ship moving forward collectively. In the absence of this critical role, no one was engaged to keep the big picture in mind and the team moving in the right direction.

With the coach reengaged, the team returned to the strengths-based leadership approach and deepened its application. Knowing that the team was at a critical point in its development, the dean team committed to a weekly team meeting and individual strengths sessions with the coach. These individual sessions allowed the team members to clarify unique strengths and areas of growth and then bring that information back to the group. The individual exploration of strengths was fuel for the team meetings—helping clarify perspectives, rethinking roles, and identifying new ways to collaborate. It also further clarified the areas where the team needed extra support. In addition, the team started to identify activities to strengthen and evolve the effectiveness of the team. For example, the very exercise of writing this chapter was used to reinforce the team, with each member assigned a different role that played to their individual, unique strengths.

Reflecting and Refueling

Leading from the middle can be a difficult, thankless job. Doing so as an interim team that was trying to fit into a traditional hierarchical organization made the shared leadership approach more difficult than it would have been otherwise. Getting the chairs to move past a department-specific mindset has also been extremely challenging, but a challenge that shared leadership is well-suited to address. Overall, the impact of the budget issues on the team cannot be overstated; those issues continue to influence how the team responds to other stressors, including the impact of the pandemic.

When the team embarked on the shared leadership journey, the goal was to change the direction of the college; however, the main outcome appears to be more closely aligned with keeping the train on the tracks. This experiment in team leadership would have been much more successful without the added challenges of serious budget constraints and lack of institutional support for the shared leadership model. These stressors (as well as others discussed before) not only affected the ability of the team to successfully engage in shared leadership but also contributed to serious stress-induced illnesses of two of the three team members. While these illnesses caused disruptions in the team's ability to work together and to get much of the necessary work done, they also highlighted and reaffirmed the foundational importance of working together as a team and of taking care of each other. All considered, our experiment in shared leadership was exactly what the college needed at this time, and despite the challenges faced the team would pursue shared leadership again.

Until now the team's focus has primarily been on managing the college through a series of challenges with little time to think about the future. Now the team is looking ahead and organizing around the inspiring future for CLAS. This time has provided critical lessons that the team has folded into a charter and set of foundational values (see Appendix 7.A at the end of this chapter). It could be argued that that this journey should have begun with a charter. However, it is only because of this journey (and the reflections on the journey) that clarity has arisen. Each of the points in the charter are based on a lesson (or multiple lessons) learned. The charter is provided in Appendix 7.A for others to consider when embarking on their own shared leadership journey.

At the time of this writing, the internal search for a dean concluded. The current interim dean and one of the other associate deans were both candidates. They both put their names in for consideration with a core goal of maintaining the team and creating an opportunity to continue the work they all started nearly 2 years before. The associate dean (not the current interim dean) was chosen as the permanent dean and began in the fall of 2020. Since one of the members of the current team was chosen, it allows the shared leadership approach to evolve and continue into the future.

Chapter 7 Reflection Questions

1. Can you identify instances of coleadership or team leadership like this on your campus? Have they been effective? What have been some of the challenges and benefits of this particular form of shared leadership?
2. What role does context play in the use of shared leadership? What does this case reveal about the challenges and opportunities that emerge during the effort to provide shared leadership of a large and complex college?
3. What challenges may arise in each stage of introducing shared leadership as an accepted leadership practice rather than as an approach to solving a particular complex problem?

References

Kezar, A. J., & Holcombe, E. M. (2017). *Shared leadership in higher education: Important lessons from research and practice.* American Council on Education.

Rath, T., & Conchie, B. (2008). *Strengths-based leadership: Great leaders, teams, and why people follow.* Gallup Press.

Wexler, E. (2016, April 6). Law school co-deans: 'Like a marriage.' *Inside Higher Ed.* https://www.insidehighered.com/news/2016/04/06/why-universities-hire-two-deans-lead-their-law-schools

Centering the success of the College of Liberal Arts and Sciences as a whole: We make decisions that center the success of the College of Liberal Arts and Sciences above everything else. In the process, we create a new narrative about CLAS both within and outside of the college. We move forward the work that needs to be done without limiting ourselves by the perceptions of others or making decisions based on fear.

Making decisions: We are accountable to each other for decisions and do not engage in individual deal-making. Strategic decisions will be made by the team. We respect each other and trust that we all are committed to the well-being of the College. We are committed to having a conversation to ensure that we fully understand each other's perspectives when we disagree. When there is a lack of consensus, a majority of two will decide.

Maintaining team health and function: We value our individual and team health above all else. To this end, we support each other emotionally and professionally. We make difficult decisions and participate in difficult meetings together. We invest in our team consistently and diligently. This is a part of our jobs, and it positively benefits the college when we are at our best individually and as a team.

Building the team beyond the team: We surround ourselves with people who are forward-thinking and center the collective good. We look to invest in and empower those who are committed to the success of CLAS.

Building the future we want: We center the inspiring future we want to build. This future is grounded in the context of where we are but not limited to or by it. While it is fine to acknowledge the challenges facing us, we do not wallow in that space or spend time making excuses.

MANY SPIDERS, ONE WEB

Distributing Leadership for Inclusive
Excellence at the University of Richmond

*Ashleigh M. Brock, Patricia Herrera, Amy L. Howard, and
Glyn Hughes with Ronald A. Crutcher, David Hale, and Jeffrey Legro*

I n 2017, the University of Richmond (UR) issued a new strategic plan
under 10th President Ronald A. Crutcher that named fostering a
"thriving and inclusive university community" (pp. 2, 4) as one of its
five pillars. Building on progress made in diversifying the undergraduate
student body over the past decade by prioritizing access and affordability,
the University identified the need to pair growing representational diversity with campus culture change to enable "students, faculty, and staff [to]
reach their full potential and thrive in an inclusive University community"
(University of Richmond, 2017, p. 4). Enlisting more than 100 faculty,
staff, students, and alumni during a 2-year span, the president charged
three groups to consider the institution's past, present, and future in rela-
tion to diversity, equity, inclusion (DEI), and thriving, which culminated
in a university report and recommendations on making excellence inclusive (University of Richmond, 2019). The report identified three critical
goals with respect to representation, belonging, and capability; outlined
an ambitious 3-year action plan; and named the university's executive vice
presidents, vice presidents, and academic deans as responsible for each
action (University of Richmond, 2019).

To advance this agenda, the university began piloting a collaborative,
shared leadership approach we refer to as the *distributed leadership* (DL)
model to advance our commitment to making excellence inclusive. This
approach aims to embed DEI broadly and deeply across our campus, and
has yielded successes and insights during its inaugural year. The DL model

apportions responsibility for and ongoing attention to the university's DEI work among the president and his leadership team—the executive vice presidents, vice presidents, and academic deans; a senior administrative officer (SAO) for equity and community, who serves on the president's cabinet and reports jointly to the executive vice presidents (the provost and chief operating officer); and the Institutional Coordinating Council (ICC) for thriving, inclusion, diversity, and equity, composed of 20 faculty, staff, and students from across the university. Together these "nodes" of the DL model collaborate to engage the campus in the ongoing work of making the UR an equitable, inclusive community.

Characteristics and Intentions of Distributed Leadership

A new and important experiment in process for the university—a predominantly White institution in the former capital of the Confederacy—the DL model centers collaboration and accountability for DEI efforts while simultaneously expanding the networks of faculty, staff, and students engaged in the ongoing work of culture change. Put simply, responsibility for attending to DEI work at UR does not fall to a single person. The president's cabinet, the deans, and the ICC—made up of faculty, staff, and students whose departmental and organizational affiliations support campus DEI work in a variety of ways—form a web of more than 35 faculty, staff, and student leaders actively driving toward our inclusive excellence goals and growing the capacity of others to contribute to our efforts. The model requires synchronous action on three fronts: first, senior university leadership focuses on the actions and outcomes of the 3-year campus action plan; second, the ICC brings together staff, faculty, and students to foster alignment, communications, and best practices for inclusive excellence across campus, while centering the longer-term vision for DEI at Richmond in its work; and third, the SAO serves as the bridge between these efforts and as a proactive strategist, advocate, and organizer catalyzing both the short-term actions and long-term planning. This multidimensional and collaborative approach is essential to align and embed efforts and practices that increase and sustain institutional coherency, urgency, and accountability for DEI work.

In adopting the DL model, we seek to address a perennial problem in higher education: Systemic DEI work becoming siloed and losing momentum because it is seen as the responsibility of a central authority or individual, rather than the responsibility of all. Inevitably efforts get derailed in the wake of evolving campus interests, crises, and leadership changes within the institutional hierarchy. These problems, as well as others associated with the ways colleges and universities traditionally approach their DEI work (Witham et al., 2015), persist and include: institutional decision-making that is insulated from the experiences and priorities of groups underrepresented in the hierarchy; default preference for short-term strategizing tied to academic calendars, strategic plans, annual rankings, capital campaigns, and the tenures of senior leaders; discontinuities and reinventions linked to leadership turnover; the tendency to compartmentalize problems/challenges so that they match the timetables and existing structural capacities; a relative absence of DEI in "discussions of 'core' management operations" (p. 34); and an overall lack of institutional urgency to propel second-order, transformative change.[1]

The shared leadership approach of the DL model seeks to address these impediments to sustaining DEI focus and efforts by introducing "new goals, structures, and roles that transform familiar ways of doing things into new ways of solving persistent problems" (Cuban, 1988, p. 341, as cited in Sturm et al. 2011, p. 9). A t-shaped distribution of leadership and accountability *across* the institutional leadership structure and *down* into departments, units, and organizations, the DL model is designed to: encourage and sustain long-range thinking, inform short-term actions; pull from a wider range of DEI expertise on campus in the process; and generate a sense of ownership for DEI goals and work within departments and units. The model is therefore intended to generate institutional capacity for pursuing transformative change in which DEI values and goals inform "not just the design of individual components...but the entire operational structure" of the university (Witham et al., 2015, p. 33). In enacting the DL model, we seek to enable equity-minded change by overcoming persistent tendencies in higher education to focus only on "boutique programs or isolated [DEI] initiatives" (Witham et al., 2015, p. 33) and instead weave DEI into the fabric of institutional decision-making on a day-to-day basis.

Building Capacity for Distributed Leadership

Distributing leadership for the work of DEI across a complex, interconnected institution requires ongoing capacity-building among individuals, departments, and leaders. In higher education, centralized, hierarchical leadership structures, often led by a chief diversity officer or vice president (and often accompanied by an advisory committee) represent the most recognizable form of DEI leadership (Leon, 2014; Williams, 2013). The summer of 2020 and a new era of civil rights activism across the United States has forced many institutions, including colleges and universities, to reexamine these structures for pursuing DEI goals to better understand their successes and shortcomings.

Building capacity for DL at UR is a fledgling and ongoing effort, but in particular, we have focused time and attention on multidirectional trust building, thought partnership and dialogue, and amplifying a diversity of voices. Putting the DL model in place was an important step, but creating the conditions conducive for practicing shared leadership is even more vital. That is, how we work and learn together in the DL model matters. A central goal of our efforts is to build a model that is woven deeply in the fabric of how the university operates and engages in collective action for change.

Trust Building

In piloting the DL model, we have found that trust building—in multiple directions—is foundational to our work and a necessary action step toward cultivating an inclusive and equitable community. Establishing and strengthening trust among DL stakeholders fosters a culture of respect for each other's talents and expertise, promotes collaboration, and most importantly, creates a stronger collective that can address the pressing social, cultural, economic, and environmental challenges we face as an institution. At present, we are focused on building relationships rooted in trust and reciprocity among the SAO, ICC members, deans, and the president's cabinet, and we are paying close attention to how we interact and work together in order to learn from each other's differences and draw upon one another's talents, expertise, and experiences.

Faculty, staff, and students engaged across the model are working side-by-side with university leaders, and vice versa, on DEI issues. In the case of the ICC and its members, colleagues—some who have worked at Richmond for many years—are being asked to reconsider notions of how DEI work on a college campus is done. Trust building within the ICC has entailed engaging its members in the coconstruction of a shared identity as a council, one that delineates their efforts from that of a typical, task-oriented campus committee and reorients members toward the long-range planning and cultural transformation work we believe is required to reach our vision. Creating bonds of trust fosters a culture of respect for expertise, a propensity for collaborative programming, and more importantly, a strong, diverse institutional team positioned to address our most pressing challenges.

Thought Partnership and Dialogue

We embrace the notion that the knotty, intersectional complexities of DEI issues we face as an institution require dialogue and deliberation that necessitate a multitude of perspectives from a range of institutional altitudes, and thus dialogue is critical to our capacity building. To practice DL means embracing the idea that all campus community members are agents in creating an inclusive culture at UR, regardless of position or discipline. The ICC actively invites individuals, departments, and units to engage the council as thought partners as a mode of working and sharing ideas, expertise, and experiences to assist in navigating complex DEI challenges. From reviewing inclusive language style-guide drafts with the university communications team to offering feedback on a draft "employee resources group program" through Human Resources to brainstorming program ideas with university museums, the ICC serves as a sounding board and a source of dialogue and information for campus partners addressing DEI challenges within their units across the institution.

Facilitating ongoing dialogues across campus on our goals of representation, belonging, and capability and how they manifest in different units was a key focal area in the DL model's 1st year. The cochairs of the ICC, in partnership with the SAO, were invited to numerous departments and offices during the 2019–2020 academic year. They facilitated dialogues with over 300 faculty and staff about how their units contribute to institutional DEI efforts, as well as identified areas of action to improve the climate within their own departments and spheres of influence. These discussions yielded rich qualitative data that have assisted us in identifying which components of our DEI agenda are best understood by the campus or feel most urgent, as well as gaps and areas that require more attention.

Amplifying Voices

Effective DL arises from participation and interactions among diverse individuals and challenges the idea that an individual leader alone can shape action. Instead, DL, by design, draws attention to the larger number of actors who contribute to the process of leadership in shaping collective action (Van Almeijde et al., 2009). Like many institutions of higher education, UR was not well-situated at the outset of our work to consider a multitude of voices in day-to-day decision-making. As such, we have made concerted efforts to amplify a diversity of voices in building our institutional capacities for DL.

In particular, the ICC is structured to magnify a range of voices, experiences, expertise, and backgrounds in its assembly and in interactions with university leaders and the broader community. Designed with the widest possible institutional representation in mind while keeping the group small enough to be nimble (20 members, including offices such as athletics, communications, student development units, academic schools, and current students), the council elevates perspectives from underrepresented groups and people with on-the-ground knowledge and expertise of DEI work in a range of university offices and academic departments, as well as via its student members. The DL model brings people from across campus engaged in DEI work together to ensure those efforts are well-coordinated and mutually reinforcing, and centers the ICC within its structure to ensure the council has direct input and influence in institutional DEI decision-making.

Our desire to listen to more voices has also created space for more candid and open conversations between university leaders and our students, in particular. For example, immediately following a spate of racist and xenophobic incidents on campus in January 2020, the president invited student leaders into dialogue with the executive vice presidents, SAO, and ICC cochairs to ensure their voices were heard quickly and their feedback incorporated into the ongoing institutional response. One outcome of these dialogues was the creation of a president's student cabinet meant to bridge the gap between students' lived experiences and institutional decision-making and ensure their feedback and opinions are shared more consistently with senior leaders. By working to amplify voices across campus, we aim to encourage and facilitate wider participation in DEI work, and to bring a diversity of ideas and experiences to bear on institutional practices, policies, and decisions in a mutually beneficial manner. In so doing, we cultivate spaces for communities of practice and collaboration on DEI efforts.

Benefits of Distributed Leadership

Although the DL model at Richmond is still in its infancy, we have begun to see some positive changes that we believe may have long-term effects on our DEI goals moving forward. In particular, distributing leadership has resulted in increased transparency and mutual understanding on DEI issues and efforts, an embrace of critical introspection as we do our work together, and the development of a team mentality that deemphasizes hierarchy and separation. We believe these benefits contribute to propelling our work forward and will help the university to embed this approach to leadership more deeply into the culture of the institution.

Transparency

Changing the way Richmond leads DEI work requires a level of administrative transparency that is perhaps atypical in higher education institutions.

As we have worked to build relationships among the nodes of the model—the president, executive vice presidents, cabinet, deans, and the ICC—we have also worked to develop new ways of communicating about our efforts. For example, in the wake of the aforementioned campus incidents that threatened DEI goals and values on campus, our approach to shared leadership encouraged us to bring *more* people to the table at the outset of crisis response, rather than a select few. Within hours of the incidents, leaders and members of the ICC, the president, the executive vice presidents, and other campus leaders were convened by our Bias Resource Team to consider next steps. Those first moments of response were messy, yet senior leaders, midlevel staff, and faculty voices from across the institution were heard and their perspectives used to inform the development of a comprehensive university response. Because participants came to the discussion open, ready to listen to different perspectives, and trusting of others, our response was faster, more cohesive, and more representative of the collective wisdom needed to respond creatively to our challenges. It is risky for institutional leaders to allow others to view "the mess" of a campus crisis in progress, but in this and other examples, we have found being more open and transparent has benefited us and created better responses and outcomes.

Clear communication with the wider community about our DEI efforts has also been critical to the early stages of the model. Built on precedent created by the 3-year university effort that preceded launching the DL model, where unredacted committee reports and documents were shared publicly on the president's website, we have aimed to share as much information as possible about our work on a public-facing inclusive excellence website. This includes painstaking work updating and revisiting our action plan and ensuring its details reflect our progress underway, even as the actions themselves evolve (University of Richmond, 2020). As other university initiatives unfold, we expect this more open and transparent way of working may positively influence our colleagues across campus to do the same.

Critical Introspection

Taking inspiration from the American Association of Colleges and Universities' (AAC&U) report *America's Unmet Promise* (Witham et al., 2015), we strive to uphold DEI practices and equity-mindedness "as a pervasive institution-wide principle" (p. 33). This means that an essential part of our DL work is critically reflecting on our practice and process in the moment (Youngs, 2017). This reflective work is a vital action. We regularly pose questions among the DL model's members, as well as within its nodes, about existing power dynamics and how power is distributed (or not), the kind of change that is needed, how we imagine change happening, and how we can enact it.

Our focus on critical introspection proved beneficial when the university embarked on pandemic contingency planning for the 2020–2021 academic year. In keeping with its charge to foster alignment, communication, and best practices for inclusive excellence, the ICC created and shared the following equity-minded guiding questions to cultivate critical introspection among the groups charged with developing plans for operations during the pandemic:

> Who benefits? Who is burdened? Who is missing? How do we know? In other words, how are the perspectives and interests of underrepresented groups centered in each aspect of the planning and the possible outcomes?

We understood the pandemic was and is disproportionately affecting people of color and other vulnerable groups, and it is crucial that our own responses serve to mitigate such inequities. In posing these questions, we sought to encourage one another to become *more equitable* in this moment, rather than backsliding on equity gains.

As we do this work, we also recognize that in practice, DL can create an illusion of participation by calling various stakeholders for advice when decisions have already been set into motion (Kezar, 2012). We are intentionally working to ensure our DL model does not become a utilitarian tool of work activity meant to simply dissolve tensions, resolve problems, or otherwise continue with business as usual. Doing so can legitimize division and exclusion and reify the inequities that we are working so hard to reduce (Bolden et al., 2009; Josyln, 2018; Youngs, 2017). Critical reflection on current actions and intentionality around future actions ensures more integrated, concerted, and supportive work. This reflexivity fosters synergies; encourages us to connect theory and practice; enables and encourages actions to be critiqued, challenged, and developed; and grounds our work in long-term cultural change. Paying close attention to how we work increases DEI leadership quality and capacity (Joslyn, 2018), and distributing leadership for DEI intentionally creates a campus social network engaged in equity-minded practices.

Cultivating a Team Mentality

One of the surprising benefits of our DL approach has been relational; across the model, we are seeing a team mentality starting to develop, where ownership for our DEI goals is truly shared, and reciprocal relationships flourish in perhaps unlikely places. Because the model involves many people and decision-making is driven by a combination of expertise, dialogue, and consensus, the work can be messy. It also requires us to constantly, repetitively communicate about what we are doing, both among the model's nodes and outward to the university community. This process of shared repetition ensures all of us, from the president to the student members of the ICC, are practicing and refining our shared message: that each person on our campus has a role to play in DEI work that is important and unique, and that our goals are for the whole institution, not just those whose roles or offices focus explicitly on DEI.

An offshoot of this work has also been the close working relationships that have developed among university leaders who might otherwise find themselves somewhat isolated from one another. For example, the DL model brings together the university's provost and chief operating officer in their shared supervision of the SAO, but it also enables them to wrestle with the intersections of DEI issues that affect faculty, staff, and students. We recognize that relationships in higher education that cross academic and operational boundaries in pursuit of DEI is unusual, and are proud that the DL model is forging more of them across, down, and among various parts of our campus. The early benefits we have seen from these developing relationships suggests the potential utility of DL designed for other purposes—such as leading strategic planning efforts or other cross-institutional initiatives.

Challenges and Reflections

We have, of course, also faced many challenges in our 1st year standing up and practicing our DL model, some from inside the university and many from beyond its boundaries. In addressing these challenges, we have also learned important lessons that may help others seeking to share leadership on critical, ongoing university initiatives.

Steering Through Crisis

Almost from the moment we announced our DL approach, we have been battered by crises, both on the campus and off. Within a few months of launching our work together, the aforementioned racist, xenophobic incidents on campus threatened to derail us by calling into question our stated goals and actions and destabilizing the ICC and campus leaders' focus on our longer term aims. Off campus, the nation and world have presented a set of almost inconceivable, interconnected challenges with major DEI implications: an unprecedented global public health crisis, a summer of continued violence against people of color, protest, and widespread civil rights activism;

an economic downturn; and a contentious presidential election. In times of crisis, it is an understandable response to demand more of institutional leaders at every level. And, our philosophical and structural approach to leading cultural change and executing DEI objectives demands both a steady hand guiding toward our long-term goals *and* the ability to re-evaluate and reprioritize in the face of crises.

We have learned, and sought to reinforce, that the ICC is not a crisis or bias response team, nor is it directly responsible for immediate action in the wake of crises. Similarly, among the university's senior leaders, we work to stay the course, rather than let campus and national crises immediately call into question the goals and actions to which we have committed. At the same time, we have also worked to remain nimble within our DEI framework, adding new action steps and reprioritizing our efforts to address the most urgent and salient needs of underrepresented groups on our campus. Of late, we have had to work even harder to stay grounded given the tempestuous political and cultural landscape in which we are situated, returning frequently and purposefully to the goals we have set as the right goals for our institution.

Communication

As we have referenced throughout this chapter, communication is critical to our work and to the enactment of DL. While we have experienced some key gains, especially with regard to transparency on DEI issues and expedient, university-wide messages in response to DEI challenges on campus and beyond it, we have also experienced missteps along the way. For example, at the outset of our work, we released a comprehensive report outlining our approach to leadership, University-wide goals, and a 3-year action plan (University of Richmond, 2019). While the report remains the keystone of our work, our failure to embed it within a comprehensive and institution-wide communication strategy has meant that enormous time has been spent—across the DL model—communicating and recommunicating our goals and planned actions. As a result, much of our 1st year was spent both trying to do the work outlined in our plan while simultaneously explaining to a range of audiences what the plan entailed. This challenge has served as a constant reminder to us to plan and overcommunicate (to the extent that is possible) about the work we are now doing.

More importantly, frequent and fluid communication within and across the different nodes of the DL model are critical for building its capacity. The SAO has proven a pivotally located catalyst for this boundary spanning work. While we anticipated the need for building intentional structural communication links, we did not anticipate the extent to which the actual practice of communicating across these boundaries has built trust and increased our collective capacity to communicate and to act.

Keeping Students at the Center

Last, we have experienced an ongoing challenge around ensuring our students' involvement and investment in our DEI work, while also navigating a desire not to overburden by engaging them in uncompensated labor on behalf of the institution; in other words, we deeply desire their involvement but believe the difficult work is ours, as faculty, staff, and administrators. This tension led to an early oversight in developing the DL model and its key nodes; we failed to imagine a permanent place for students within it. For example, when launching the ICC, we aimed to build a new structure that works differently than normative committees. We intended to add student representatives the 2nd year, once the council had solidified its structure and work. This was a mistake. Having student representation from the beginning would have made our work better, more connected, and more inclusive. The ICC now has two student representatives, and the president has since created the president's student cabinet to amplify the voices of our students in university decision-making and DEI work. The ICC student representatives are also ex officio members of the student cabinet. We will likely continue to struggle with how best to engage students in our DEI work, but these early missteps have cemented our intention to keep them at the center—in spirit, if not directly in practice—of all we are doing.

Conclusion

Early in our work together, the authors developed a shared principle that has guided us through these early and challenging days of adapting to and enacting a shared leadership approach: *We are making the path by walking it.* This phrase reminds us that we are forging new pathways together, seeking to disrupt and dismantle impediments to a more diverse, equitable, and inclusive university community, while simultaneously developing skills, capacities, modes of work, and approaches to collaboration that are new and sometimes anxiety-inducing for us and for our institution. While we have not yet "arrived," so to speak, we believe we have positioned UR to more fully embrace shared imperatives that are in keeping with our values of diversity and equity, inclusivity and thriving, and to demonstrate to ourselves and the wider community that all of us have unique and critical roles to play in pursuit of those values.

Chapter 8 Reflection Questions

1. Is leadership for DEI work at your institution broadly shared? If not, what lessons can you draw from this case that might help more leaders on your campus engage in equity work?

2. The use of DL to instill shared responsibility for a deep, cultural change within a campus community requires several steps: (a) synchronous action across several fronts; (b) structures and roles that can address long-standing and embedded problems; and (c) a focus on trust, partnership, and dialogue that includes a broad range of voices. What capacity do you have now within your institution to tackle these steps, and what initial steps might you take at your institution to create a supportive environment for collaboration at this scale?

3. How can you build trust at your institution and what challenges will you face in doing so? Are there areas you can identify where trust is clearly lacking? Or areas where trust is well-established and offers a firm foundation for collaboration or shared leadership?

Note

1. Second-order transformational change alters the culture of an institution by changing underlying assumptions and institutional behaviors, processes, and products. It is deep and pervasive, affecting the whole institution, and is intentional, occurring over time. For more, please see Eckel et al. (1998).

References

Bolden, R., Petrov, G., & Gosling, J. (2009) Distributed leadership in higher education: Rhetoric and reality. *Educational Management Administration & Leadership, 37*(2), 257–77. https://doi.org/10.1177/1741143208100301

Cuban, L. (1988). A fundamental puzzle of school reform. *Phi Delta Kappan, 69*(5), 341–342.

Eckel, P., Hill, B., & Green, M. (1998). *On change: En route to transformation.* American Council on Education. https://eric.ed.gov/?id=ED435293

Joslyn, E. (2018). Distributed leadership in HE: A scaffold for cultural cloning and implications for BME academic leaders. *British Educational Leadership, Management & Administration Society (BELMAS), 32*(4), 185–191. https://doi.org/10.1177/0892020618798670

Kezar, A. (2012). Bottom-up/top-down leadership: Contradiction or hidden phenomenon. *The Journal of Higher Education, 83*(5), 725–760. https://doi.org/10.1080/00221546.2012.11777264

Leon, R. A. (2014). The chief diversity officer: An examination of CDO models and strategies. *Journal of Diversity in Higher Education, 7*(2), 77. https://doi.org/10.1037/a0035586

Sturm, S., Eatman, T., Saltmarsh, J., & Bush, A. (2011). *Full participation: Building the architecture for diversity and public engagement in higher education* [White paper]. Columbia University Law School Center for Institutional and Social Change.

University of Richmond. (2017). *Forging our future, building from strength: A plan for the University of Richmond.* https://strategicplan.richmond.edu/common/strategic-plan.pdf

University of Richmond. (2019). *Making excellence inclusive: University report and recommendations.* https://president.richmond.edu/inclusive-excellence/report-pdfs/making-excellence-inclusive-final-report-2019.pdf

University of Richmond. (2020, March). *Making excellence inclusive. Work plan update.* https://president.richmond.edu/initiatives/inclusive-excellence/report-pdfs/mei-work-plan-march-2020.pdf

van Ameijde, J. D. J., Nelson, P. C., Billsberry, J., & van Meurs, N. (2009). Improving leadership in higher education institutions: A distributed perspective. *Higher Education, 58,* 763–779. https://doi.org/10.1007/s10734-009-9224-y

Williams, D. A. (2013). *Strategic diversity leadership: Activating change and transformation in higher education.* Stylus.

Witham, K., Malcom-Piqueux, L. E., Dowd, A. C., & Bensimon, E. M. (2015). *America's unmet promise: The imperative for equity in higher education.* Association of American Colleges and Universities.

Youngs, H. (2017). A critical exploration of collaborative and distributed leadership in higher education: Developing an alternative ontology through leadership-as-practice. *Journal of Higher Education Policy and Management, 39*(2), 140–154. https://doi.org/10.1080/1360080X.2017.1276662

9

CHANGING MINDS

Integrative Tutoring and Institutional Transformation at SUNY Geneseo

Joe Cope, Robert Feissner, Beverly Henke-Lofquist,
Gillian Paku, and Lisa Smith

The State University of New York at Geneseo (SUNY Geneseo)'s project focuses on better cohering academic support services in tutoring, learning centers, and supplemental instruction (SI) by providing common training in professionalism and ethics, cultural humility and inclusive pedagogy, mental health awareness, and metacognitive strategies. In the midst of growing institutional concern about student success and particularly retention, Geneseo has been moving to better connect siloed academic success initiatives. Over the years, grassroots efforts in several academic departments including English, math, and physics prioritized student-centered approaches to learning and had led to the development of department-based tutoring programs and other supports. In a shared leadership context, our project required finding common ground between the administrative priorities and those grassroots efforts, leveraging administrative support to identify resources and increase the visibility of programs, and empowering program coordinators to pursue strategic change.

SUNY Geneseo is a public, residential liberal arts college with approximately 5,000 undergraduates and 100 graduate students. Like many northeastern regional colleges and universities, SUNY Geneseo is responding to rapid demographic changes, a decline in college-age students, and changing student expectations regarding academic and personal support. An important part of this work focuses on maintaining strong retention and completion rates. Although Geneseo has been successful in retaining 1st-year students, the retention rate has gradually declined over the past decade.

For the 2009–2010 entering cohort, 1st-year fall-to-fall retention rates were 92.0%; by 2018–2019, that rate had fallen to 84.4%.

Geneseo's identity as one of the most selective SUNY institutions over the past 30 years has been closely tied to assumptions about a naturally talented and high-achieving student body. As a result, the college did not invest proactively to support student success infrastructures such as 1st-year seminars, a professional advisement office, or comprehensive tutoring. While some faculty are outspoken in their "sink-or-swim" attitude to student success, several stakeholders at Geneseo have gradually built out grassroots support resources. This fairly ad hoc approach has, however, meant that student success initiatives tend to be broadly dispersed and disconnected, and programs tend to guard their support services against top-down interference. The nexus between an institutional focus on improving retention and these grassroots initiatives made the enhancement of academic support services an excellent candidate for a shared leadership project.

The creation of an associate provost for academic success (APAS) in the 2017–2018 academic year enabled a single office to connect independently functioning initiatives and programs, including our four largest tutoring and academic support centers: the Writing Learning Center (WLC), the Math Learning Center (MLC), Access Opportunity Program (AOP) tutoring, and Supplemental Instruction. In fall 2017, the APAS collected information that clarified existing tutoring practices on campus and the centers' goals, including ideas for streamlining processes to reduce workload and increasing impact via a more cohesive message. Anecdotal evidence of a lack of consistency and inclusivity in some department-based tutoring programs also led the APAS to assemble a shared leadership team across the four largest student support centers to build a comprehensive, universal training course. This approach to shared leadership has many characteristics typical of Kezar and Holcombe's (2017) model. This group included a management/confidential position, three faculty with reassignments to coordinate academic support initiatives, and a full-time professional staff member. The group functioned collaboratively and was structured to allow efficient communication, alignment with campus strategic objectives, and peer engagement with critical staff and faculty allies.

One exciting component of Geneseo's shared leadership approach is that students were intentionally brought into leadership in a serious and sustainable way. Students serving in academic support roles are strong in their content area, but not all have a fully developed sense of themselves as facilitators of student learning. Some see their ability to provide a correct answer as their primary function. We wanted tutors to understand, in addition, that the professional, inclusive, and metacognitive way they enact their role is a major locus of retention. The value of our model depends on the fullness of tutors' understanding of themselves as agents of student success.

Shared Leadership and Goal-Oriented Planning

Every member of our core shared leadership, five-person team brought expertise regarding their own domain, but we all positioned ourselves as learners when it came to the best material to incorporate into our joint tutor training course. In constructing the course, we extended the shared leadership best practice of engaging multiple people through mining resources and expertise already on campus. The leadership team collaborated, for example, with the Department of Student Health and Counseling to incorporate the mental health interactive software Kognito. The college's chief diversity officer directed us to relevant readings and connected the team with the student facilitators of the Diversity and Inclusion Community Educators group (DICE) to integrate a Wokeshop on cultural humility. An adviser from the Office of Academic Planning and Advising helped us coordinate with the approach for 1st-year programs, while the APAS also brought resources from a faculty–staff learning community on student self-reflection that he had coordinated. Our student tutors were, of course, the ultimate resource: We invited the experienced tutors who were enrolled in the first iteration to digest, reflect on, and evaluate the course curriculum and format. We asked them to take on a leadership role and share their insights in the knowledge that they were effecting change.

Mirroring our own fluid roles, the tutors' ability to see themselves inhabiting a leadership role as well as their more familiar role as learners was vital to dismantling the usual hierarchies that work against a shared leadership model. This fluidity was the embodiment of the metacognitive material in our training curriculum and reflects the claim that "When students use metacognition, they become tremendously empowered as learners because they begin to be able to teach themselves" (McGuire & McGuire, 2015, p. 16). We excerpted Saundra Yancy McGuire and Stephanie McGuire's *Teach Students How to Learn* (2015) and *Teach Yourself How to Learn* (2018). Geneseo's Teaching Learning Center had recently hosted a reading series on such metacognitive strategies, as well as on Carol Dweck's (2006) concept of growth mindset—people's belief that their most "basic qualities are things you can cultivate through your efforts" (p. 7). Also linking growth mindset to metacognitive strategies, the AOP has for many years collaborated with a professor from the psychology department who, with the assistance of an instructional designer from our computing and information technology department, recorded a video on working and long-term memory functions for our project. In many ways, this broadly inclusive team, which pooled the talents and skills of an ever-widening circle of campus experts and stakeholders, reflects the principles of shared leadership planning outlined by Bolden et al. (2015) in which planning draws together

> a broad range of leaders in positions of institutional authority (termed formal leaders), employees respected for their leadership but not in positions of institutional authority (termed informal leaders), experts in learning and teaching, and formal and informal leaders and experts from various functions, disciplines, groups, and levels across the institution. (p. 17)

Just as we were encouraged by the shared leadership model to move beyond hierarchical thinking, so, too, we embraced a nonproprietary approach to intellectual property. We plan to create an instructor's guide for the nondiscipline-specific training course with tips, assessment rubrics, and FAQs so that any supervisor of peer academic mentors can adapt the course effectively. To facilitate distribution, we made our online course available in the Canvas Commons area of our learning management system, while a webpage will enable the campus community and groups beyond Geneseo to engage with our project. We will continue to present our work at events both on and off campus, taking advantage of the centralized offices—particularly the provost's office and the Office of Academic Planning and Advising—as sources of support for outreach. This multidirectional approach stresses ongoing collaboration at all levels: Student input shapes the training, faculty and staff leaders assess and improve the curriculum, and administrative staff support the project and help build institutional visibility.

Building Capacity and Engaging Allies

Prior to the shared leadership approach to this pilot, the WLC and AOP had attempted a similar coordination in 2015, inviting tutors to participate in those parts of each other's training that were not subject-specific. The attempt was mildly successful, but without support for building a truly general training course, some center-specific details inevitably crept in to confuse tutors, and we needed financial support to pay tutors to attend because the coordination exceeded our tight, individual budgets. Such support was not willingly forthcoming when we "asked up" for it, so we could only run the training once, using an unsustainable funding source. In other words, the shared understanding and desire for outcomes already existed, but nothing could come of the plan until its leadership became more horizontal across units and a better mechanism existed to communicate the relevance and importance of the project and to secure institutional funding support.

Another attempt at coherence was the creation of a Center for Academic Excellence (CAE) between 2010 and 2016, which cast a much wider net across college units, but not a more productive one. While the WLC and AOP had been unable to bring together the necessary players, the CAE had the opposite problem, with too many members but no empowered leaders or well-defined deliverables, demonstrating ably the difference between effective shared leadership and what Elrod et al. (2020) describe as "task forces that involve lots of people without clear definition of the problem or development of shared goals" (p. 1).

The CAE eventually disbanded, but more recently, in connection with a 5-year institutional strategic plan developed in 2016, senior leadership has taken steps to better cohere, support, and assess student success programming. In the 2017–2018 academic year, the provost and vice president for academic affairs repurposed an administrative line into an associate provost for academic success (APAS) position that included responsibilities in overseeing the Office of the Dean for Planning and Advising, tutoring and learning centers, and academic affairs-based high-impact practices. Additionally, the provost assembled a cross-divisional team to focus specifically on issues related to retention. Drawing on the vision for strategic change outlined in McChesney et al.'s *The 4 Disciplines of Execution* (2016), this team has met weekly since December 2017 to track progress on strategic initiatives intended to improve the college's already strong 1st-year retention rate, implement strategic change in advisement, revise 1st-year and transfer orientation, expand delivery of introductory course offerings (including 1st-year seminars), implement an early alert system, and enhance professional development. Weekly meetings make accountability for student-centered retention efforts a high priority, and monthly memos to the entire campus community keep this work visible.

The creation of the APAS position and the wider institutional focus on retention efforts set the stage for a deep connection between the administration and faculty and staff leaders of tutoring and learning centers. This reflects Kezar and Holcombe's (2017) model in which strategic change "[capitalizes] on the importance of leaders throughout the organization, not just those in positions of authority" (p. v). This coalition led from the middle in synthesizing what the president's cabinet and provost's office wanted in terms of improved retention rates with what the directors found desirable in tutoring. The provost funded our trip to the Association of American Colleges and Universities (AAC&U)'s 2019 Institute on High-Impact Practices and

Student Success, which not only helped us define our collective goals, but also created space—a retreat from distractions—for the leaders to become acquainted with each other.

Geneseo's Teaching and Learning Center generously awarded each member of the team an Innovation Grant for continuing this work. More generally, the TLC solicits and hosts workshops that clearly signal the campus's openness to experimentation, and it routinely offers opportunities for faculty, staff, and administrators to come together around topics of interest so that forming a shared leadership group is an easy step from the many reading groups or interested parties that convene regularly.

A further important aspect of institutional support is recognition of this work as valuable service to the college and an acknowledgement that this work is valued by not just the SUNY Geneseo administration, but also by the faculty members' and professional staff's department supervisors, personnel committees, and colleagues as evidence to be considered in performance reviews and to be included in promotion portfolios.

Integrating Academic Support Services

Our central achievement was to create and run a pilot version of the tutor training course by the start of the fall 2019 semester. Every collaborator's contributions were integrated, and we were able to enroll—and pay—all the tutors. The various emphases of the shared leaders dovetailed: retention, student success, the streamlining and coordinating of resources (and reducing workloads), the ability to advertise services more broadly because of invitations to participate in campus-wide events, higher campus recognition for tutors, tutors gaining valuable tools, and students benefiting from tutors being more alert to the whole student.

Overall, we solved the problem of decentralized tutor training and the lack of coherent diversity, equity, and inclusion training in ways that clearly improved on previous efforts. Several departments on campus already employed peer academic mentors in some capacity, be it as TAs, one-on-one tutors, or tutors in drop-in centers. The content-specific training was already handled by the faculty supervisors, but some supervisors trained tutors in their free time, others ran credit-bearing training courses, and some offered no training at all. The online tutor training course focuses on the common competencies that every student academic mentor should have. The coordination of our team's efforts helped us integrate tutoring into student success and retention more successfully than before and increased the satisfaction of all stakeholders as we all achieved our goal of defining tutoring as a high-impact experiential learning experience in which well-prepared students have the opportunity to apply knowledge and skills in largely unstructured problem-solving with their peers.

This shared, horizontal structure worked where previous bottom-up efforts had not: With the administration on board, both directors and tutors were compensated for the undeniable work involved, and administrators also saw more clearly that the goals of the centers aligned with the central college desire for greater retention and student success. But equally, a top-down approach would not have worked: Administrators did not force anything that directors did not choose or facilitate, so no one felt that their autonomy was threatened. In previous years, some departments had resisted top-down invitations to even advertise their presence at student success information sessions; other departments had not been proactive about presenting tutoring as more than a method to disseminate correct content and would have been dismayed to imagine themselves the recipients of a targeted inclusivity intervention.

Our shared approach to the setup was swift and efficient, but the real test was whether our tutors understood themselves also as part of that same student success initiative and felt that the problem we had perceived with an absence of coherent training was also something they experienced as a lack and wanted to remedy. We hoped to shift that "fix what's wrong" mindset to one where the tutor conceives of their main role as helping students understand themselves as growing learners through sharing metacognitive strategies that will apply beyond any specific question or problem. While addressing metacognition, the tutors approach their work through an equity lens and are sensitive to student well-being. This approach makes them more alert to the "whole student," which both aids empathy but might also help explain why a student is struggling with certain material in the first place: for example, a woman struggling in a STEM course because of stereotype threat.

Similarly, we wanted to shift the student perception of tutoring from the unequal dynamic of "tell me / get me to the right answer" to one where they see tutoring as a place to talk over approaches and acquire new learning strategies. When tutoring is viewed as not solely about gaining content, it becomes a process that students recognize more easily as common to—and a best practice of—successful academics at every level: Discussion clears a path forward rather than fixing something that was "missing" from or should have been covered in the past, as *re*-mediation suggests. Using a model easily adaptable to other institution types, this training expands our capacity to offer high-quality tutoring experiences and also destigmatizes students' use of academic support resources.

One central measure of success was whether tutors responded positively to the modules. Based on survey results, the tutors felt that the content was practical and useful, and they were interested in pursuing more tutoring opportunities. On a Likert scale of 1 to 5 (strongly disagree, disagree, neutral, agree, strongly agree) the fall 2019 and spring 2020 responses to "I felt that the topics covered in the tutor training program were appropriate" averaged 3.73 and 4.27 respectively, while responses for the same period to "I believe the training has helped me to become a more effective tutor" averaged 3.27 and 3.81. While the effect on retention is yet to be fully assessed, and remote instruction due to the COVID-19 pandemic negatively impacted usage by students, we nonetheless have some positive indicators via the tutor feedback and reflections.

The satisfaction of the tutors might have been less uniform than that of the directors and administrators but is still clearly trending toward feeling that the training had occupied their time meaningfully. We anticipated iterations while we were in the pilot phase, but already groups at every level feel more cohesive: The directors met each other and feel recognized, backed, and compensated by administrators; administrators know that the directors share their goals for the college rather than solely for their own fiefdoms; tutors know we value them as a vital resource and that we see them as a community; tutors met each other and the directors, felt that their performance improved, and reached out across the centers to ask questions or discuss their work. By realizing that previous boundaries between groups were largely artificial, and by having a clearly articulated sense of shared purpose, interactions were more confident and trusting, and thus more constructive.

Challenges

The shared leadership approach was crucial to the creation of the tutor training course and engagement with the problem of student retention and success but was not without its challenges. Collaborating across departments and offices was difficult logistically. The team was composed of faculty members from English, biology, and mathematics, and a professional staff member from the AOP Office, each with multiple demands on our time. One way we created time was by traveling to the AAC&U Institute together: Dedicated time away from other responsibilities allowed us to engage in learning together so that we could share a nuanced understanding of our key terms and begin the work of sketching our plan under the gentle pressure of its public presentation on the final 3 days. This time also allowed us to get acquainted, which made the inevitable need for an individual member to be able to focus more or less at any given moment during the semester easier to manage.

Even with the time dedicated to this project, we needed to multitask: We were building the system, including getting meetings with—and sometimes products from—other equally busy people across campus, while fitting with external deadlines for public opportunities to advertise the new course, plus needing to coordinate with the school's new early alert system and the larger campus effort regarding retention. We needed others to take time from their usual responsibilities to meet with us and then to determine the best course of action, sometimes with a quick turnaround. For example, the Office of Diversity and Equity tailored Wokeshops specifically to our needs, provided trained student leaders, and coordinated four sessions to handle over 100 tutors within a 3-week timeframe.

In addition to the logistics, because program development on campus typically occurs in silos, we were trying to mine the best practices and respect the individuality of multiple programs. Comparisons were inevitable: There were differing models of compensation and expectations for the directors, and discrepancies between how directorships counted toward promotion for a lecturer versus a tenured faculty member. Similarly, some student support services are well established and funded, while others run on department budgets decided by department chairs. Therefore, pay to the tutors also varied between rates of hourly wages and nonmonetary compensation in the form of institutional credit. There were also varying expectations around the number of hours tutors would work, whether they would have job security or need to reapply, whether they needed to pass some entry-level vetting process, whether they would work for varying amounts of money or credit or glory, if they would be more or less tightly attached to a specific class, and if they would be able to have immediate recourse to a faculty member or supervisor to handle either content or professionalism issues. Some students approach tutoring as an industrial-type job, where they arrive, give students the answers they want, then leave, while other tutors were expected to consider the power differentials inherent in tutoring centers or to consider themselves also as learners in the tutoring situation. Clearly, bringing these many perspectives together was not an easy task, and while most tutors did recognize the benefit of shared leadership, some remonstrated against the added responsibility.

While most tutors understood that tutoring is more than just improving content competence, some claimed the equivalent of colorblindness across race, gender, ability, or socioeconomics, backing away from the need to consider those factors unless students explicitly raised them (a scenario they found unlikely). They possibly felt condescended to or attacked by a perceived implication that only someone "failing" in the areas of diversity, equity, and inclusion required instruction in them (an ironic echo of the metacognitive parallel that tutoring is only useful for remediation), and even wondered if such training was a "check the box" move designed to create a superficial display of inclusivity for college marketing purposes. Furthermore, these responses appeared in reflective essays, a new genre for some students, which they perceived as either unwillingly sharing their personal diary or as soliciting praise for the course.

While we are confident that we can refine our course content and messaging, the most significant challenges we foresee revolve around funding. The COVID-19 pandemic hit during our pilot year, and the ensuing budget crunch highlights that funding is never guaranteed. We anticipate exploring micro-credentialing to reward tutors if we cannot pay them, but we also need a system for scaling up to the larger campus community, when instructors will need to take responsibility for assessing the performance of tutors they invite to the course. Geneseo makes use of approximately 200 upper-level students in tutor-related positions per year, with perhaps 60% of those employed by the four largest centers. The other 40% may enroll in the course, but the founding leadership team cannot reasonably take on that workload every semester for no compensation; other faculty and staff members across the campus will need to share the work, or the course will require a central coordinator.

Although the curtailment of in-person instruction in spring 2020 disrupted many operations, the foundations of our shared leadership model played an important role in smoothing the transition. Because the core group of coordinators had been collaborating closely and successfully for many months in advance, they were able to move in a coordinated way to deliver tutoring and academic support services online. As the college rapidly accelerated the timeline for rolling out advanced features of the campus early alert system, the coordinators were in the vanguard of adoption and implementation. Although this was partially driven by the complex circumstances surrounding COVID-19, the collaborative relationships and trust that had emerged within this group as a result of common efforts toward the tutor training project facilitated this critical work.

Lessons Learned

We were fortunate to be able to harness the energy behind the college-wide goal of increased retention. Those conversations repeatedly returned to the importance of building robust opportunities for peer-to-peer engagement, normalizing the use of academic support services, and incorporating growth mindset approaches in a range of learning opportunities. Tutoring reflected these aims, with the added benefit of providing a broadly accessible opportunity for the tutors themselves to participate in a high-impact, integrative learning experience. Situating tutoring in the context of institutional efforts to reverse declining retention rates helped justify the strategic investment of resources and empowerment of campus champions.

Nonetheless, we learned that a good team needs dedicated, hard workers who take individual responsibility for aspects where they have clear competence, such as in securing funding, handling statistics, framing content, or reaching out to personal contacts. The decision-making authority was clear when needed, and in other areas, most decisions were reached fluidly because we were in the same room.

We also learned that careful messaging matters, and not only to tutors about the course content. As a result of the homegrown services model, many departments are very protective of their student support programs and were at first reluctant to be part of a larger community. Explaining that we want to add to what they already have, not to change their programs, mattered. One challenge we still face, though, is the extra work it takes for the directors and coordinators to administer the course to their tutors. Going forward, with the continued support of administration both financially and by valuing the contributions of those faculty members doing the extra work, and with a comprehensive instructor guide to help them, we foresee several departments training their tutors with this course.

Our campus already holds events that elevate visibility for new projects: TLC presentations, workshops, and reading groups; Academic Affairs summits and assessment events; Office of Diversity and Equity programs; Department of Health and Counseling presentations and town halls. We took and will continue to take advantage of those to increase collaboration and inclusion across campus. With increased competition for decreased funds, it is imperative that stakeholders get a clear picture of the effect that tutoring as a high-impact practice can have on the campus as a whole.

Students who benefited from the revision of these programs as both tutors and users have played a role in campus activism, pushing campus leaders to standardize training and to expand tutoring in academic areas that are underserved. The tutors themselves are empowered as campus leaders by SUNY Geneseo's shared leadership project: Since their interests and talents align with campus priorities, they are a wealth of information about the challenges facing our student body. Having gained the common competencies within the training course, they recognize themselves as both instructors and learners and can continue SUNY Geneseo's drive toward high-impact practices grounded in our commitment to inclusivity and equity. Investing in peer academic mentors as a pathway toward improving student success and retention needs to remain the core message for this program to be sustained and grown.

Chapter 9 Reflection Questions

1. Shared leadership can be applied to many kinds of problems. Your own institutional context may shape which form of shared leadership works best and how ready the institution is to employ this model. Would this example of shared leadership work well for the problem(s) you want to work on? Are conditions right to support the use of shared leadership? If not, what steps might you take to generate momentum and capacity before you begin to introduce a shared leadership approach? Is there anything happening now that you might build upon?

2. This project resulted in a spread of leadership thinking and participation beyond the original leadership group attributed to the way they were learning together. Has anything like this happened on your campus and, if so, what triggered or supported that shift?

3. This case illustrates the importance of allies. As you think about the issues you are responding to at your institution, what allies do you already have and what additional allies might you seek to cultivate?

References

Bolden, R., Jones, S., Davis, H., & Gentle, P. (2015). *Developing and sustaining shared leadership in higher education.* Leadership Foundation for Higher Education.

Dweck, C. S. (2006). *Mindset: The new psychology of success.* Ballantine Books.

Elrod, S., Holcombe, E. M., Kezar, A. J., & Ramaley, J. A. (2020). *A short primer on shared leadership* [Unpublished manuscript].

Kezar, A. J., & Holcombe, E. M. (2017). *Shared leadership in higher education: Important lessons from research and practice.* American Council on Education.

McChesney, C., Covey, S., & Huling, J. (2016). *The 4 disciplines of execution: Achieving your wildly important goals.* Free Press.

McGuire, S. Y., & McGuire, S. (2015). *Teach students how to learn: Strategies you can incorporate into any course to improve student metacognition, study skills, and motivation.* Stylus.

McGuire, S. Y., & McGuire, S. (2018). *Teach yourself how to learn: Strategies you can use to ace any class at any level.* Stylus.

PORTLAND STATE UNIVERSITY'S HOMELESSNESS RESEARCH AND ACTION COLLABORATIVE (HRAC)

A Shared Leadership Journey

Maude Hines, Jacen Greene, Greg Townley, Marisa Zapata, and Todd Ferry

P ortland State University's (PSU's) Homelessness Research and Action Collaborative's (HRAC's) commitment to shared leadership is represented in the use of *collaborative* in our name, and has been important from our earliest discussions of our mission and goals. This chapter discusses our journey in shared leadership. In it we outline the history and development of the research center, the process of designing a shared leadership structure, and how challenges encountered along the way led to our current approach. The collaborative approach among the research center leadership team to writing this chapter integrates a diverse set of perspectives and enables a more transparent analysis of the HRAC model.

Origins and Development of Our Shared Leadership Model

HRAC came together around the wicked problem of how to end homelessness. We wanted to effect *transformative change* by providing models for ending homelessness that can be adapted elsewhere. Two former administrators used PSU's annual Winter Symposium to bring faculty together across disciplines to create ideas for campus-wide centers of excellence that would address large, complex social problems. The event was designed to include the humanities and social sciences, as well as STEM disciplines, and to synergize interdisciplinary, collaborative endeavors. Some of us met for the first time while devising a pitch we delivered to our colleagues at the symposium. We then had 1 week to prepare our initial proposal.

Unlike an existing hierarchical organization electing to shift to joint leadership, HRAC evolved a shared-leadership strategy from its environment. The competition-based format of the proposal process with its tight deadlines, the collaboration between strangers who had roles at the university whose relative hierarchy was not apparent, and our interdisciplinary perspectives and expertise all demanded a "we-based" approach (Elrod et al., 2020, p. 1), while the problem of homelessness requires the kinds of complex solutions that demand shared leadership strategies. An early name for the collaborative (The Center to End Homelessness) foregrounded the complex problem; the current name that evolved from early discussions (The Homelessness Research and Action Collaborative) foregrounds the complex interplay of ideas and solutions, the individual and institutional capacity, and the leadership style that addressing the problem demands.

Conceptualizing the new center, we had the opportunity to develop a shared leadership structure from the ground up. There is no way a single one of us could have moved this forward alone. The five research areas that became core to our mission reflected the expertise and interests of the multidisciplinary team that cowrote the original proposal. Early language described "a truly collaborative approach" to "leverage overlap between our five research areas."[1] The new center formed a shared leadership structure among the original cofounders that emphasized consensus-based decision-making and values-driven governance models, with a strong commitment to racial equity.[2]

While we were in the position to think about our shared goals, values, and leadership structure as a new center, we were doing so in larger contexts that created unique challenges. The university had political and financial reasons to announce the new center immediately after it was selected for funding, while we would have preferred time to build our relationships internally, get our house in order, and protect foundational staff from the immediate spotlight cast upon this new research center addressing such a pivotal community issue. Even a month or 2 would have given us time to write a strategic plan and prepare for a launch more systematically. Being very transparent with each other about our feelings was of primary importance in this context. Venting our frustrations in a safe environment helped us navigate the tensions between our vision for the center and the political exigencies of its existence: We may have come together around the project of ending homelessness, but we did so in a context that defined the problem differently. In subsequent stages of the process, pitches to the university foundation, to administrators, and to community stakeholders brought into relief this difficulty: Was the goal funding our center, ending homelessness, or creating income for the university? The expectation that we match the university's initial investment made autonomy difficult, as external funding was linked to external priorities. Our commitment to shared leadership required that we spend many hours in meetings discussing, committing to, and strategizing how to stick to our shared values, all while hitting the ground running and working to quickly secure external funding. A senior staff member in the Office of Research and Graduate Studies provided important support in this context, going out of their way to be on call for us. This experience underlines the importance of identifying allies in the institutional hierarchy early on.

Bureaucratic organizational procedures in the university context favored a single center leader, even in the submission of the original proposal, despite the university's goal of catalyzing synergistic collaboration. We found that in the absence of one formally designated leader, the default was too often for university administration to defer to a White male member of the team, even when the person with the greatest depth of knowledge about policy issues and connections to potential partners and donors (the university's target) was a Latina. Community partners and donors also expected a clear organizational hierarchy. Had we operated as a pure collective with no hierarchy, it would have been impossible to keep up with sharing of relevant information without some kind of information clearinghouse. For all of these reasons, and because she emerged during the initial stages of proposal creation as the person who coordinated assigning work and clarifying steps and roles, Marisa Zapata became the center's director, with Greg Townley sharing leadership as director of research. These positions and titles empowered each of them to represent the center in meetings with internal and external stakeholders. Some of the remaining eight cofounders took over HRAC's research areas.[3]

The structure that developed—a coleadership model with team leadership elements (Kezar & Holcombe, 2017)—let the director face outward, while preserving freedom for the other members to percolate ideas, a freedom of intellectual exchange that was important to all members. Major decisions are made by a larger group of eight cofounders through a consensus-based decision-making model. Cofounder involvement continued as planned, with weekly planning meetings involving all cofounders and smaller meetings of those with relevant experience around specific topics or projects. Individual cofounders lead research projects linked to their disciplinary expertise, bringing in other cofounders and faculty or staff from across the university as needed. The relative length of the various "work reports" became more and more unequal, a sign that Marisa's calendar was quickly filling up with meetings in an amount that was both impossible to keep up with and impossible to keep the rest of the group apprised of. How could we keep our values of shared leadership in an environment that forced lack of information and put unequal accountability on participants?

It was in this context that we created a third coleader position, an assistant director to oversee daily operations and financial management. This role was designed to function within a shared leadership framework from the start, described as a "managerial, administrative, and intellectual colleague" of the director and research director, part of a three-member leadership team. With no one dictating orders, colleagues in these three administrative positions are able to step back and provide help when requested, letting those most suited for the task at hand decide how to tackle it. What we've ended up with is two levels of leadership: the three coleaders in formal positions, and a larger group that operates through shared decision-making and consensus, depending on one another to lead based on expertise and familiarity with problems.[4]

Our Shared Leadership Characteristics

Our shared leadership endeavor is characterized by several practices that we strive to implement regularly. These include engaging a greater number of people in leadership roles, creating interchangeable leader and follower roles, incorporating multiple perspectives and expertise, providing opportunities for informal leadership roles, and emphasizing collaboration across the organization.

Engage a Greater Number of People

We attempt to keep the eight cofounders engaged and provide opportunities for synergy with regular weekly meetings where center staff, including a program assistant and communications specialist, are valuable contributors. The current structure of the team benefits from a diverse skill set and knowledge base, supplemented to fill gaps and improve competitiveness for external funding. For example, Maude Hines, an English professor, has overseen the *changing narratives, creating action* research area in close collaboration with a linguist. She has decided to develop a larger team in that area, which now comprises colleagues from sociology, public administration, urban studies, theater arts, and education. Expanding the disciplinary expertise of the research area has transformed the core goals of the area and the very definition of narrative.

Another important way the center has worked to engage a greater number of people is by offering faculty membership and grant opportunities to university colleagues who are not part of the founding team but who share interests and expertise pertaining to homelessness. This has created opportunity and expanded intellectual resources, but it has also challenged our ability to make sure we are living our values as we work to make sure others are committed in ways we think articulate the center's values.

Create Interchangeable Leader and Follower Roles

It is important to have a consistent point person for community partners, policymakers, and university administration; the three administrative positions are not interchangeable, especially as regards connections outside HRAC to campus and community leaders. But we do take turns leading and following depending on which research area is being highlighted. Ideally, we would all like to learn more about the different strands of the center. Different leadership opportunities emerge because of our different strengths and skill sets. These occur collaboratively or on a volunteer basis, rather than being decreed from the top down.

There are some institutional and cultural barriers to truly interchangeable roles, such as requirements for terminal degrees, disciplinary differences, and different research requirements for fixed-term and tenure-track faculty. However, there are typically formal or informal ways to address these barriers that still allow for shared and interchangeable leadership. For example, a center member with a PhD must serve as the principal investigator (PI) of record alongside a co-PI with a master's degree in order to satisfy requirements for a grant or institutional review board (IRB) application, even if the co-PI may have more responsibility for leading the project.

Incorporate Multiple Perspectives/Expertise

The center's eight cofounders represent a broad range of perspectives and expertise indicative of the multidisciplinary challenge of homelessness. Cofounders come from seven different departments and disciplines: architecture, social entrepreneurship, community psychology, English, land-use planning, public health, and social work. We represent tenured and non-tenure-track faculty and staff, with primary assignments in six of PSU's 10 schools and colleges. Shared leadership is essential here because complex problem-solving requires collaborative, coordinated thinking. We can leverage our very different perspectives and expertise to produce outcomes we work toward together. Sometimes our differences are complementary. For example, Marisa's greater attention to homelessness prevention and doubled-up populations complements Greg's focus on unsheltered homelessness, chronic homelessness, and serious mental illness, giving a fuller picture of the problem we are addressing together.

Other times we challenge one another to think differently. For example, cofounder Todd Ferry and his collaborators worked with a local neighborhood, offering housed residents the opportunity to vote on hosting a "village" of tiny homes they had designed for women experiencing homelessness. Marisa's critique of this voting process as potentially illegal and exclusionary gave new insights to the work, and informed Todd's research for a major grant. While buy-in was a core component of the success of the village from a design and development point of view, HRAC's larger view of issues relating to housing and homelessness that is possible because of our different perspectives sheds new light on our practices. This type of interface is something we are working to build on as we challenge one another to grow individually and collectively, especially in our attention to racial equity.

Provide Informal Leadership Roles

In addition to the more formal positions of director, research director, and assistant director, each of the center's five research areas is headed by a cofounder, although there can be quite a bit of movement and flexibility in these informal leadership roles. Individual projects, activities, and initiatives have also benefited from informal leadership. Tania Hoode, our program assistant, led the development of the center's policy for compassionate response to visitors in distress, including those who might be houseless. Stefanie Knowlton, our communications specialist, coordinates HRAC's participation in major university-wide events,[5] soliciting specific participation from cofounders and other staff members. Marta Petteni, a designer and researcher with the center, codesigned the exhibit "Houseless" that Todd coordinated with the Anchorage Museum. These are not projects delegated to staff. Rather, they tend to originate from staff members, who often delegate to cofounders. Who takes the lead on projects is determined collaboratively—at weekly meetings, by self-appointment, and by suggestion. In addition to informal leadership roles within the organization, part of HRAC's value system requires that we lift up the work of others, fostering leadership opportunities for students and community partners.[6]

Emphasize Collaboration Across the Organization

The initial request for proposals (RFP) was, in many ways, an attempt to catalyze collaboration across PSU, and HRAC embodies that collaboration. A recent successful grant application is an example of this. Evaluating the "village" model of transitional housing and producing a "how-to guide" for best practices relies on collaboration across our research areas and disciplines. Todd, an architect whose students construct tiny homes for villages, is a known and trusted stakeholder in local village-model housing communities. Greg, a community psychologist, is an expert in interviewing techniques and works in the areas of mental health and homelessness, and Marisa works in public policy solutions, an area the research is designed to inform. The project is informed by HRAC's interdisciplinary racial equity lens, evaluating the village model specifically with an eye toward communities of color.

Lisa Hawash, a social worker with expertise in waste and hygiene, convenes meetings with representatives of local government, business, and nonprofits in collaboration with Jacen Greene, who brings perspective from his role as assistant director, considerable organizational skills, and background in business administration. Lisa also collaborated with Todd on a hygiene project connected to the tiny home village work described previously.

In each of these cases, shared leadership facilitated the collaboration, with roles and intersections determined according to content expertise, methodological expertise, and job portfolio. This type of collaboration is not limited to formal or informal leadership. HRAC's 2019 Summer Institute, designed to involve graduate students in primary projects aligned with center research areas, evolved into collaboration across multiple projects as faculty identified additional needs, and this helped to further tie together different research areas. Continuing to build ties between our research areas and creating opportunities for synergy is an important goal, but one that needs more work. We will discuss barriers to this as well as ways to strengthen it in the "Challenges" section.

Building Capacity

While our shared leadership journey was catalyzed by coming together in a format strategically designed by university leadership to create synergy, with a common desire to end homelessness, we have worked hard to achieve our shared leadership model. We have consciously recognized its necessity and worked toward sharing leadership with concerted intention. In the proposal stage we built a shared understanding of the problem of homelessness, which we regularly revisit and refine as we make decisions about priority areas and new projects.

Early on we researched best practices for leadership models, including shared leadership and participatory governance. We looked into a coleadership model utilized by the PSU College of Liberal Arts and Sciences deans, and talked to PSU President Emerita Judith A. Ramaley, one of the coeditors of this volume, about emerging best practices in higher education shared leadership. We also researched models for our equity lens.[7] We were thoughtful about decision-making structures, and settled on governance models jointly. We decided as a group to cultivate two external boards of directors: a local board consisting of service providers, advocates, non-profit directors, and people with lived experience; and a national research board consisting of nationally known experts in housing and homelessness research. The entire team weighed in on board structure and membership, creating a shared vision of external guidance. Hiring an assistant director was also a team decision.

Meeting notes from early in our work together show weeks of deliberation and contributions from the team around constructing a philosophy statement, methods for consensus-based decision-making, participatory budgeting, and research priorities. Conversations were sometimes tabled until the entire team was available. We reminded each other of the importance of applying an equity lens to all we do, and links to our preferred racial equity models topped each agenda. While top-down decision-making would have moved things along more quickly, our deliberative process resulted in a richer and longer-lasting outcome that benefited from multiple perspectives. The results empowered each member of the team, supported autonomy, and strengthened our relationships to one another. Every idea is open to contributions and editing from the rest of the team.

Our early work set the stage for future decision-making. Weekly cofounder meetings continue to be an important place to share information and work collaboratively. Early this year we began a strategic planning process that, like our retreats and regular meetings, was designed collaboratively. Because the organization of how to say things often determines what can be said, leaving our (racial) equity lens atop each agenda reminds us to ask important questions of one another, and guides our work. We saw this recently as we sought to build collaborative capacity and diversity of expertise through an expanded membership structure and grant opportunities for the PSU community. We required a racial equity statement in membership applications, and research grant proposals were awarded extra points for incorporating a clear racial equity lens. Not all potential members addressed racial equity, even when invited to submit an updated application.

This surfaced a potential conflict in fundamental values before engaging in deeply collaborative work, and we rejected applications that failed to meet this requirement. But these approaches raised additional questions: What are the limits to shared leadership and collaborative problem-solving? How do we retain our values while remaining open to challenges and different ideas? We will tackle these in the "Challenges" section.

Benefits and Outcomes

It is difficult to imagine trying to tackle a problem as multifaceted as homelessness together without some kind of shared leadership structure. Some of us find the very idea to be disingenuous and self-serving. We have found that shared leadership promotes the opposite effect, upending the academic model of individual credit and vitae lines. This is especially important in our work, since homelessness is exacerbated by systems that are set up to address single issues; between these systems are the proverbial "cracks" to fall through. Our collaborative model creates a web of approaches, resulting in improved problem-solving. Here the example of Greg's focus on mental illness and chronic homelessness has wider reach when coupled with Marisa's focus on doubled-up and sheltered homelessness.

Two of the center's highest impact projects resulted from this commitment to focusing on diverse experiences of homelessness. First, Marisa conducted a study of homelessness in the Portland tri-county area which estimated that 38,000 people experienced homelessness in 2017, a number that was nearly seven times higher than the point-in-time estimate for the same year (Zapata et al., 2019). This study sparked local and national awareness of the critical need to expand our definitions and counts of unhoused people to include not only unsheltered people, but also those living in doubled-up situations out of necessity. Meanwhile, Greg led a study in partnership with numerous community stakeholders examining the experiences that unhoused individuals have with police and other first responders (Townley et al., 2019). The findings were instrumental to the development and eventual city council approval of the Portland Street Response, an alternative first responder program aimed at reducing the amount of contact police have with people experiencing homelessness and mental health distress. A social issue as complex as homelessness demands an ability and a commitment to crafting research and policy recommendations that respond to the diversity of ways that people enter into and exit out of homelessness; shared leadership inspires us to be flexible and far-reaching in our approach.

Likewise, most of what we have accomplished in team-building could not have been done had we come at this with a perspective of leadership as a solo enterprise. Our collective construction of our structure, identity, and scope of work has opened up space for all of us to make meaningful contributions at every stage, leading to increased satisfaction, confidence, and trust. Calling each other back to our focus on racial equity is easier for building stronger group cohesion. Watching our ideas be taken seriously and incorporated into the group effort establishes trust and enhances engagement, ultimately allowing us to better address homelessness in Portland and on our campus.

Challenges

Most of our challenges relate to our two-tiered leadership structure. While responsive to a real need for "clear delineation of decision-making authority" and "leadership from a positional or hierarchical leader . . . with a particular set of skills/capacity" (Elrod et al., 2020, p. 3), it comes with challenges to all involved. We elaborate these as follows.

Lack of Clarity Around Decision-Making Authority

Decision-making authority is an area where we have found shared leadership takes special patience. Marisa describes herself as a "front-facing person" and as someone who "likes to tell people what to do." It takes trust to transfer external relationships to others, and it is difficult to come back to the group for assessment, especially when it would be easier to make decisions on the spot, and when there is pressure from outside (both PSU and the broader community) to do more controlling. For those in the larger group, there is a tension between engagement and passivity: Some people might desire to be consulted in most decisions, but show a lack of engagement with meetings or are unresponsive to group outreach. We need to think carefully about how we decide whom to engage, when, and for which issues.

Unequal Access to Information and Community Partners

Differential access to decisions and their justification leaves some members uncertain about how much those in outward-facing leadership positions are willing to push back against funders and other types of power to ensure we are living within our values. Without room for everyone to be at the table in these conversations, it is hard to know what the trade-offs are. While unequal access to information limits collaboration (a topic we discuss in the following sections), setting up structures to bring back every piece of potentially relevant information from outside meetings would be impossibly unwieldy.

We also believe that our different gifts equip us for different responsibilities. We need to continue our work building trust and create channels for making group opinion clear and representable. We have worked on this with our investment in shared values.

Emotional Strain for Externally Facing Positions

The mayor, county chairs, and joint office call Marisa first—having a point person is a necessity. In the early days of the center, the director was in the unenviable position of negotiating the unpredictable and inconsistent mix of micromanagement and a hands-off approach by university administrators. At the same time, a large component of early meetings with external stakeholders (community partners and activists) was talking people down, allaying suspicions about the new center, and demonstrating our values and convincing others that HRAC was committed to engaging the issue of homelessness for "good" reasons. Guarding against cooptation by White supremacist power structures—which privilege and benefit White people at the expense of people of color—is a continuing struggle. For instance, chronic and unsheltered homelessness garners a lot of public attention and political interest, and in Portland the most visible unsheltered populations tend to be White. We have to resist pressure to privilege homeowner concerns, which risk overlooking other homeless populations (e.g., people in doubled-up situations), homelessness prevention, and racial equity issues. We are often asked to identify the "most vulnerable" people experiencing homelessness, or the people "most likely" to become homeless without intervention. These questions accept as given that we have few resources to serve many people in need, in a project that aims to spend the least amount possible. A racial equity lens focuses on who is in need, why, and how to resolve it, with cost secondary. At the end of the day, as director and signatory, Marisa is the one of us called on most often to resist these pressures, and who has most on the line. Coleaders support each other informally, and a cheering section is good to have, but perhaps we need something more formal in place to empower and support those on whom the work takes an emotional toll. One example is a recent suggestion from Marisa that center staff take time for self-care during the work day, as needed.

Obstacles to Collaboration

There is a tension between "accountability structures" and interdisciplinary, collaborative exchange of ideas. Establishing accountability and clear roles can result in pushback from faculty used to setting their own research agendas. While freedom to develop organic partnerships and projects can be generative of synergies, some structure may be needed to catalyze collaboration for academics used to working in isolation and to direct energies toward concerted efforts that meet practical needs. Other challenges to intensified collaboration include tight timelines that make soliciting collaborators less appealing; the intrusion of "one-off" projects the center picked up but did not plan for; and, especially for the directors, an overwhelming number of meetings and decisions. We still need to work on building ties between our research areas and creating opportunities for collaboration, which was one of our early goals. Hiring an assistant director was good to help lead this process. To continue building capacity here, we will need to manage different communication styles and preferred modes of communication, continue to build trust, and make creating those opportunities a group priority. We will need more of a framework for connecting projects and goals.[8]

Time

A central thread through all of the challenges previously discussed is the problem of balancing ideology and practicality. Addressing this tension in the context of shared leadership requires difficult conversations—and a lot of time. Some of the central tensions we have found we need to address include:

- **Tension between bringing in research money for the university and a focus on homelessness,** where promising approaches may not align with available funding. We are pressured to pursue funding in areas less relevant, meaningful, or impactful as those we would choose from our values.
- **Tension between the need for institutional infrastructure and the pressure it puts on a shared leadership model,** especially as it regards future plans and supporting current staff. Institutions demand accountability for individuals. They also want clear and easy procedures and protocols, and a clear sense of who is in charge.
- **Tension between recommitting to racial equity and moving quickly,** which constrains the time needed for an effective equity analysis. Advancing racial equity often requires going slowly, unpacking assumptions, examining biases, and locating more data or information.
- **Tension between different research priorities and preferred methodologies** when working with a truly multidisciplinary core group of faculty and staff. Learning to translate across disciplines requires coeducation and patience.
- **Tension between a commitment to transparency and delicacy of discussing finances with those whose livelihoods are impacted by the center's future prospects.** Cofounders from different ranks

bring different levels of financial security to the discussions. Our early discussions about preferring obsolescence to chasing contracts ring very differently now that we have staff funded by the center.

- **Alignment with community partners and elected officials**, who as individuals and groups may bring opposing perspectives and expectations regarding homelessness solutions and priorities.
- **Balance between a group commitment to certain strategies and the flexibility of acting in the moment** in response to rapidly changing circumstances or emerging opportunities. Our work with the strategic plan includes conversations about a sustained strategy and other important decisions and processes designed to ameliorate this tension.

Taking the time to negotiate these requires serious commitment, flexibility, and a safe environment for risk-taking and learning.

Reflection

Writing this chapter together has reminded us of the powerful journey we have been on together, often without the aid of a map. It has solidified our commitment to shared leadership and also drawn our attention to areas for further work (including continuing the conversations listed in the previous section). We are reminded of the lessons we have learned along the way and offer them here for others to learn from:

- Honest, inclusive conversations at the beginning were essential. They helped us strengthen our shared commitment and laid the groundwork for trust.
- Listening to one another and lifting up each other's accomplishments and skills is a must for team-building.
- Strive for autonomy for your leadership team, even within more traditionally hierarchical bureaucratic structures. We have found that the more we are connected to the university community, demonstrating our value through various projects on campus, providing seed funding to researchers across campus, and so on, the more autonomy we are granted.
- Shared leadership requires checking your ego and even intellectual independence at the door, which can be counterintuitive for academics. But focusing on the success of the center rather than on individual success is rewarded with more impact in our collective work.
- Shared leadership is incredibly challenging—and incredibly fulfilling.

We hope our experiences can help others who decide to embark on the journey of shared leadership. Enjoy the ride!

Chapter 10 Reflection Questions

1. This case illustrates how the concept of shared leadership can shape the approach you take to creating the capacity to work on a complex problem, as well as how you actually work together to address that problem. Can you identify places in your institution that already have a pattern of strong collaboration or of people working well together? Are there any structures in place that facilitate that collaboration? If not, how might you build a workable structure?

2. In this case, requirements for a single accountable leader for the new center led to impossible demands on this individual. How can you keep your values of shared leadership in an environment that demands a single leader?

3. How does this account of the challenges that this center faced and how the group dealt with them relate to your own situation?

4. Often experiments like this one can become a basis for a broader use of shared leadership (see chapter 13). Can you think of any centers or programs on your own campus that you can learn from or build on to help generate a richer culture of shared leadership?

Notes

1. We discuss the difficulty nurturing that overlap in the "Challenges" section.

2. Shared leadership aligns with HRAC's broader commitment to equity and inclusion. As Kezar and Holcombe (2017) have demonstrated, team leadership cultivates "inclusive organizational environments that tap into the unique perspectives and experiences of historically marginalized social groups" (p. 13).

3. The five core research areas are *reducing homelessness at PSU; changing narratives, creating action; innovative approaches to supporting people experiencing homelessness; housing as health care;* and *policy and program evaluation.*

4. At least one of our members thinks these are at odds, calling our leadership model "shared between three; collaborative among eight." We take this up in the "Challenges" section.

5. These include Portland State of Mind events and the Portland State Day of Giving.

6. A key example of this is HRAC's support of the AfroVillage, an initiative to create a village specifically for Black women in Portland who are experiencing

homelessness. The village can also serve as a gathering space for the larger African American community. The effort's visionary, LaQuida Landford, is supported by HRAC with funding, resources, and HRAC staff time, but maintains full leadership of the project's trajectory.

7. An equity lens is a decision-making tool that poses a series of questions about a proposed plan, policy, program, project, action, and so on. The lens helps people identify who may "win" or "lose" because of the decision, and then either rethink their decision or change course completely based on the analysis. Using a "racial" equity lens prioritizes considerations about race. Racial equity lenses play an important role in advancing conversations about race and highlighting racial disparities across other groups that experience systematic disparities (e.g., other protected classes, sexual orientation). See Zapata (2017) for an overview of racial equity lenses, and an example for higher education institutions.

8. Our situation is in many ways opposite to the "groupthink" (Elrod et al., 2020) that can challenge shared leadership efforts.

References

Elrod, S., Holcombe, E. M., Kezar, A. J., & Ramaley, J. A. (2020). *A short primer on shared leadership* [Unpublished manuscript].

Kezar, A. J., & Holcombe, E. M. (2017). *Shared leadership in higher education: Important lessons from research and practice*. American Council on Education.

Townley, G., Sand, K., & Kindschuh, T. (2019). *Believe our stories and listen: Portland Street Response survey report*. Street Roots.

Zapata, M. A. (2017). *Creating an equity lens at institutions of higher education*. Portland State University.

Zapata, M. A., Liu, J., Everett, L., Hulseman, P., Potiowsky, T, & Willingham, E. (2019). *Governance, costs, and revenue raising to address and prevent homelessness in the Portland tri-county region*. Portland State University.

CREATING THE CAPACITY
TO WORK ON COMPLEX
PROBLEMS AT WINONA
STATE UNIVERSITY

Judith A. Ramaley

Each institution has its own list of issues that it must address if it is to survive and thrive, but we share many of these issues across the larger higher education community. In 2008, the largest challenge that we were facing at Winona State University (WSU) had been created by the economic downturn that was placing financial stress on the state of Minnesota and its ability to support its higher education institutions. As a consequence, we faced another round of deep budget cuts. The institution had faced a series of budget reductions in recent years and it was clear that we had to find a different way to manage that painful process. At the time, the campus had a fairly typical siloed structure in which different academic and support units were loosely coupled, if connected at all. To respond differently to the challenges we faced, we needed to find a way to change the traditions of the academy with its emphasis on individual achievement, individual disciplinary and professional perspectives, and individual choices. Our academic programs and support units were held together by an equally loosely coupled internal structure in which each unit tended to function independently.

There were several reasons why our budget problem was especially hard to address. While budget cuts were nothing new to the institution, there were definitely no well-practiced ways to solve it other than to make cuts across the board. We set out to find ways to do better with less, not more with less. We already were stretched to our limits and people were tired of taking on yet more work as our hiring freeze lasted longer and longer. We set out to create a culture that embraces collaboration and mutual problem-solving within the context of the institution as a whole. We wanted to weave the different units together in ways that would allow for better ways to serve our students and our community. In that way, we could use our resources more wisely and withstand at least some of the impact of further budget cuts.

This chapter will describe our efforts to engage people across the campus and the strategy we used (Educational Lean) to incorporate a diversity of experiences and ideas into the task of solving campus problems, ranging from the design of the undergraduate nursing curriculum to a plan to address the needs of transfer students to the management of supplies and replacement parts in information technology (IT). These efforts created a natural opportunity for professional growth as well as a path toward creating a sense of shared purpose and responsibility for the well-being of the institution and its role in society. We were learning ways to work together to address the realities of a *new normal*, a term that was just beginning to show up in the literature. At the same time, we were learning ways to use our own resources more effectively as we faced a series of budget cuts. It was also my first experience with intentional shared leadership.

Learning New Ways to Think and Work Together

We all know that how people think affects what they pay attention to and how they interpret their experiences. I wanted WSU to find a way to learn to see issues in new and more creative ways and to find effective solutions to those problems. Many of our procedures were overly complicated, involved too many steps, were designed more for the convenience of our faculty and staff than for our students, and many steps did not add any value to the outcome for anyone. George Marshall (2015) captures the problem succinctly when he asks, "What explains our ability to separate what we know from what we believe, to put aside the things that seem too painful to accept?" (p. 1). Marshall's words help illuminate why we seem to be so slow in responding to the societal changes that are affecting higher education. First, we tend to dismiss criticisms of our institutions as too expensive and often insensitive to the extreme social and economic divides that are shaping our nation today. We are, after all, committed to the public good and to preparing our graduates to lead meaningful lives. As a result, these criticisms are not seen as requiring immediate actions. Second, dealing with these challenges requires us to accept very clear short-term costs and changes in how we perform our roles in order to adapt to changes that seem to many of us to be far into the future. Finally, the information we have about that future is often uncertain and contested, and we tend to deal with that uncertainty by drawing on our own unconscious biases and intuitions about how the world works and deciding that there is nothing we can do about it (Kahneman, 2011).

As universities and colleges react to a rapidly changing world and seek ways to contribute to the understanding and management of the complex problems that communities face today, institutions themselves must change. As Arthur Levine forecasted in 1997 in an essay in *The Chronicle of Higher Education*, our nation's colleges and universities have become a "mature industry." If our efforts were to succeed, we had to find a way to realize the goal articulated by Poleman et al. (2019), who have argued that we must transform higher education "from a linear, hierarchical, competitive organizational model to a distributed, interdependent and collaborative one" (p. 97). In short, all of us at WSU had to figure out how to move out of our silos and work together. Doing so would have implications for who would take part in setting our goals, who would contribute to the design of actions we might take to achieve those goals, and how we would work together to achieve them.

Choosing a Strategy: Engaging People Across the University

Given the complexity of the problems that cabinet members and I were being called upon to address while cutting our budget at the same time, we wanted to find out how to change our ways of recognizing issues and working together to address them as we sought to lead our university to respond to the changing societal context in which our institution was embedded. We brought together the entire senior management team that consisted of not only the cabinet but also all the deans, as well as directors of our support units for a 1-day retreat and asked ourselves several key questions: Do we have a robust learning environment? How do we respond to questions and concerns that affect the ability of our community to function at a high level? How can the experience of working together to identify "glitches" in our policies and practices that create problems and frustrations for our campus community lead to better results? How can we understand and work on the unspoken and often unconscious assumptions that contribute unintentionally to whether newcomers to our campuses, whether faculty, staff, or students, feel welcomed and included and whether they feel that their experiences, ideas, and interests will be valued and supported?

By the end of the day, our management group decided that the best way to answer some of those questions was to create a leadership academy to engage members of our campus community in solving problems together in a new way. At the time, the director of our Institutional Research and Planning

Office, Theresa Waterbury, was working on her doctorate. As her dissertation topic, she was studying how to adapt an industrial process improvement model called "Lean" to an educational environment. She was in the process of conducting an experiment using Lean in solving some problems in our Continuing Education Program. Impressed by that story and after talking with people who were participating in that pilot project, the president's cabinet asked Theresa to draw upon her experience to design the first leadership academy using Educational Lean as a framework to guide the work of each leadership academy cohort.

The locus of leadership in this process shifted from the cabinet members, who agreed to undertake this approach to shared solution-finding, to Theresa Waterbury, who designed the process based on her dissertation work, to the members of each leadership academy cohort who studied the issues at WSU and decided which topic to work on. At the conclusion of each year, the leadership academy members submitted a set of recommendations to the cabinet, including proposed funding for aspects of their proposal where needed. I will start by talking about Educational Lean itself, followed by the launching of the leadership academy and the lessons we learned from those experiences.

What Is Educational Lean and Why Did We Choose It?

As Waterbury and Holm (2011) explain it, "Educational Lean is a quality methodology that uses the strength of collective knowledge, a scientific approach and a shared understanding of value to redesign administrative and academic functions to operate from the student perspective" (p. 31). The goal of this approach is to deliver core functions such as student services and the curriculum in the best possible way by drawing upon disciplined inquiry and collaboration, two qualities that are highly valued in the academy. In the terms we are using in this book, it is an example of *shared leadership*.

In essence, Educational Lean initiates deep organizational learning, engages people in new ways to share expertise and to address problems and opportunities, and becomes a way to explore below the cultural surface to uncover the deeper workings of the organization (Waterbury & Holm, 2011). The Educational Lean process consists of four principles, according to Hughes (2019):

1. The focus is generally on the student experience. Gather data on how well the current system is working. Define exactly what value will mean for the people who will be affected by the changes you are proposing to make.

2. Begin by mapping out the processes that are currently in place, what Educational Lean calls the "value stream," in order to figure out the specific steps that are required to deliver the value you want to provide.

3. Once you have figured out what exists now, it is time to imagine a simpler, more streamlined way to reduce the number of steps or signatures needed and work on the inefficiencies in the process that exist and the ability of the campus to address the needs of students it serves.

4. Design your more effective approach by using a data-driven approach to problem-solving. Once the improvements are in place, gather data on how the newly designed process is working and assess whether the design is better than the one that existed before.

The Educational Lean model of shared problem-solving was introduced in an environment of urgency created by several years of state funding cuts and the need to maintain momentum and integrity in the face of reduced resources and the malaise that years of diminished funding can create. We wanted to learn how to operate in a reflective mode and how to create an environment that can support the kind of learning and informed actions that are now expected of us and our graduates as we respond to a changing world. To pave the way to a better future, each cross-constituency leadership academy was asked to find better ways to use our resources to become a community of learners improving our world.

The Leadership Academy: Creating Opportunity for Professional Growth

The leadership academy engaged members of our campus community from all employee groups in the analysis of current practices and the design of new ways of doing things with fewer resources. We proposed that working across our traditional boundaries would not only create new habits of practice but also allow us to develop leadership throughout the organization in order to become more resilient and to help us respond to the unanticipated challenges and opportunities that might be ahead of us. We were trying to create a culture of *shared leadership* before we had heard of that term.

The introduction of the leadership academy model and the use of Educational Lean allowed us to create a shared capacity to understand the problems we encountered, work together to design solutions for them, and then implement those solutions using teams made up of a cross-section of faculty, staff, and students with interests in the issue and knowledge and experience relevant to the task of addressing that issue. The result was our own form of shared leadership.

A quick caveat is needed here. We chose to tackle only complex problems that required people to work together in a new kind of way. It is important to recognize that only some kinds of problems are complex enough to require this kind of collaborative approach (Baer et al., 2008). The kinds of issues we were facing required new ways of thinking, new sources of insight and experience, and new approaches to working together. It is this kind of problem that we set out to address by using Educational Lean. We wanted as a community to expand the way we thought together about really difficult problems.

Launching the Leadership Academy: Developing a Sense of Shared Purpose and Responsibility and New Ways of Working Together

Our intention in launching the leadership academy was to foster a pattern of organizational learning together by identifying and addressing issues that were affecting our ability to support our vision of becoming a community of learners improving our world. The goals of the academy matched up with the overall direction that our budget crisis and societal changes dictated. The provost and I wanted our campus community to: (a) learn how to read our own environment more accurately; (b) engage more members of our campus community in helping us adapt to changing political, social, and economic pressures and the growing concerns about climate change and our environment; (c) provide opportunities to practice new habits that would serve us well as we continued to respond to a rapidly changing world; and (d) to develop leadership throughout the organization so that we could become more resilient and work together across our departments and our traditional roles to deal with the challenges, many of them hard yet to anticipate, that would surely confront us in the future.

This experiment unfolded in three phases. In the first phase, we provided some support for Theresa Waterbury to use our Outreach and Continuing Education unit as a test case for developing a full Educational Lean model and to complete her doctoral dissertation on the application of Lean principles to higher education. The participants included staff from Continuing Education and support staff from each of the colleges whose faculty designed and offered courses through the division. Dr. Waterbury served as the guide and mentor for the team that was assembled to work on issues of importance to the unit. The next step took advantage of the growing interest and momentum created by our experiments with using a cross-functional leadership model to create the stage for becoming a truly resilient learning organization that could recognize and solve problems before they grew into more difficult and wicked issues. This momentum was created by positive comments that participants in this trial run made about their experience on working together to find solutions to problems that were faced in the Continuing Education Program.

In the second phase, we launched the leadership academy. The first academy was made up of a mix of people from the faculty, the staff, and the student body. Later academies also included key members of the surrounding Winona community. People were invited to apply for the opportunity and to secure the recommendation of a colleague or supervisor. For this first academy, the administration chose the topic for the year—support for transfer students. We used the experience of this first leadership academy year to shape our subsequent approach to creating shared leadership experiences to address especially complex problems. All subsequent academies were given the opportunity to study the campus and select their own focus for the work. In this way, the academy shifted toward the model many cities used to develop leadership among their residents. As in the case of the city of Winona, we were seeking to prepare the next generation of leaders for our own community.

In the third phase, the use of Educational Lean began to expand from the administrative side of the house to the academic core. The focus of this next stage was to revisit our curriculum and begin to build our academic programs on a more coherent and compelling educational philosophy that yields clear expectations and learning goals. The first project using this approach was undertaken by the faculty of our Nursing Program who used Lean principles and a mixed team of people including faculty members, nursing students, and community preceptors to rethink the undergraduate nursing curriculum.[1]

Lessons Learned

The launch of this effort to create new capacity to solve problems met with the usual start-up problems. As Waterbury (2015) reflected back on the process, she identified several challenges. These include the time it takes to work in this collaborative way, the question of which projects to select, the difficulty of stepping outside our usual frame of reference and seeing problems in new ways and the realities of the effort it takes to coordinate, facilitate, and implement the improvements.

To address the time barrier, the senior leadership team set the vision for improvement and used multiple communication channels to disseminate these goals and to ask unit leaders to encourage their colleagues to participate on the improvement teams. As more people began to participate, they began to see that the time spent was paying off in better support for students. As an indicator of the initial impact of this approach, we saw our retention numbers begin to go up, and we expected that we would soon see increases in graduation rates as well. A couple of years later, graduation rates did begin to climb from approximately 79% to approximately 82%.

Project selection was another challenge. Initially, there was a tendency to focus on projects that were easier to manage and that might affect a small number of students. When the decision was made to focus on projects that had the potential for university-wide impact, Theresa Waterbury as the facilitator of the leadership academies faced a new issue, namely the competing interests and values of people at different levels of the organization. Although the overall goal was to select projects suggested by faculty and staff rather than the administration, not all of the projects could be supported with the resources available. Given that limitation, projects needed to have the potential for a broader impact. This brought into play two incompatible issues: first, to provide faculty and staff with the opportunity to gain critical leadership skills and learn how to solve problems in a systematic and collaborative way, and second, to have the limited resources directed toward projects with significant organizational impact (Waterbury, 2015).

Another challenge was the difficulty of dealing with the status quo mindset of some of the faculty and staff who had begun to lose hope in the face of steady reductions in state support. As Waterbury (2015) explains it, "Employees are immersed in day-to-day chaos with routine work. It is challenging to abandon the chaos for creativity" (p. 944). A strategy that worked well in this situation was to start with a couple of questions to help a newly formed team shift from one set of lenses to another:

1. What could we learn from others?
2. Are there promising ways to handle this problem that we might adapt to our own situation?

Efforts were also made to use various tools that encourage people to examine a problem from different angles and compare multiple perspectives.

All of these issues illustrate the need for both clear support and encouragement from senior administration and midlevel leadership and the absolute necessity of having skilled facilitators. During the early years of this project, two positions were provided to the Office of Improvement and Leadership to train people in Lean-thinking and its tools and to coordinate the projects. At its peak, the office supported four or five projects each semester. Each project needed a coordinator who was skilled enough to know which tools and concepts would best serve each project.

Despite the many challenges we faced in launching and sustaining the leadership academy model, the first cohorts that participated in the leadership academy clearly developed a diverse community of interest that continued to operate informally after the project ended and the recommendations were implemented. It became clear that our institution had developed much more capacity to identify and work on mission-critical issues than we had ever thought would be possible.

When I left WSU in 2012, we were starting to think about a fourth phase of efforts to create a resilient learning community as a way to generate the capacity to achieve our vision as a community of learners. At that point, a significant number of people had been involved in one of the leadership academy cohorts and there was early anecdotal evidence that those experiences had created a new pattern of interaction across support units. When someone encountered a problem that might originate in another unit, instead of complaining about that unit's incompetency, the more common response became to pick up the phone and call a colleague in that unit or walk across campus to talk with someone to figure out what could be done to remove the logjam or correct the problem.

In preparing to write this chapter, I got back in touch with Theresa Waterbury, who is still at WSU, now as the chair of the Leadership Education Department in the College of Education. In 2012, due to a change in leadership, a midlevel administrator with many other competing priorities was assigned to oversee Lean. At that time, the university still had six Lean facilitators, but over the next 18 months the number of projects declined steadily and the administrators who had been originally assigned to this effort between 2008 and 2012 had new roles and responsibilities. As a result, the capacity to identify projects and support cross-functional teams to address them declined significantly.

Today, WSU still practices the Educational Lean approach to identifying and solving problems but on a much smaller scale and largely through its connections to external organizations. Theresa Waterbury teaches a graduate course on the use of the principles of Lean. In this course, the class first observes an authentic Lean session and how the art of facilitation blends with the science and practice of Lean. Prior to that session, the students participate in planning that event. After they complete the course, the students have 7 weeks to select a process that spans at least three departments either in their own organization or at WSU and that should be redesigned to remove aspects that do not add value to the outcome of that process. This design gives them an opportunity to see the necessity for collaboration among multiple departments or areas. During the past 8 years, this graduate course has been responsible for improving over 160 processes in higher education, nonprofit organizations, and health-care organizations.

Final Thoughts

More often than not, each institution has some project or experience that could create the basis for a fresh and engaging way to work together and make decisions. At WSU that was the early experience with a more broadly shared leadership approach through the use of Educational Lean. Building on the lessons and working relationships that arise from those experiences can enable a campus community to respond to the totally unexpected. This example from WSU offers some insights into why shared leadership is so important today, as well as the challenges that an institution may encounter when it decides to create the capacity to draw upon the experience, expertise, and ways of looking at problems of a broader range of participants. We must develop this capacity if we are to address the kinds of complex challenges that all of our colleges and universities are facing. As in any other form of collaboration, these efforts change how we identify and think about problems. Among those changes are: (a) Who cares about the problem?, (b) Who will work together to understand the problem?, (c) Who will help design responses that can address the issue?, and (d) Who will work together to implement the response, interpret the results, and decide what to do next? It is not easy to change the culture of our institutions to support and encourage this way of working together, but the outcomes are worth the effort.

Chapter 11 Reflection Questions

1. Pressing problems like the prospect of severe budget cuts can generate some fresh thinking and create solutions including the use of shared leadership. If you have a wicked problem to address, how might this become a catalyst for further collaboration?

2. Given the changing nature of the problems and opportunities that are emerging, how effectively is your institution reviewing its traditional ways of decision-making, distributing resources, and measuring the impact of the efforts you make?

3. How might you use a tool like a leadership academy to build capacity for shared leadership on your campus? Are there existing leadership development programs you can identify that you could connect with or work with to train leaders in the skills or capacities necessary for shared leadership?

Note

1. For a detailed look at how another Educational Lean process unfolded, see an article by Honken and Janz (2011) that describes how an information technology department used Educational Lean to solve problems. To see an example of how a Lean project was presented to stakeholders, see Winona State University (2011).

References

Baer, L. L., Duin, A. H., & Ramaley, J. A. (2008). Smart change. *Planning for Higher Education, 36*(2), 5. https://www.scup.org/resource/smart-change/

Honken, R., & Janz, K. (2011, November). *Utilizing educational lean to enhance the information technology project intake process.* Proceedings of the 39th annual ACM SIGUCCS Conference on User Services. San Diego, California. https://doi.org/10.1145/2070364.2070413

Hughes, J. (2019, September 24). *A beginner's guide to lean management in higher education.* Keystone Academic Solutions Blog. https://www.keystoneacademic.com/news/lean-management-in-higher-education

Kahneman, D. (2011). *Thinking, fast and slow.* Farrar, Straus and Giroux.

Levine, A. (1997). Higher education's new status as a mature industry. *Chronicle of Higher Education, 43*(21), A48–A48. https://www.chronicle.com/article/higher-educations-new-status-as-a-mature-industry/

Marshall, G. (2015). *Don't even think about it: Why our brains are wired to ignore climate change.* Bloomsbury.

Poleman, W., Jenks-Jay, N., & Byrne, J. (2019). Nested networks: Transformational change in higher education. *Sustainability: The Journal of Record, 12*(2), 97–99. https://www.liebertpub.com/doi/full/10.1089/sus.2019.29152

Waterbury, T. (2015). Learning from the pioneers. *International Journal of Quality and Reliability Management, 32*(9), 934–950. https://doi.org/10.1108/IJQRM-08-2014-0125

Waterbury, T., & Holm, M. (2011). *Educational lean for higher education: Theory and practice.* Lulu Publishing.

Winona State University. (2011, July 11). *COE Lean Event Stakeholder Presentation.* https://www.winona.edu/education/media/14_project_lean_event.doc.pdf

12

SHARED TRANSFORMATION

The One Door Approach at Cuyahoga Community College

Alex Johnson and Karen Miller

Cuyahoga Community College (Tri-C) has long been known nationally for its committed and visionary leadership. While community college presidents nationally serve for an average of 5 years, by 2013 Tri-C was facing only the third presidential transition in its 50-year history. It would be the first change in executive leadership in 20 years, closing a chapter on a president who had served for nearly half of the college's history and had propelled the college to national prominence. The college, with four campuses and several centers in and around Cleveland, Ohio, also enjoyed a strong local reputation and faithful support from the community; the institution's operating levies, which comprise a significant portion of its revenue, almost always passed with a substantial margin. Nationally, Tri-C was among the first Leader Colleges of Achieving the Dream, an organization dedicated to community college student success, and was a long-standing board member college of the League for Innovation in the Community College.

As the college prepared to welcome a new president in 2013, however, many national and internal challenges loomed. Across the country, the educational attainment of Americans aged 25 to 34 years old was ranked 16th among developed countries; Ohio placed 39th among the 50 states in degree attainment. In Cleveland, the largest city the college serves, the skills gap meant that only about 67% of available workers could compete for more high-wage, high-tech jobs and achievement. President Barack Obama's American Graduation Initiative shone a spotlight on these trends, as well as low official graduation rates at many institutions. In 2013, Tri-C's graduation rate through the Integrated Postsecondary Education Data System (IPEDS) was just 4.5%. Despite great achievements in many areas, and strong outcomes for many students, this figure hindered both the institution's fulfillment of its mission and its message in the community. What's more, Ohio was shifting from funding public higher education based on enrollment to funding based on performance.

These were the strengths and challenges Alex Johnson embraced as he became Cuyahoga Community College's fourth president in the summer of 2013. He was not new to the institution or the community, having served as president of the college's Metropolitan Campus for 11 years before undertaking college presidencies in New Orleans and Pittsburgh. This familiarity proved to be an advantage as he sought to thoughtfully transform the culture of the institution to meet the needs of a new era.

Even in the interview process, however, President Johnson clearly articulated that this transformation could not be undertaken by the administration alone. Ed Foley, then president of the American Association of University Professors' local union, noted that President Johnson discussed not only the importance of building relationships with the college's faculty but also articulated specific ideas about how he planned to involve faculty in strengthening student success and the student experience at the institution.

This was the genesis of a transformative approach to leadership at Tri-C, an approach that not only would enable the college to meet the challenges of student success and completion, but also would equip us to address new challenges by shifting the institution's culture toward change. This approach would involve the entire institution, not just a secondary initiative. As such, we have come to define *shared leadership* more broadly than simply having faculty and administrative cochairs of a program or center. Such insular approaches, while certainly helpful in our college operations for many years, had not resulted in the transformed organization we desired and needed to address the existential challenges facing the institution.

Rather, we have pursued a *shared dialogue* approach, seeing the necessity of involving not only all levels of administrators and faculty members but also campus staff, students, community members, employers, and government leaders in establishing priorities, identifying innovative approaches to solving problems, and ultimately increasing success for our students, our college, and our community. This goes beyond a single initiative or program, seeking instead to transform the way the organization operates and the way diverse groups interact with one another. To begin, however, we had to expand the leadership conversation at the college in order to move forward from a position of trust and solidarity.

Expanding the Conversation of Leadership

The incoming president immediately took steps to increase communication at the institution and to build a sense of urgency around the key priority of student success and completion. To begin the feedback process and establish early emphases in a systematic way, within his 1st month on the job we administered the Culture's Contextual Elements (CCE) survey to senior administrative leadership at the annual President's Retreat. President Johnson had previously used this instrument in both New Orleans and Pittsburgh to identify and overcome cultural roadblocks within organizations. The survey rates institutional effectiveness in the categories of involvement, consistency, adaptability, and communication by tallying the anonymous rankings of participants.

The results of this assessment were reported back to the President's Retreat participants, and groups were quickly formed to develop recommendations to improve the lowest ranked elements within each category. The recommendations of these four teams were implemented broadly, and specific cultural elements showed substantial increase as we repeated the assessment several times over the next few years and expanded its scope to include lower-level administrators and faculty at the campuses as well. This expansion included many new voices in the process of setting priorities and improving the institutional culture.

Rather than a "top-down, bottom-up" philosophy to organizational development, President Johnson intended for collaboration, decisions, and work be carried out on middle ground. To accommodate this approach, he had to flatten a particularly hierarchical organizational structure to create one that ensured greater connection and communication. A form of *matrix management* is evident at the college, which means some programs are operated by individuals who only have a "dotted" or indirect reporting line to the administrator at the program site. This nonsupervisory arrangement requires productive relationships between the parties to work effectively.

Reflective of this matrix approach, he expanded membership of the president's cabinet to include not only the three executive vice presidents but also the four campus presidents and the heads of key departments. Although the campus presidents directly report to the executive vice president/chief academic officer, their inclusion on the president's cabinet promoted greater coordination and consideration of the varied culture and circumstances at each campus at the top level of leadership at the college.

In addition, more flexible pathways increased the permeability of the traditional barriers between the faculty and administrative ranks. Two of our current campus presidents were previously faculty members, and faculty also stepped into leadership roles of a new scholars academy and the Office of Faculty Professional Development, among others—some permanent, some shorter-term. Administrators from the campus level have also risen to senior leadership, and there has been increased movement among the formerly siloed administrative divisions of the institution. These hires have brought fresh perspectives and new voices to administrative leadership.

As indicated, Tri-C administrative leadership traditionally met each year for the President's Retreat and monthly during the academic year. However, the membership of this group was expanded to the assistant and associate dean levels at each campus, as well as central administrative leadership. This body, a college-wide cabinet, provides key updates to midlevel leaders and an opportunity for feedback. It has served to make messaging more consistent from executives through to faculty and front-line staff. Much of the substance of these meetings informs the priorities and messages at departmental and divisional meetings across the college.

We also transformed the traditional President's Retreat. Now including both the college-wide cabinet and faculty leaders, it has become one of the keystone moments in our annual planning cycle, providing an opportunity to reflect on advancements toward the goals of the past year, to learn from business and educational thought leaders, to identify priorities for the coming year, and to actively begin the process of developing campus, divisional, and departmental goals to align with those priorities.

To promote transparency, we also overhauled the college's Marketing and Communications (now Integrated Communications) Department; introduced a biweekly president's newsletter distributed to all employees via email; began sharing weekly updates with the college's board of trustees; and introduced town hall meetings each semester at every campus and administrative location. The format of these town halls has evolved over time, moving from primarily informational to much more of an open forum with opportunities for faculty, staff, and students to ask questions of senior leadership and engage in dialogue.

Beyond these changes within the administration, the root of our efforts to develop this middle ground of collaboration was the creation of President's Council. Previously, faculty leadership would meet with executive administrative leaders primarily during times of crisis or transition, such as union contract negotiations. President's Council, however, became a standing body comprising the president's cabinet, the Joint Faculty Senate Committee, and faculty union leadership.

More than just an informational meeting or a venue seeking faculty buy-in for predetermined administrative initiatives, this monthly gathering became a forum for discussing key priorities at the college and brainstorming ways to meet challenges collaboratively. Faculty and administrators share the floor with an emphasis on transparency and synergy. The intention is to use data and relevant individual expertise to discuss and decide on approaches by consensus. This group has been responsible for designing many pilot initiatives and identifying successful pilots that can be scaled across the institution. President Johnson also prioritized time at the end of each meeting to dismiss administrative leadership so that he could meet privately with the faculty members. This opportunity for faculty leaders to speak frankly and directly with the president proved helpful in promoting transparency and maintaining open dialogue.

President's Council complemented 25 existing shared governance committees comprising faculty, administrators, staff, and students at various levels. For many years, these committees have addressed key topics from academic disciplines and curriculum development to campus safety and information technology. These groups, with shared faculty, staff, and administrative leadership, recommend and implement changes in procedures and operations through regular meetings. While these groups have real authority and have made substantive improvements within their spheres of influence, and while they would remain a significant part of the organization moving forward, these committees nonetheless fell short of the true high-level partnership that President's Council would come to represent. President's Council provided faculty leadership the opportunity to regularly connect with administrative leadership to provide input, guidance, and real leadership on important, strategic, college-wide issues such as facility planning, budget priorities, strategic planning, and human resources processes.

One Door, Many Options for Success: Identifying the Cause for Action

The foundational work of expanding and strengthening the leadership conversation at Tri-C took place during President Johnson's 1st year, although many elements continued to be implemented and refined for years to come. During that 1st year, the president's cabinet, President's Council, and the college-wide cabinet focused their conversations on beginning to develop our response to the needed increase in degree attainment. This response was focused on improving students' access to the college and increasing their success in a learner-centered environment characterized by superior programs and services.

We arrived at this cause for action based on a thorough analysis of evidence derived from data on student outcomes, including test scores and grades. President's Council was particularly formative in this process—administrators presented institutional and national data that helped to bring the student-focused expertise of faculty members to bear in identifying patterns and trends. This process resulted in six strategic priorities around the call to action of student success and completion:

1. Create a holistic student experience that contributes to increased retention and completion rates.
2. Increase engagement with the community.
3. Establish more short-term workforce education programs.
4. Keep tuition affordable.
5. Reduce the equity gap experienced by students of color, students from low-income backgrounds, and nontraditional students.
6. Enrich the brand and image of the college.

These strategic priorities were introduced to broader administrative leadership at the 2014 President's Retreat, along with a presentation by Delos "Toby" Cosgrove, then president and CEO of the Cleveland Clinic. His book *The Cleveland Clinic Way* presents a model benchmark system based on national standards and best practice. The system rates services identified by patients as important to them, measures the effectiveness of day-to-day operations, and determines the extent of the clinic's compliance with various regulatory agencies.

Based on the clinic's model, and beginning with breakout sessions at the 2014 retreat, each of the college's three divisions—academic programs, workforce offerings, and financial and administrative services—identified benchmarks for measuring progress against the six strategic priorities. These benchmarks are extensive, but the ones most critical are those that measure our progress against vanguard colleges, such as the recipients of the Aspen Prize for Community College Excellence and the Awards of Excellence from the American Association of Community Colleges (AACC). These benchmarks include graduation rates and overall numbers, student retention rates, and pass rates in college-level mathematics and English.

Identifying Strategies and Techniques for Leading Together

In order to effectively meet the challenge of student success and completion, however, faculty and administrative leadership could not simply create tactical plans from on high. Achieving real results would require the involvement of every campus, department, office, and employee at the institution. Our approach relied heavily on the theory of appreciative inquiry, as the college invited all college constituencies to participate in creating the blueprint of the way forward for Tri-C through discussion, identifying institutional strengths and weaknesses, establishing priorities, and creating strategies. To accomplish this type of inclusive leadership, the college began its "One Door, Many Options for Success" project.

During the fall of 2014, open working sessions at each campus helped employees at all levels to understand the six strategic priorities and began the process for departments and individuals to identify specific processes, initiatives, and goals to support them. These processes then became part of the broader campus and division plans.

In turn, faculty members and administrators outside the regular membership of President's Council and college-wide cabinet would jointly present on certain promising process improvements and initiatives at the meetings of these leadership groups, with opportunities to provide advice and support while identifying practices that should be scaled college-wide. Data were also employed to determine which initiatives were not succeeding and change course where necessary.

Among the initiatives implemented jointly by the faculty and administration at the campus level and then scaled college-wide, success centers were established at local high schools to prepare students for the college experience. As students arrived, a new First Year Experience (FYE) program, featuring two semester-long student success courses and other intentional and mandatory activities, provided students with a more structured start to college. Efforts to improve grades in English and mathematics helped students to remain on a more dependable "guided pathway" to earning a degree. Each campus created Care Teams to provide individualized attention to students, tracked using specially designed software called One Record. And a paid internship experience at our college or a local business partner location kept students connected to their education during the summer months.

Lost momentum during the summer was not only a student phenomenon but also applied to college initiatives, particularly those that featured strong collaboration between faculty and administrators. Faculty leadership also recognized that progress on many mission-critical projects was delayed or even forgotten during the summer months. As a result of discussions at President's Council and throughout the existing committee structure, the college and faculty agreed to introduce summer work teams. Faculty members were compensated for their valuable input and hard work during the summer, when they would normally be off-contract. The first summer work teams focused on service and development credits; a second-semester experience to expand the initial FYE program; Care Teams; college-wide academic pathways; prior learning assessment; and DegreeWorks, a tool to create academic plans for all students as they moved toward their educational goals. These summer teams preserved true faculty–administration partnerships and permitted important work to continue without a gap in progress between academic years.

Undergirding these student-facing activities were the administrative units of the college. "SMART" (specific, measurable, agreed-upon, realistic and time-based) goals now populated an employee evaluation system that recognized and rewarded individual and collective contributions to student success. Expanded scholarships, tuition incentives, textbook affordability, public transportation passes, and other measures kept costs low for students. And technology, including an expanded social media presence, a redesigned website, and a strengthened information technology infrastructure, improved students' online connections to the college.

Some of these initiatives were new; others were already in progress when One Door was announced. However, the One Door framework provided a mechanism for connecting all of them to the overall priorities of the institution. As a result, every department and employee—administrator, faculty, or staff—was invited to reconsider individual responsibilities and operations in light of the emphasis on student success. In turn, everyone was given an opportunity to influence the college's overall operations as successful improvements and initiatives were adopted broadly. As such, the scope of leadership at the college extended far beyond central administrative meetings or isolated governance committees. This shared dialogue perceptually flattened the structure of a large organization, promoting greater synergy across the college.

Measuring Success

President's Council and the college-wide cabinet identified 51 performance measures to test the effectiveness of responses to our six strategic priorities developed through the newly implemented shared leadership structure. And our response was in fact effective. For example, the number of Tri-C students completing degrees and certificates increased from 2,380 in 2010 to more than 4,000 by 2015. The College's IPEDS graduation rate increased from 3.7% in 2010 to 22% in 2019.

Unprecedented collaboration between the academic and workforce divisions brought together credit and noncredit programming into six newly identified Tri-C Centers of Excellence that structured industry credentials, short-term certificates, and degree programs into tiered pathways grouped by critical industry sectors. These programs got individuals into quality jobs with family-sustaining wages quickly and resulted in an explosion in the number of workforce credentials earned by students—an increase of more than 2,000%.

According to the magazine *Community College Times*, these accomplishments place Tri-C among the top ranks of the nation's 1,108 community colleges. At the same time, students continued their education at increased levels and exhibited improved success in mathematics and English courses that serve as "gateways" to degrees and certificates.

In recognition of these achievements and the college's overarching success, Tri-C received numerous awards that provided moments to celebrate our achievements and to think about how we could use our momentum to take Tri-C to even greater heights. While we had made substantial strides toward many aspects of the original One Door vision, some areas would still require revision or renewed focus. However, the most significant achievement of this process would in many regards prove to be the process itself.

Reflections on Transformation and Lessons for the Future

As originally envisioned, "One Door, Many Options for Success" referred to the experience of incoming students: They would be able to enter the institution by any office or program and receive the same quality and scope of service directing them toward and along the best educational pathway for them. This was an ambitious goal for an institution serving more than 50,000 students annually through 190 career and technical programs across four campuses and several educational centers, each with a unique student demographic and distinct culture.

What became evident, however, was that the *process* of the One Door initiative was in fact far more flexible than we had initially realized. The method provided college-wide impetus for change in a way that inspired the creation of new initiatives while naturally incorporating existing programs and promoting continuous improvement in processes to benefit the student experience. And it effectively expanded the influence of individuals from every corner of the institution, whatever their roles. Thus, One Door came to refer not so much to an initiative as to a process. It came to refer not to a door traversed by incoming students but to a common gateway to transformation at the institution.

The flexibility of One Door began to be seen in the summer of 2015, when we celebrated the progress made during the yearlong emphasis on student success. Yet even as we marked our achievements, we realized that not all students were seeing equal gains. As a result, while maintaining progress toward our overall student success goals, we embarked on a parallel and very similar process, this time with a focus specifically on equity in outcomes. In following years, the One Door framework was utilized to identify and shape the College's response to improving college access and develop a new strategic plan.

Now familiar to most employees at the institution, the title has become shorthand for a collaborative, inclusive process to address top priorities of the college. Faculty and administrative leaders, through President's Council and the college-wide cabinet, will identify emerging priorities based on analysis of data coupled with input from individual campuses, departments, and offices. Listening and work sessions across the college then give faculty, staff, and administrative employees, students, and often community stakeholders opportunities to shape and refine actions and goals to address the challenge. And promising initiatives or process improvements at the individual department, office, or campus level are shared and implemented college-wide.

One Door is no longer just an initiative at Tri-C. Instead, it gives a name to the integration of change and continuous improvement into the culture of the organization in a way that includes everyone in the shared conversation of leadership and transformation. One Door has provided Tri-C with the freedom to incorporate and evaluate new and existing programs, track progress, adjust course where necessary, and celebrate achievements while continually looking to the future. The One Door framework has become an ingrained part of how Tri-C plans for large-scale changes, reacts to challenges and opportunities, continues to obtain feedback in order to support the community, and creates innovative programs that enhance students' experience from their first connection to the college through graduation.

Benefits

As a process for expanding the conversation of leadership at Tri-C, One Door has successfully involved employees across the college, at all levels of the organizational chart, and across the administration, faculty, and staff. One Door does not just include faculty leadership in decision-making that is still completely centralized. Instead, it promotes organization-wide influence on what priorities need to be addressed and how to address them most effectively. This has resulted in stronger initiatives that solve real problems more effectively. One Door has contributed to a focus on clear outcomes, ones that are visible throughout the community. A five-fold increase in the IPEDS graduation rate, for example, demonstrates a commitment to student success far more succinctly than any policy speech. Voters have responded with nearly unprecedented levels of support for both a major capital improvement bond, the first in the institution's history, and the renewal and increase of an operating levy just 2 years later.

The One Door process has also incorporated a mechanism for change into the rhythm of the institution. Its flexibility and adaptability to different priorities has provided an effective and accepted tool for planning and continuous improvement. Regularly reevaluating processes in light of the college's priorities has helped to make the institution more nimble in adapting to new challenges. This proved particularly valuable in the spring of 2020. Like the rest of higher education, Tri-C had to adjust to the massive shift in educational delivery and operational processes brought on by the COVID-19 pandemic. As the institution closed its classrooms and facilities, and employees began working from home while faculty transitioned to remote instruction, the culture of change nurtured by One Door presented a more flexible college to the ongoing crisis. Even as some of the formal structures were hindered with the inability to meet in person, the environment One Door fostered kept faculty voices, and those of others across the college, central to the development of innovative solutions to the challenges of the pandemic.

Challenges

These benefits are not to say that One Door has been without its own challenges. At an institution the size of Tri-C, it is not easy to actually involve everyone in the process of change, or to effectively and equitably promote successful initiatives college-wide. It would be unrealistic to suggest that there has been no dissention or disagreement along the way, particularly when initiatives that reflect significant personal investment are determined not to be succeeding. Increasing flexibility and internalizing change is always difficult, especially for long-term employees who may be more entrenched in existing processes and patterns.

The size of the college introduces another difficulty due to the scope of Tri-C's programs. With 190 programs of study from liberal arts to public safety, nursing to manufacturing, it would be impossible to introduce a one-size-fits-all approach for every program. Yet even adapting a range of approaches to the distinct character and circumstances of such divergent fields requires great attention to communication and a steady hand by leadership groups such as the president's cabinet and President's Council in order to maintain focus on the broader institutional priorities.

Similarly, while one of the primary assets of the One Door model is its incorporation of a broad spectrum of viewpoints into the decision-making process, it can prove nearly impossible to completely reconcile contradictory or conflicting viewpoints from across the diverse range of stakeholders internally and externally. In addition, it is all too easy on the one hand to unintentionally leave out an important stakeholder group, or on the other to create committees of an unwieldy size out of a desire to give everyone a seat at the table. These cases are somewhat mitigated by the large number of opportunities to hear from diverse constituents provided by the One Door model, but increasing the number of meetings can easily slow the pace of progress.

Lessons

One Door has become integral to the culture of Cuyahoga Community College. It speaks to the importance of establishing a "brand" for change as part of the culture of a thriving organization. This must go beyond mere buzzwords and reflect an earned respect for a process that relies on data and respects the contributions of individuals regardless of title or pay grade. The principles of this model would certainly be applicable to other contexts. Any attempt to replicate elements of One Door, however, must keep several lessons in mind.

First, the effectiveness of the approach depends on transparent, honest leadership from those with formal leadership roles. Employees and other stakeholders who cannot trust that they are hearing the truth from the president and other administrative and faculty leaders will not trust that they are being heard. The success of One Door as a process for change at Tri-C was built on a foundation of open dialogue and an honest assessment of the current situation.

Second, in addition to listening and honesty, leaders must establish a clear context and sense of urgency around a discrete issue. A scope that is too broad or vague will result in confusion and ineffective involvement across the organization. Consistency in vocabulary and talking points reinforces strategic priorities and keeps everyone on the same page.

Third, the call to action must reflect the mutual interest of all stakeholders. In Tri-C's case, this was based on our shared commitment to our students, and the belief that a self-regarding institution must take student outcomes seriously.

Finally, the One Door process relies on developing mutually agreed-upon goals and objectives. While direction and oversight from senior administrative leadership is necessary, the process must be delegated to a broad base of involvement. Leaders must trust that departments and offices will use their own expertise and imagination in the course of meeting goals. In fact, they will develop uniquely innovative solutions when given the freedom and support to do so.

"One Door, Many Options for Success" may have begun as a singular initiative to address the challenges of student outcomes at a particular point in Cuyahoga Community College's history. What it has become, however, is a process for sharing leadership, adapting to change, and meeting challenges that has transformed the institution. This evolution reflects the organic nature of an organization and the importance of each part of it. The lesson of One Door is that shared transformation can be the gateway to a successful future.

Chapter 12 Reflection Questions

1. The context for practicing shared leadership can be set by the senior administration, in this case by a newly appointed president. Has that stage been set at your institution and, if so, how and by whom? If not, how might you get support from senior leaders—or if you are a senior leader, how might you demonstrate your support for shared leadership?
2. What changes could you make at your own institution, depending upon your current role, to provide a more supportive environment for working together and leading in more productive ways?
3. Shared leadership includes "shared dialogue" in which the core group benefits from interaction with the broader community. Do you have a way to do that now and, if not, what already exists that you might use to create more input?
4. How can you use various forms of communication to generate buy-in and build a sense of urgency about the issue you are addressing?

SHARED LEADERSHIP IN A NATIONAL-SCALE NETWORK

The Center for the Integration of Research, Teaching, and Learning (CIRTL) as a Case Example

Ann E. Austin and Robert D. Mathieu

Within the context of higher education literature and consistent with the theme of this book, shared leadership is defined as an approach to leadership that involves collaboration, the inclusion of a number of people, attention to multiple perspectives and expertise, and the involvement of informal as well as formal leaders (Kezar & Holcombe, 2017). This case example of shared leadership focuses on a North American network of research universities with a shared goal of preparing a future science, technology, engineering, and math (STEM) faculty skilled in teaching and learning. Context is essential for understanding shared leadership. Thus, this chapter begins with a description of the nature and mission of the Center for the Integration of Research, Teaching, and Learning (CIRTL). The chapter then describes CIRTL shared leadership, key design features, how shared leadership contributes to the sustainability of CIRTL, and challenges and lessons learned.

The CIRTL Network: Purpose and Mission

The Center for the Integration of Research, Teaching, and Learning (Mathieu et al., 2020) is a network of universities, all working together to prepare a generation of STEM faculty who are both excellent researchers and skilled teachers. CIRTL began in 2003 in response to a call for proposals from the U.S. National Science Foundation (NSF) to create national centers of teaching and learning in higher education. Three universities—Michigan State University (MSU), the Pennsylvania State University, and the University of Wisconsin–Madison (UW)—collaborated to build CIRTL on the foundational idea that future faculty—that is, graduate students and post-doctoral scholars aspiring to teach as a part of their careers—should be prepared to do so before stepping into such roles. Over the years, the CIRTL Network grew to six member institutions, then 25, and now 41 research universities in the United States and Canada that prepare substantial numbers of STEM future faculty.

Specifically, the mission of CIRTL is to develop future faculty who are able to implement and advance evidence-based teaching practices for diverse learners. Three core ideas guide the work of CIRTL. First, *teaching-as-research*, which prepares future faculty to bring their skills as researchers to their teaching: to understand how to frame questions about their own teaching and their students' learning, to gather data to answer those questions, to use the resulting answers to revise and improve their teaching and to thereby enhance their students' learning in an ongoing way. Second, *learning-through-diversity*, which acknowledges that learning is enhanced when teachers and learners respect diversity, and when both are able to use the diverse perspectives, knowledge, and abilities in a group to strengthen and advance the learning of all. Third, the core idea of *learning communities* emphasizes that shared discovery and generation of knowledge in groups that nurture functional relationships among its members can create learning that exceeds what individual learners can achieve alone. In the CIRTL Network, learning communities of future faculty occur both within each member university and across the CIRTL Network.

CIRTL's mission is fulfilled through initiatives and programming at the institutional level and the national level. Each member institution creates a *local CIRTL learning community* to provide professional development opportunities for future faculty. Within these local learning communities, participants interact with faculty, academic staff, and peers to grow in their knowledge and expertise as teachers. In addition to these local learning communities, the entire CIRTL Network provides learning opportunities in a *cross-network learning community*. As part of the shared expectations of membership, each university contributes learning opportunities, such as workshop series, courses, and MOOCs, available to future faculty across the CIRTL Network. This cross-network curriculum is robust and dynamic, providing a range of exciting and innovative options for CIRTL participants seeking to broaden their development as teachers and valuing opportunities to interact with their counterparts at often very different member institutions.

A range of evaluation studies (Hill et al., 2019a, 2019b; Schein et al., 2018) have provided evidence that CIRTL participants gain specific knowledge important in implementing and advancing effective teaching, enhance their self-confidence as teachers, and deepen their career aspirations to include teaching-related work. At the same time, evaluation and research studies have demonstrated that the partner universities also benefit. Their leaders gain ideas and inspiration helpful in their local planning; the affiliation with a project having major grants from the NSF and other funders raises prestige and visibility for their graduate education; and the individual CIRTL leaders at the institutions value the collegial relationships, professional development, and career advancement that they experience.

Rationale for a Shared Leadership Approach

From its beginning, the CIRTL Network has taken a shared approach to leadership. Several factors have contributed to its sustained success. Most fundamentally, shared leadership and decision-making aligns with CIRTL's core ideas, and in particular the principles of learning communities. One of the founders of CIRTL came from the field of social work and brought a keen understanding of the factors that enable learning communities to function effectively and reach desired outcomes. His contribution was to help the founders see that simply establishing a group is not sufficient. Rather, an effective group is one in which there are functional tasks that require mutual connection to accomplish the overarching mission, and participating members see their specific opportunities to make key contributions. Given CIRTL's broad commitment to the power and potential of collaborative learning communities, organizing around a shared leadership model has been quite natural for the CIRTL Network. In fact, members of the network sometimes explicitly reference CIRTL's core idea of learning community as part of their rationale when they make recommendations for refining how the network engages in shared leadership.

A second reason for shared leadership recognizes that a collaborative network of universities needs a leadership approach that aligns with that structure. Each university has its own culture and context, its particular organizational structure, and its own way of defining preparing future faculty for their careers. The sentiment of a senior-level university leader at one of the original three universities articulated at a CIRTL convening in the 1st year highlights the following: "Our university has its own approach to graduate student development and has enjoyed considerable success. We want to collaborate; we do not want to simply adopt what another university is doing."

This clear statement foregrounded the importance of institutional autonomy among the partners of the CIRTL Network. Each member university sees value in working with others and in sharing and adapting successes, but each also wants to maintain its own decision-making, culture, and identity. Further, each partner wants to have a valued voice as the work of the network proceeds. In this context, shared leadership makes much sense.

Third, the expansion of the CIRTL Network over time has contributed to valuing the shared leadership model. Over the course of almost 2 decades, as the network has expanded steadily toward its current membership of more than 40 university members, the activities and work to be accomplished have increased. The curriculum of the cross-network activities of CIRTL have expanded over time as the numbers of universities and participants have increased. The process of planning for twice yearly in-person network meetings and monthly online network meetings has become more complex. The rich possibilities for new directions have increased with the ideas brought forward by more institutions. The related interest in writing and applying for grant funding has required more coordination. While three universities could operate initially in an informally connected way, expansion created both the need for and interest in broad sharing of talents, leadership, decision-making, and responsibility for network activities.

Shared leadership has fit well with the activities, philosophy, origins, and growth of the CIRTL Network.

The Nature of the Shared Leadership Model in the CIRTL Network

Structurally, the commitment to shared leadership permeates the whole CIRTL Network. Each university partner has two CIRTL leaders who guide the development and growth of their local CIRTL learning community. The *CIRTL institutional leader* has primary responsibility for the success of the local CIRTL learning community. The institutional leader typically is a STEM faculty member, respected by colleagues and students for both research and teaching. The institutional leader advocates and develops presence and resources for the learning community, and so needs to be knowledgeable of campus cultures and systems, especially around STEM and graduate education. Often a CIRTL institutional leader also holds a position within the university's graduate school. The *CIRTL administrative coleader* leads the operation of the local learning community and its programming. Activities of the coleader might include hiring and mentoring of staff, marketing of opportunities to future faculty, acquisition and reporting of evaluation data, and facilitating in-kind contributions to the CIRTL Network. Many coleaders also work in centers for teaching and learning. The CIRTL leaders at each university are "linking pins," looking inward to their own institutions to plan and implement opportunities for their local CIRTL learning community and looking outward in monthly meetings to discuss issues relevant for CIRTL at large. Hill (2018, 2019) sees these CIRTL leaders as indispensable bridges whose shared leadership is essential to the functioning and aligned success of the network and of each of its member institutions.

The CIRTL Network has a leadership team, consisting of a director, an associate director, a lead of evaluation and research, and CIRTL leaders from four of the university members. Even within a shared leadership structure, it remains necessary to have a director as the person holding fiduciary responsibility for the network (Historically, this position began as and evolved from the principal investigator role in the initial core funding grants.) The associate director has primary responsibility for the daily operation of the network and supervises several staff in "CIRTL central" who handle coordination of cross-network programming, internal and external communication issues, support of meetings, and so on. The leadership team, which is advisory to the director, meets weekly to discuss the well-being of the network, make tactical decisions that guide immediate work and long-term plans, develop strategic directions and policy for consideration of the network and advance engagement of the whole network in the work of CIRTL. All members of the leadership team contribute actively to the ongoing conceptual development of the CIRTL Network.

Importantly, most CIRTL universities have local leadership teams in addition to the two formal CIRTL institutional leaders. These teams include faculty and staff, and often future faculty as staff as well. The members of these teams are also part of the CIRTL Network shared leadership community, including serving in the operations groups, for example. And future institutional leaders and coadministrative leaders also grow from these team members, occasionally moving into such positions at other CIRTL Network campuses.

The partners of the CIRTL Network share the leadership of network operations through operations groups. For example, the CIRTL network operations group (CNOG) is responsible for the curriculum offered within the cross-network learning community. The CNOG receives proposals from universities for various curricular ideas, evaluates them in the context of CIRTL learning goals, and puts together a set of online opportunities. The membership operations group is responsible for recruiting, selecting, and onboarding new university partners. The CIRTL Network also creates ad hoc committees for specific needs. For example, currently such a committee, called CIRTL 2.0, is developing new structural and financial plans for a growing and sustainable CIRTL Network.

While these structures form the skeleton of the CIRTL Network's shared leadership, equally important are the processes that enable a vital community that is so critical for successful shared leadership. One such process is frequent convenings that connect the many members of the CIRTL Network community. Twice a year, CIRTL holds an in-person meeting attended by at least the two institutional leaders from each member campus, the leadership team, the operations groups, and, most recently, invited future faculty. The location of the in-person meeting rotates to different partner campuses to make visible their homes and cultures, and to highlight the local learning communities and teaching-as-research work of their future faculty. These meetings are designed to build connections across the network, to enable exchange of ideas, and to provide the venue and time for important network-level decision-making.

In addition to the semiannual in-person network meetings, the network meets online twice monthly. An administrative meeting is held monthly with the CIRTL institutional leaders and members of the CIRTL operations groups. These meetings are organized by the director, the associate director, and the leadership team. A monthly network meeting functions as a learning community time for the entire network with the purpose of sharing lessons learned and new ideas. All of these meetings serve to foster the cross-university exchange and to build the kind of connected community that establishes the foundation for trusted shared leadership.

Valuing Diversity as a Key Characteristic of CIRTL's Approach to Shared Leadership

From the start, CIRTL built on diverse abilities, skills, and perspectives across many people. The development of the original proposal to the NSF was initiated by a mid-career UW professor of astronomy who, from personal experience, felt the need for preparing future faculty with understanding and expertise in teaching along with strong disciplinary research skills. From an informal teaching and learning network on campus, the idea nucleated a UW core team comprising faculty and staff across all STEM domains (except mathematics) and from social science fields. For example, he was first joined by a UW professor of social work who shared these goals and brought deep knowledge and experience with learning communities. The UW team invited the collaboration of colleagues from MSU and Penn State with extensive research expertise in higher education, including research on teaching and learning, graduate education, professional development, and research and evaluation. Thus, the conceptualization and preparation of the proposed Center was built on deep and broad cross-disciplinary collaboration.

In the early years of CIRTL, the founders were often surprised and excited when they learned from each other's individual disciplinary and field experience. For example, during the founding years, those from the STEM fields were enthusiastic to incorporate teaching and assessment strategies well-known by their colleagues in education who were part of the movement to encourage active, engaged learning in STEM higher education. Similarly, the leaders from the field of education appreciated learning about the disciplinary-related habits of mind that related to the challenges of involvement of STEM graduate students in CIRTL activities (such as cultural expectations for an extensive investment of time in research).

Thus, as CIRTL grew into a network, it was natural to extend its commitment to diverse perspectives into all that the CIRTL Network does. For example, the cross-network opportunities are provided by members of each local CIRTL learning community, ensuring that a range of topics, approaches, and perspectives are available in the professional development provided for future faculty. These characteristics of sharing responsibility and utilizing diverse talents and perspectives echo the guiding core idea of learning-through-diversity that is at the heart of CIRTL's identity. They also embrace shared leadership, in which principles of distributing responsibility and tapping into different kinds of expertise or institutional strengths serve to enhance the overall effectiveness of the work of the CIRTL Network.

How CIRTL Integrated Decision-Making and Shared Governance Into Shared Leadership

While the founders of CIRTL envisioned and planted the seeds of a shared approach to leadership, the practice of shared leadership within the CIRTL Network has expanded and evolved over the almost 2 decades since. One way in which CIRTL has evolved in its approach to shared leadership is in its decision-making and governance processes.

Major policy and strategic decisions typically occur at in-person meetings. In the first years of the CIRTL Network while it was funded by external core grants, decisions about significant issues occurred through discussion and emergent consensus of network members. Strictly, this consensus was advisory to the NSF principal investigator, although that authority was seldom engaged. As the CIRTL Network moved off NSF funding and into a dues-based financial structure, and as the network experienced greater organizational maturity, interest developed in formalizing such decision-making to reflect and ensure the network's commitment to being a collegial, diverse, and equitable community. With this motivation, an ad hoc committee explored possible approaches to decision-making appropriate for networks and proposed the method of sociocracy (Endenburg et al., 1998; Rau & Koch-Gonzalez, 2018). This approach to decision-making foregrounds structured and respectful opportunities for every member of an organization to voice perspectives, questions, and concerns as part of a well-defined process. A key feature of sociocracy is an iterative process that creates space for multiple views, encourages active listening to alternative perspectives, and provides opportunities for concerns to be addressed. These steps refine proposed decisions and lead to a final decision that can be owned and respected throughout the organization. The CIRTL Network adapted sociocracy for major policy and strategic decisions, with the primary variant being that the final decision is made by a vote in which each university has one vote and a 90% majority is required for acceptance. While the network continues to refine its adaptation of sociocracy and to develop opportunities for members to become proficient in facilitating the sociocratic method, there has been wide appreciation for the ways in which sociocracy reflects CIRTL's commitment to shared leadership and inclusive decision-making processes.

In addition to refining its processes and structures for decision-making, the network has formalized transparent and regular processes for membership on committees in order to ensure that everyone has an opportunity to engage in the shared leadership opportunities. In the early years, the membership of such committees took place on an ad hoc volunteer and appointment basis. Elections are now held annually to select members for the leadership team and operations groups, with candidates nominated by others or themselves. Members serve single staggered terms in order to ensure wide knowledge about the ways network leadership functions.

The CIRTL Network also fosters shared leadership by encouraging individuals within the CIRTL Network to deepen their involvement over time. Often those from universities relatively new to the network will take on assignments to speak at or facilitate particular conversations in network online or in-person meetings. They may offer to assist in ad hoc committees and new initiatives. Through these opportunities, they can work with and get to know others in the network and become recognized as emerging leaders. Over time, those who have enjoyed modest assignments may decide to self-nominate when elections occur for network leadership roles. This kind of informal pathway of gradually increasing leadership responsibilities means that those on the leadership team and other major standing committees are knowledgeable about CIRTL history, core ideas, and practices and well-connected with others across the network.

Finally, the CIRTL Network cultivates shared leadership by providing numerous opportunities for all involved to develop respectful and comfortable professional relationships—ones that, for many, evolve into strong professional and personal friendships. The twice yearly in-person network meetings and the monthly CIRTL online meetings are intentionally organized to foster interaction and opportunities for attendees to get to know each other. Presentations that explicitly feature different members of the community and carefully designed small group break-out conversations and work sessions (including in the online setting) have been very successful over the years in creating spaces for people to connect across the institutions. At in-person meetings, informal social gatherings punctuate the structured meetings, and attendees always enjoy occasions for coffee, early morning breakfast, or evening get-togethers as opportunities to foster what for many have become highly valued personal and professional relationships. (The disappointment when the 2020 in-person CIRTL Network gathering was moved to a shorter online meeting due to the COVID crisis partly reflected the sadness over giving up the chance to connect with friends.) The strength of personal connections cultivated informally is critically important in creating the respect and trust that are necessary for smooth shared leadership processes.

Shared Leadership as Part of Building a Sustainable Network

Sustainability is a goal and challenge for any network. The large number of people invested in contributing to the CIRTL Network means that responsibility for ensuring vitality rests on many shoulders. Furthermore, the range of ideas generated across multiple people opens possibilities for innovation and evolution; at the same time, stability benefits from experienced leaders who can guide those who are newer.

Shared responsibility for leadership and deep commitment to CIRTL's mission has meant that many individuals speak up on behalf of the CIRTL Network in national venues. CIRTL Network leaders who are graduate deans participate in the Council of Graduate Schools, where they have given formal presentations about CIRTL Network projects and impact, hosted gatherings of deans of prospective member universities, and encouraged interest in the CIRTL Network during informal conversations. Similarly, CIRTL Network members often give presentations at national conferences and professional and scholarly meetings, where they spark interest in what

CIRTL does. Connections with funding agencies, prospective member institutions, and organizations with aligned missions increase when a number of people have the knowledge and confidence to speak about the network. The expansion of CIRTL over the past 2 decades demonstrates that CIRTL goals and programs are recognized within the national landscape of efforts to strengthen graduate education and improve undergraduate education.

Another way in which habits of shared leadership contribute to long-term stability is through the personal connection that members feel to each other and to the network. Many people have found a home in the CIRTL Network in terms of their commitment to strengthen how graduate preparation prepares the next generation of faculty and the value they place on evidence-based teaching practices. Participating in a network of like-minded colleagues who share deeply held values, enjoy working in collaboration with each other, and feel a sense of shared ownership and leadership means that individual members are likely to work hard to ensure the long-term sustainability of the CIRTL Network.

Challenges to Shared Leadership

While shared leadership is integral to the way in which the CIRTL Network carries out its work, this approach also has brought some challenges that are opportunities for reflection and adjustment. First, embracing shared leadership must be balanced with the responsibilities of those who hold formal organizational and fiduciary responsibility. For example, when CIRTL had core funding grants from the NSF and other organizations, an important task was creating a sense of "we" in terms of responsibility. Balancing the formal roles of the PI and co-PIs with the importance and benefits of much wider responsibility and ownership of network directions and decisions required many conversations, quite a bit of time working together, and a sense of patience to not rush the process. While the CIRTL Network no longer relies on external funding, financial and organizational responsibilities to the partners remain through memoranda of understanding and continue to require clear fiduciary responsibilities.

A second challenge was investing substantial energy and time into developing formal and structural processes to support the shared leadership model. The processes described in the prior section required major investments of social capital from all of the leaders across the network.

Shared leadership processes also require managing diverse personalities and styles. As in any group, context, perspectives, and approaches vary across individuals. Effective shared leadership requires a commitment from all involved to approach the process with a spirit of generosity, humility, and respect for others. Occasional frustration can be balanced against ongoing commitment to the value of shared leadership, recognition that outcomes are usually better when based on collaboration, and a belief in the good intentions of all involved.

One challenge CIRTL has faced has become an opportunity. In recent years, many within CIRTL have looked for ways to create a more inclusive community that explicitly welcomes and encourages the involvement of those whose identities bring more diversity to the network. Those involved in CIRTL recognize that the aspiration to create such an explicitly diverse community takes time and effort and is ongoing. This challenge, however, has become an opportunity for network participants to learn together and for some CIRTL participants to step into leadership roles around diversity, equity, and inclusion that draw on their expertise, knowledge, and value orientation. This commitment to a stronger multicultural organization has both required shared leadership and broadened opportunities for shared leadership.

Lessons Learned and Advice for Others

Throughout this chapter we have explained how a commitment to shared leadership has been woven throughout the history of the CIRTL Network. While our telling of the CIRTL story includes embedded lessons, here we offer explicit advice:

- First, engaging in shared leadership does not occur simply through a decision that can be instantiated immediately. Rather, shared leadership requires long-term effort and nurturing. From its conceptualization and early days, the CIRTL Network has had a vision of shared leadership. Fully bringing that commitment to fruition is an ongoing process.
- Second, shared leadership is enhanced when organizational values align with this approach. In the case of CIRTL, the underlying core ideas of learning communities and learning-through-diversity aligned well with and supported efforts to develop shared leadership.
- Third, advancing practices of shared leadership requires attention both to structure and relationships. Over time, CIRTL has formalized structures and processes, such as an operations group structure, a process to elect people to committees, and the sociocracy approach

to decision-making. Equally important, however, CIRTL holds regular network meetings, both in-person and online, that provide the occasion and venues within which individual CIRTL members come to know and trust each other, attributes essential to establishing effective shared leadership.

Shared leadership requires organizational values and principles that are aligned with shared leadership, relevant structures and processes, and opportunities for creating trusted relationships. When these organizational characteristics are in place, efforts to advance shared leadership are on fertile ground.

Chapter 13 Reflection Questions

1. This case illustrates ways to set up a broader network across a collection of different institutions. Do you know if your institution is a part of any multi-institution collaborative efforts like this that could support and reinforce your approach to shared leadership on your own campus?
2. How can shared leadership work within a distributed network? What challenges have you faced in using this model across institutions either within other higher education institutions or with community partners?
3. The practice of shared leadership can develop over time. If you can identify existing examples of shared leadership on your campus, how have they evolved since they began? What can you learn from those changes about what to do next to strengthen your capacity to work in this way?

References

Endenburg, G., Lindenhovius, J., & Bowden, C. (1998). *Sociocracy: The organization of decision-making: 'No objection' as the principle of sociocracy*. Euburon.

Hill, L. B. (2018). *The key role of institutional representatives in networks* [Research Brief #5]. Center for the Integration of Research, Teaching, and Learning (CIRTL).

Hill, L. B. (2019). Understanding the impact of a multi-institutional STEM reform network through key boundary-spanning individuals. *The Journal of Higher Education, 91*(3), 1–28. https://doi.org/10.1080/00221546.2019.1650581

Hill, L. B., Austin, A. E., Bantawa, B., & Savoy, J. N. (2019a). Factors of success: building and sustaining teaching professional development opportunities for doctoral students and postdocs. *Higher Education Research & Development, 38*(6), 1168–1182. https://doi.org/10.1080/07294360.2019.1616677

Hill, L. B., Savoy, J. N., Austin, A. E., & Bantawa, B. (2019b). The impact of multi-institutional STEM reform networks on member institutions: A case study of the Center for the Integration of Research, Teaching, and Learning. *Innovative Higher Education, 44*(3), 1–16. https://doi.org/10.1007/s10755-019-9461-7.

Kezar, A. J., & Holcombe, E. M. (2017). *Shared leadership in higher education: Important lessons from research and practice.* American Council on Education.

Mathieu, R. D., Austin, A. E., Barnicle, K. A., Campa, H., III, & McLinn, C. M. (2020). The Center for the Integration of Research, Teaching, and Learning: A national-scale network to prepare STEM future faculty. In K. Saichaie & C. H. Theisen (Eds.), *Approaches to graduate student instructor development and preparation* (New Directions for Teaching and Learning, no. 163, pp. 45–63). Jossey-Bass.

Rau, T., & Koch-Gonzalez, J. (2018). *Many voices, one song: Shared power with sociocracy.* Sociocracy for All.

Schein, J., Hill, L. B., Austin, A. E., & Rollert-French, K. (2018). *The impact of high-engagement teaching-as-research programs* [Research Brief #4]. Center for the Integration of Research, Teaching, and Learning (CIRTL).

REFLECTIONS ON SHARED
LEADERSHIP IN ACTION

Elizabeth M. Holcombe, Adrianna J. Kezar, Susan Elrod, and Judith A. Ramaley

I n this final chapter, we take the opportunity to reflect back on the various
case study examples and consider how they illuminated key points from
the opening chapters about the nature of shared leadership, when to
use shared leadership, the benefits of shared leadership as well as the challenges, and capacity-building lessons learned from experience in the field.
We also want to thank our chapter authors for their honesty, deep reflection,
wisdom, and enthusiasm to help promulgate shared leadership which they
found so valuable to their efforts of institutional transformation and managing complex issues.

Types of Complex Challenges Shared Leadership Can Address

Our chapters highlight the rich array of complex challenges that can be
addressed through shared leadership. The sheer ambitiousness of the projects signals the value of shared leadership and is encouraging for the future
of higher education as an enterprise. Perhaps not surprisingly, many of the
initiatives focus on improving student success. With decades of critiques of
higher education for its failure to improve retention and success rates, we
must make progress on this vexing challenge.

The University of Wisconsin–Whitewater worked on improving the
1st year for students and improving their retention rates (chapter 6). Their
work on the Re-imagining the First Year project was the perfect opportunity
for harnessing expertise across the institution and making a difference for
students. Similarly, the State University of New York (SUNY) at Geneseo
team focused on implementing an integrative tutoring approach that aimed
to dramatically improve student retention and success (chapter 6). Such

an initiative required unprecedented work across a variety of units that are engaged in advising and to connect this work. Cuyahoga Community College also ambitiously engaged the "one door, many opportunities for success" approach that had a six-pronged strategy to increase access and ensure student success (chapter 12). And lastly, Humboldt State University worked on the challenge of getting more low-income, first-generation, and racially minoritized students to succeed in science, technology, engineering, and math (STEM) disciplines by integrating three high-impact practices during the 1st year focused around a thematic experience (chapter 5). All of these student success initiatives move beyond many of the simplistic, fragmented, and siloed approaches to student success that have been largely unsuccessful in moving the needle on retention and graduation and show the promise of shared leadership for tackling this most urgent challenge.

Related to student success but slightly different is the challenge of ensuring diversity, equity, and inclusion (DEI) are prioritized on campus. The University of Richmond illustrates how their move to shared leadership was a concerted attempt to move forward their DEI efforts that had been stalled for many years (chapter 8). They noted that "systemic DEI work [had become] siloed and [lost] momentum because it [was] seen as the responsibility of a central authority or individual, rather than the responsibility of all" (Crutcher et al., p. 11, this volume). Even though their initiative is new, they are seeing great success. Other campuses are also experimenting with a shared leadership approach to DEI work and are finding similar successes in meeting their goals and including more voices in leadership (Kezar et al., 2021).

Another area that has been a perennial challenge is improving the teaching and learning environment in higher education. The Center for the Integration of Research in Teaching and Learning (CIRTL) has been working on this important challenge in STEM fields over the past several decades (chapter 13). Their initiative works to reimagine graduate education as well as faculty socialization in an effort to move the needle and make teaching quality more central on campuses. This ambitious effort, which relies on shared leadership, also shows how multiple institutions can work in a shared fashion to engage the most complex challenges of our time. That broader collective action was not limited to individuals within institutions working together but multiple institutions working collectively and learning from and with each other.

Other chapters took on external or community-based issues, such as the Homelessness Research and Action Collaborative (HRAC) at Portland State University (chapter 10), which looked at addressing homelessness in the Portland regional area. Shared leadership is ideal for this type of challenge that many college campuses will be engaged in with their communities. We imagine many other challenging community-based issues such as poverty, mental health, or racial justice, among others, could be excellent candidates for college campuses that do work in the community engagement space to utilize a shared leadership approach.

The Portland State University College of Liberal Arts and Sciences (chapter 7) and Winona State University (chapter 11) cases highlight the challenges of budgetary constraints and ways that leaders can use shared leadership to continue to meet their important missions even as they face fiscal challenges. Having only recently emerged from a worldwide recession, and now emerging from a global pandemic that also has had significant economic repercussions, understanding how shared leadership can help campuses innovate while addressing significant budgetary constraints is also an important takeaway from this book. The diversity of settings on display in this book demonstrates the versatility and flexibility of shared leadership and how it can be used and adapted to solve a variety of complex challenges.

Shared Leadership Models

In chapter 2, we described three primary models of shared leadership: coleadership, team leadership, and distributed leadership. Many times, faculty, administrators, and staff struggle to envision exactly what shared leadership looks like, or else they may have a narrow vision of one approach, such as a president's cabinet. This book offers examples of a variety of ways that shared leadership can play out in practice, highlighting multiple examples of coleadership, team leadership, and distributed leadership (see Table 14.1). As we noted in chapter 2, in practice shared leadership often does not fit neatly or perfectly within one model; indeed, many of our case studies show elements of multiple types of shared leadership. For example, three of our case study chapters demonstrate elements of all three models. In chapter 5, the Humboldt State project featured coleaders (the project's co-PIs), several leadership teams (one for each place-based learning community), and elements of a distributed leadership structure, as they had leaders from multiple administrative and academic units at varying levels of the organizational hierarchy. The University of Wisconsin–Whitewater example (chapter 6) also described a complex project with elements of all three models of shared leadership—coleaders of the project and of some teams, four teams for different aspects of the project, and distributed leadership seen in how flexible configurations of leaders popped up to solve different problems like the creation of the campus emergency fund or the development of the institutional growth mindset framework. The CIRTL case (chapter 13) also contains elements of all three models of shared leadership, with coleaders at CIRTL Central, multiple teams or subgroups running various elements of the project, and leadership teams on each campus as well as at the central project level.

The other chapters can be categorized a bit more easily into one of the three models of shared leadership. The Portland State dean team (chapter 7) offers an example of coleadership, with the three associate deans who took on the functions of the dean after she left the University.

TABLE 14.1

Models of Shared Leadership in Case Study Chapters

Coleadership	Team Leadership	Distributed Leadership	Elements of All Three Models
			Chapter 5: Humboldt State University
			Chapter 6: University of Wisconsin–Whitewater
Chapter 7: Portland State Dean Team			
		Chapter 8: University of Richmond	
	Chapter 9: SUNY Geneseo		
	Chapter 10: Portland State HRAC		
			Chapter 11: Winona State University
		Chapter 12: Cuyahoga Community College	
			Chapter 13: CIRTL

Three chapters described a distributed leadership model: the University of Richmond's distributed leadership for DEI (chapter 8), the Winona State leadership academy (chapter 11), and the One Door approach at Cuyahoga Community College (chapter 12). And two chapters described a team leadership approach: SUNY Geneseo's APAS team for academic support services composed of five people (chapter 9) and the Portland State HRAC composed of eight people (chapter 10).

Common Characteristics of Shared Leadership

It is notable that regardless of the model or approach, all of the case studies featured similar characteristics and processes as the authors described what shared leadership looked like in practice. For example, almost every chapter highlighted the importance of understanding that shared leadership needs to be nurtured over time and cannot happen instantaneously, at least not at any meaningful scale or in an authentic, high-quality way. In terms of what shared leadership looks like on the ground, most chapters emphasized the importance of creating a common vision to help center and ground the work. For example, the Portland State dean team created a team charter to help ensure team members all understood the vision. The HRAC at Portland State University also describes this process and provides an excellent example for others to follow.

Additionally, many chapter authors describe the importance of considering the right structures or models to support shared leadership. At Winona State this was a leadership academy; at the University of Richmond it was a council; at SUNY Geneseo it was a team; at Cuyahoga it was a matrix organization connecting existing units; at University of Wisconsin–Whitewater it was "birds of a feather" meetings similar to professional learning communities, as well as several teams and flexible groups that formed as issues arose. The Winona State chapter provides an excellent example of a more unusual structure for the higher education context to consider. Many campuses have likely utilized teams, councils, and other similar shared structures before so they will not be entirely new, but there are many other structures we should be considering that can be borrowed from outside of higher education like Winona State's leadership academy. Cuyahoga Community College's matrix structure is another example of this type of innovative structure that shows immense promise. The CIRTL case also underscores how structures need to be responsive to particular campus contexts and cultures. In this case, leaders allowed shared leadership structures to evolve locally to fit different campus cultures rather than impose a single structure on all their member campuses.

The same might also be relevant for units within a larger decentralized campus, and leaders might want to consider providing general guidelines and allowing units to evolve structures that best fit within their norms around working together.

Every chapter described the importance of fostering relationships both formally through structures such as the meetings, subgroups, or town halls, and also informally. The Humboldt State University example of holding happy hours for their shared leadership group is an example of one of the ways to informally build relationships that help deepen shared leadership, as well as the CIRTL examples of breakfast and dinner gatherings at their annual meetings. Central to developing relationships is trust-building, which was a key feature of the University of Richmond story; trust allowed them to work seamlessly across divides that are often challenging, such as faculty and administrators, academic and student affairs, or faculty from different disciplines. At University of Wisconsin–Whitewater, trust-building paid off in terms of helping the group change a policy fairly easily. Elrod et al. noted:

> Because many of these faculty, staff, and administrators had spent so much time together in RFY team meetings, getting this accomplished was not as difficult as it might have been if we had not already built these relationships. It took just a few meetings of the Academic Policy Committee for the RFY team to share information, data, answer questions, and empower the committee to come up with a reasonable solution. (p. 102, this volume)

In addition to trust, many chapter authors emphasized the importance of listening and setting up enough structures and processes to ensure that significant changes can happen.

Each of the chapters explored the processes that helped them in sharing leadership, ranging from regular meetings and convenings, to ways to orient and socialize new members of the group, to episodic retreats or town halls. Each process helped leaders achieve their goals in different ways. For example, the Portland State dean team increased the department chair meetings at their college from monthly to weekly "in order to share, in real time, the information received from the University budget office and the team's budget calculations" (Beaudoin et al., p. 111, this volume) to promote transparency and collaboration around the budget process. Cuyahoga Community College created a President's Council, consisting of the president's cabinet, the Joint Faculty Senate Committee, and faculty union leadership, which meets monthly and is "a forum for discussing key priorities at the college and brainstorming ways to meet challenges collaboratively" (Johnson & Miller, p. 172, this volume). The Humboldt State University authors described multiple meetings of different subgroups, as well as regular meetings of the broader project leadership team, which helped ensure that as many people as possible could have a voice in decision-making.

To that end, one of the core processes reviewed by our chapter authors was decision-making, and they underscored the need for decision-making processes to be thoughtfully established. CIRTL, for example, used a method of sociocracy: "This approach to decision making foregrounds structured and respectful opportunities for every member of an organization to voice perspectives, questions, and concerns as part of a well-defined process" (Austin & Mathieu, p. 189, this volume). Cuyahoga Community College used a process of appreciative inquiry to help move forward their shared leadership. The Portland State dean team created shared criteria for decision-making and decided that consensus among their three codeans was necessary before finalizing any decision. The team set "shared priorities and us[ed] data to inform decisions" and "was more immune to the emotional appeals of individuals and focused on making decisions that benefit the college as a whole" (Beaudoin et al., p. 113, this volume).

As more people are part of the leadership process, it is also important to build appropriate communication venues and structures. CIRTL leaders described their work to change and evolve their communication structures as they grew over time. Humboldt State leaders described the challenge of very different styles of communicating among faculty and administrators, as well as among faculty from different disciplines. Many of the chapters spoke to the needs of careful consideration of the diverse set of individuals who come together for shared leadership and catering communications to these various groups. The University of Richmond chapter noted the importance of over-communicating and ensuring that a strong communications plan is in place. Cuyahoga Community College worked to develop a robust communications infrastructure—they "overhauled the college's Marketing and Communications (now Integrated Communications) department; introduced a biweekly president's newsletter distributed to all employees via email; began sharing weekly updates with the college's board of trustees; and introduced town hall meetings each semester at every campus" (Johnson & Miller, p. 172, this volume).

On the ground, shared leadership required a rethinking of the processes and structures of working together, relationships between groups, and forms of communication. These significant institutional changes also led to significant benefits for the campuses and groups engaged in shared leadership. In the following sections, we review some of these benefits, along with challenges to implementing shared leadership and important lessons for needed capacity-building.

Benefits of Shared Leadership

Shared leadership created an assortment of benefits for the campuses featured in this volume. Most importantly, of course, shared leadership helped campuses meet their goals and tackle the complex challenges outlined in the previous paragraphs. The institutions in this book made progress on student success, equity, improved teaching and learning, budgetary constraints, and the other critical challenges that they set out to address. Campuses saw additional benefits as well, ranging from an improved campus climate and culture; to better relationships among different groups on campus; to more engagement of faculty and staff in problem-solving on campus; to broader ownership of complex challenges; to increased organizational learning among faculty, staff, and administrators. For example, the University of Wisconsin–Whitewater team noted that shared leadership improved problem-solving skills across units and formed stronger cohesion and relationships among people and departments that would not normally interact. Nearly every other group featured in this book also remarked upon improved relationships and increased collaboration across campus (or multiple campuses, in the case of CIRTL). Further, both Humboldt State and the Portland State HRAC described how shared leadership that included community partners strengthened relationships with the local community and local stakeholders in addition to improving internal cross-campus relationships. The University of Richmond and the Portland State dean team both highlighted the increased transparency that shared leadership brought to their organizations. And several of the case study authors mentioned the flexibility and adaptability that shared leadership provides, which has been especially helpful as they have navigated the COVID-19 crisis and the shift to virtual instruction and operation. We hope that as more campuses experiment with shared approaches to leadership, researchers and practitioners can continue to catalogue the many benefits of this new way of leading.

Challenges to Shared Leadership

Given the work required to fundamentally rethink current organizational structures and processes and deep histories of working hierarchically, bureaucratically, and individualistically, it is perhaps not surprising that each chapter's authors encountered some challenges in implementing shared leadership. Several chapters identified how shared leadership is quite difficult to foster within the existing hierarchical and bureaucratic structures that are present at most campuses. Both chapters from Portland State University noted how many of their struggles related back to trying to maneuver shared leadership within a broader environment that was not supportive of the structure. This section of chapter 10 captured the challenge well:

> We found that in the absence of one formally designated leader, the default was too often for university administration to defer to a white male member of the team, even when the person with the greatest depth of knowledge about policy issues and connections to potential partners and donors (the university's target) was a Latina. Community partners and donors also expected a clear organizational hierarchy. (Hines et al., p. 145, this volume)

The traditions and philosophies that guide many of those we work with often clash with shared leadership. And even when clearly articulating one's new structure, others outside of the shared leadership structure often default to traditional hierarchies and systems. Those efforts that involved broad or overall campus shared leadership experienced this challenge of clashing systems because their whole system was being changed. In their efforts to move toward shared leadership, they certainly encountered resistance from the traditional structures and culture. For example, the Portland State dean team described the "skepticism" of their college's department chairs, many of whom "indicated that they preferred to have one dean that could be held accountable" (Beaudoin et al., pp. 109–110, this volume) It may be quicker (or more feasible) to move to share leadership within smaller units of the campus as was done with Portland State's Homelessness Research and Action Collaborative, but chapter 10 illuminates how the early ease of a smaller-scale initiative still faces long-term battles within an overall organization that may not be supportive of the work. It is certainly a lengthier and more complex process to change the entire campus to embrace or at least accept a shared leadership approach, but over the long run the shared leadership effort will likely face fewer ongoing challenges if these changes are made more broadly at the institution level. One way that faculty and midlevel leaders who wish to facilitate broader engagement with shared leadership structures across campus may make progress is by communicating the successes they have achieved in their smaller spheres of influence.

Each chapter's authors noted the importance of respecting and fostering diversity but also noted how they wrestled with managing diverse voices and conflict. The CIRTL authors noted that "a commitment from all involved to approach the process with a spirit of generosity, humility, and respect for others" (Austin & Mathieu, p. 192, this volume) was essential for managing this challenge that was shared by many chapter authors. The Cuyahoga Community College group also noted that no matter how open you are to diverse perspectives, it is nearly impossible to reconcile what are often competing voices, and that this challenge will be ongoing for those involved in such a process.

Time to do the work of shared leadership when institutions are organized so that individuals are responsible for work designated within a certain role means shared leadership is typically an extra expectation on top of existing work. The Portland State University HRAC authors provided important insight about the issue of the additional time it takes to conduct shared leadership. These authors note that taking the time to negotiate various tensions in shared leadership work requires "serious commitment, flexibility, and a safe environment for risk-taking and learning" (Hines et al., p. 155, this volume). While they note that it can take additional time to work through some of these issues up front, in the long run the effort will have a time-saving effect, as several of the other chapter authors noted as well. The Winona State University case also highlighted how leaders can build in time for shared leadership so that it is not work on top of one's existing role.

Several chapters mentioned that existing attitudes or routines often get in the ways of doing shared leadership. Shared leadership requires people to let go of themselves as individuals and embrace the collective, act in new ways, and change old habits. At Winona State University, for example, people struggled to behave in the new manner required by shared leadership, which prevented some of their forward movement. Campuses also struggled with collaboration and "silo-busting," as individuals routinely defaulted to traditional ways of operating without constant guidance and reinforcement of shared leadership values and practices. This challenge featured quite prominently in the examples from Portland State University, specifically their dean team, as well as at SUNY Geneseo and University of Wisconsin–Whitewater.

Accountability was also mentioned as a common challenge. When responsibility is shared, it is often not fully clear who is responsible for what work. A variety of chapters described trying to identify means for ensuring or measuring accountability because our traditional structures tend to be focused on individual achievement instead of collective accountability. The Portland State HRAC team described their struggle to ensure that individuals knew what work they should be focused on and ultimately what work they would be responsible for. These authors also identified the ways in which formal accountability and clear role definition can clash with faculty cultures of autonomy and flexibility. Especially when faculty are included in shared leadership arrangements, leaders must find a balance between holding each other accountable and honoring faculty culture and traditions. Even those examples of shared leadership which primarily included administrators struggled with shared accountability, however, and offered examples of how they worked to overcome this challenge. For example, the Portland State dean team intentionally worked to "develop transparent accountability structures" (Beaudoin et al., p. 110, this volume), especially around the college's budget process, in order to circumvent some of these challenges. In the University of Richmond example, specific goals and responsibilities were built into the formal job descriptions and goals of the executive vice presidents to ensure shared yet specific accountability. Similarly, several authors noted the challenge of how to budget for or reward formal shared leadership arrangements, especially in more formal or coleadership structures.

Several authors also emphasized the importance of senior leaders being able to "check their egos at the door" and relinquish some control of both the process and the outcome when they are opening up leadership to share with more people. The University of Wisconsin–Whitewater example described difficulties when this did not occur; chapter authors emphasized that senior leaders needed to be able to check each other. Similarly, many of the cases discussed the need for diminishing hierarchy and minimizing power differentials so that people who are lower in the organizational hierarchy or in less powerful positions can feel comfortable contributing and leading. Without attention to hierarchy, power, and ego, authentically shared leadership can be stifled.

While we described some ways in which campuses overcame challenges in this section, our case study authors had much more to say about how they built capacity to persist in spite of the obstacles to shared leadership they may have faced. In the next section, we describe some of the ways in which campuses tried to build their capacity for shared leadership.

Capacity-Building for Shared Leadership

While each chapter's authors noted the importance of capacity-building, it was not necessarily universal or easy to do. In this section, we highlight some of the ways in which campuses worked to build capacity for shared leadership as well as the limitations or challenges of building capacity within a larger organization that may or may not be supportive of shared leadership.

One strategy for capacity-building is utilizing a coach or support person who can help nurture both individual leaders and the collective, as the Portland State dean team described. The dean team engaged a coach from within the institution who knew both the individual codeans and the larger institutional context. The coach met with the team and the individual coleaders on a weekly basis, where they did strengths-based assessments and reflections and explored the research on shared leadership to ground themselves in key practices and processes, as well as discussed ways to navigate the challenging institutional environment. The dean team also engaged with an external adviser who was a shared leadership and higher education expert to advise them on their processes and practices. The team emphasized the importance of this role when they described what happened in its absence: "No one was engaged to keep the big picture in mind and the team moving in the right direction" (Beaudoin et al., p. 114, this volume). This capacity-building strategy may work especially well for coleadership arrangements or smaller teams, where it is more feasible for coaches to meet one-on-one with leaders as well as with the collective, but it is certainly worth exploring in other contexts as well.

The campuses or projects that used a team or distributed model of shared leadership—CIRTL, Cuyahoga Community College, University of Wisconsin–Whitewater, University of Richmond, and SUNY Geneseo—tended to involve more intensive efforts to refashion structures and processes and took a different approach to capacity-building. Some of the capacity-building strategies at these institutions included extensive communication strategies to navigate the inclusion of more people in leadership roles; establishing clear accountability structures; multiyear planning efforts; creating formal decision-making processes; and extensive efforts to build relationships that would help establish trust and a collaborative spirit needed to execute these ambitious shared leadership initiatives. Not all of the teams recognized the need for such extensive capacity-building at the outset, and many learned from experience and missteps. For example, the University of Richmond learned about the importance of setting up communication structures after initially struggling to communicate their distributed leadership model across campus, and University of Wisconsin–Whitewater learned about the importance of establishing accountability structures after experiencing challenges with clear accountability. Many authors refer to later realizing they should have established a "charter" or rules of engagement for making decisions, as the Portland State groups did.

While our authors provided many examples of capacity-building, most of these examples were at the team or group level, leaving several missed opportunities for capacity-building at the individual and broader organizational levels. At the organizational level, for example, campuses struggled to create rewards for shared leadership. The Portland State dean team noted this explicitly, but most other chapters did not mention it. While a couple of the campuses were able to develop clear accountability structures, most struggled to create collective accountability within their larger organizational contexts that emphasized individual accountability. Few campuses referenced development or capacity-building at the individual level, either. We noted the exception of the Portland State dean team coaches, and the University of Wisconsin–Whitewater also implemented some individual coaching and mentoring around growth mindsets to support their shared leadership work. But there are many opportunities for developing skills in individuals that support their ability to work in a shared or collective leadership environment, such as collaboration skills, managing conflict, or helping navigate diverse perspectives. Campuses that are experimenting with shared leadership should not overlook the importance of development or capacity-building at the individual and organizational levels, in addition to the team level.

Finally, building capacity for shared leadership work is not a one-time process or a one-off professional development workshop. It requires iterative engagement over time, dynamic team formation, re-formation, and even leader formation/re-formation. Several chapters describe this kind of dynamic work at capacity-building including the University of Wisconsin–Whitewater, SUNY Geneseo, and the University of Richmond. Just as shared leadership itself is a process and not a person or a single action, so too with capacity-building for shared leadership.

In Closing: Editors' Reflections

While we edited this book and wrote the opening chapters collectively, we also recognized through that process that we each had our own individual voices and perspectives on shared leadership. In closing the book, we want to allow each editor to share their last reflections and a few insights from their unique perspective. One of the lessons learned from many of the case study chapters is the value of acknowledging and celebrating individual voices as a part of shared leadership processes. With this final section, we aim to honor that process.

Elizabeth

As I read the case studies from our contributing authors, what was most striking to me was just how versatile this leadership approach is. Shared leadership can be used to tackle so many different types of issues—from DEI to remaking the 1st-year experience to academic support to community challenges like homelessness, as well as general academic leadership like the Portland State dean team or the Cuyahoga One Door approach. None of the approaches looked exactly the same, and some were very different from one another. That versatility and diversity of approaches and structures is both the biggest strength and biggest challenge of shared leadership. Because it can look so different from place to place and from one situation to the next, it can be difficult for leaders to take away lessons on how to implement it effectively in their own setting, or how to decide which model or combination of models might be the best fit for their context and the problems they are trying to solve. The nine case studies in this book provide the type of concrete examples that have been missing from the literature on shared leadership in higher education. Leaders across multiple levels, at different types of institutions, looking to solve a variety of different types of problems can take these lessons back to their own campuses and devise the structures and processes that work best for them. I look forward to learning more from our readers who experiment with shared leadership as this versatile leadership approach evolves and spreads.

Adrianna

What really strikes me is the opportunity for shared leadership and the incredible benefits that campuses experience when moving to share leadership yet at the same time the incredible challenge of maximizing these benefits within our continued hierarchical and traditional structures that make the use of it so difficult! Imagine how much more benefit will be garnered when there is not so much struggle to implement it. It also strikes me that building capacity for this work is not something that leaders generally recognize, which can also increase the struggle and challenges to implement. But I am also very cognizant that the pandemic will make investment in shared leadership approaches much more unlikely, due to the constraint of resources. In fact, we experienced a moment of increased unilateral decision-making at the very time that multiple voices were needed to ensure our campuses could successfully move forward. I have witnessed campuses moving away from equity as they make increasingly top-down decisions and ignore the breadth of expertise across campus. If there ever was a moment for shared leadership, we experienced it throughout 2020. Therefore, this demonstrates our lack of ability to see the promise of this approach and the need for leaders to really reflect on why they chose to minimize voice, differing perspectives, and the full energy of campus change agents. My hope is that courageous leaders will stand up across the country and argue for the need for shared leadership moving forward, especially as it relates to making progress on equity on our campuses.

Susan

What struck me as I was reflecting on the case studies was that many of them illustrated how a shared leadership approach can marry the passions and experiences of many across a university in ways that not only leverage those strengths but weave them together in ways that result in positive gains for the university. Some of the passions and expertise we read about rose up from individual interests and initiative (e.g., Humboldt State) while others emerged as part of a shared leadership team (e.g., Portland State University dean team). The case studies also illustrated that shared leadership can be used by any level of leader, whether formally appointed to a role or informally working to create change from their faculty or staff position. In addition to the case studies, the opening chapters of the book can serve as a guide for those interested in taking up the mantle of this form of leadership; however, that does not mean it will be easy, as several of the case study chapters also illustrate. That is an important point—the work of leadership is not easy. It takes deliberate thought, planning, patience, and focus.

I hope this book will inspire many to see themselves as leaders and give them tools to begin to shape their leadership strategy, with others, as they seek to use their strengths to improve their institutions. Beyond this guide, leaders should be prepared to face and embrace reality! While you can work to put certain structures and practices in place, you will encounter unexpected roadblocks or maybe even opportunities that will cause you to make adjustments or change course. Especially in a shared leadership (SL) approach, the system requires constant attention, tuning, and sometimes realignment. You cannot just set it up and let it go. In this way, leaders who are implementing an SL approach are more like coaches keeping their team on track with plays and points or shepherds keeping their flock safe and grazing in the right field. While mounting an SL approach may be complicated and challenging, and requires constant attention, do not shy away from it! It is through this kind of leadership approach that we will be able to address the kinds of complex challenges and issues facing higher education that we have highlighted throughout this book.

Judith

This book has brought a lot of pieces of a much larger puzzle together for me. We have been living through a remarkably disruptive and yet in some important ways transformative time as the damage that the COVID-19 pandemic is leaving in its wake becomes painfully clear. Our capacity for creativity and innovation has emerged organically during the pandemic. This ability to summon creative approaches to difficult problems facing our institution and the broader society will be critical to our future at Portland State University and at your institution as well. The key question on my mind as both president emerita and member of the board of trustees at Portland State University is how we can sustain and grow this creative capacity so that we are prepared for the set of complex challenges that are taking shape in front of us.

Earlier in this book we talked about the different kinds of problems that campuses face. Some require shared leadership and some do not. The future we face now is full of complex and potentially transformative problems. These kinds of problems cross multiple parts of an institution and require multiple perspectives and expertise (Snowden & Boone, 2007). It is difficult, if not impossible, to predict whether or when a change in one part will set up ripples that spread to other parts of the institution or create new issues (Baer et al., 2008; Camillus, 2008). To address these kinds of problems, we need new forms of collaboration. In a recent article about systems-based changemaking, Esterle et al. (2020) point out that the characteristics of organizational problems are affected by how people interact with each other. One feature of this kind of issue is that change can begin anywhere. As they describe it, "Personal relationships lie at the heart and are the drivers of complex adaptive social systems" (para. 17). Responding to them cannot be guided by top-down hierarchical structures. That has been a central theme of this book. What we need to understand and address these kinds of problems is shared leadership in its various forms.

References

Baer, L. L., Duin, A. H., & Ramaley, J. A. (2008). Smart change. *Planning for Higher education, 36*(2), 5. https://www.scup.org/resource/smart-change/

Camillus, J. C. (2008). Strategy as a wicked problem. *Harvard Business Review, 86*(5), 98. https://hbr.org/2008/05/strategy-as-a-wicked-problem

Esterle, J., Kopell, M., & Strand, P. (2020, November 22). It's all about relationships: Systems-based changemaking. *Medium.* https://medium.com/office-of-citizen/its-all-about-relationships-systems-based-changemaking-470207584bf4

Kezar, A. J., Holcombe, E. M., Vigil, D., & Dizon, J. P. (2021). *What is shared equity leadership?* American Council on Education.

Snowden, D. J., & Boone, M. E. (2007). A leader's framework for decision-making. *Harvard Business Review, 85*(11), 69–76.

Getting Started With Shared Leadership on Your Campus

1. Can you identify a particular complex problem or challenge that your campus (or your department/division) is invested in solving that might be a strong candidate for a shared leadership approach? Alternatively, are there other areas of operation that could benefit from the involvement of more people in leadership?
2. What kind of leadership structure do you think might work best for the problem or area you are targeting? Coleadership, team leadership, distributed leadership, or a hybrid structure with elements of multiple models?
3. Who/what departments or units might have a stake in solving the problem? How can you bring them into working with you? Do you have existing partner(s) or allies that are already working with you?
4. What assets do you have?
   a. Are there existing structures, committees, or initiatives you might leverage to bring people together? What assets already exist—people, funding, processes, programs, etc.? Are there new or emerging opportunities that you can leverage or align to help you work in this way?
5. What will you need to succeed?
   a. What additional resources or support might be required? What faculty, staff, midlevel, and/or senior leaders have areas of responsibility related to the problem that might lend support?
6. What aspects of your institution's culture, traditions, norms, or practices might be capitalized upon to build a shared leadership approach?
7. Identify one or more case studies that resonate with you to learn more from the practice of others. What are some of the key lessons you want to bring to your efforts?

Building Capacity for Shared Leadership

	Do we have this on our campus? (Y/N)	How strong is our capacity in this area? Rank 1–5, with 1 being very weak and 5 being very strong	How might we explore these ideas or improve capacity in this area?
Structures and Resources for Shared Leadership			
An established group or team			
Financial resources to support the team or group			
Human resources—the right mix of people to lead together			
Rewards for Shared Leadership			
Salary increase/merit pay			
Release time			
Career options and promotion			
Recognition or appreciation			
Include in service requirements			
Coconstructing Goals With Senior Leaders			

	Do we have this on our campus? (Y/N)	How strong is our capacity in this area? Rank 1–5, with 1 being very weak and 5 being very strong	How might we explore these ideas or improve capacity in this area?
Mechanisms to share ideas and vision			
Accountability Structures			
Strict performance measures			
Regular reporting			
Mutual performance monitoring			
Empowerment for Policy and Decisions			
Venue to outline decision options			
Accountability structures to communicate why options are not followed			
Developing Relationships and a Culture of Trust			
Investment in building relationships			
Intentional creation of social networks			
Environment of Organizational Learning, Risk-Taking, and Experimentation			
Risk-taking is role-modeled, welcomed, and rewarded			

PART 2
Team Capacity-Building

	Does our team have this capacity? (Y/N)	How strong is our capacity in this area? Rank 1–5, with 1 being very weak and 5 being very strong	How might we explore these ideas or improve capacity in this area?
Diverse Team(s) with Appropriate Expertise			
Clear and Shared Team Purpose			
Clear and Appropriate Role Definition			
Team Planning			
Onboarding			
Socialization			
Established group norms			
Emphasis on developing trust and building relationships			
Structures to support the team			
Anticipating and Addressing Negative Dynamics			
Team Coaching and Development			

PART 3
Individual Skill-Building

	How skilled am I in this area? Rank 1–5, with 1 being not skilled at all and 5 being highly skilled	How can I improve skills in this area? How can I support others in developing these skills?
Skills for Senior Leaders		
Creating interchangeable leadership roles		
Supporting coordination, collaboration, and consensus-building		
Promoting learning and empowerment mindsets		
Skills for All Shared Leadership Group Members		
Consensus-building and generating diverse input		
Working with colleagues with a collaborative, inclusive, and relational approach		
Coaching peers and giving feedback		
Navigating difficult conversations, managing conflict and disagreement		
Cultivating self-awareness, self-reflection, and self-leadership		

Elizabeth M. Holcombe is a postdoctoral research associate at the University of Southern California's Pullias Center for Higher Education. She earned her PhD in urban education policy with a specialization in higher education from the University of Southern California; an MA in politics and education from Teachers College, Columbia University; and a BA in political science and Spanish from Vanderbilt University. Dr. Holcombe researches organizational issues that influence student success in higher education, including leadership, faculty workforce and development issues, undergraduate teaching and assessment, and undergraduate STEM education. She has also held a variety of roles in student affairs, including running a college access partnership, managing an academic advising and mentoring program, and leading a co- and extracurricular assessment initiative. Prior to her career in higher education, Holcombe was an elementary school teacher with Teach for America in Atlanta.

Adrianna J. Kezar is Dean's Professor of Leadership, Wilbur-Kieffer Professor of Higher Education, at the University of Southern California and director of the Pullias Center for Higher Education within the Rossier School of Education. Kezar is a national expert of student success, equity and diversity, the changing faculty, change, governance, and leadership in higher education. Kezar is well published with 20 books/monographs, over 100 journal articles, and over 100 book chapters and reports. Recent books include *The Gig Academy* (Johns Hopkins Press, 2019), *Administration for Social Justice and Equity* (Routledge, 2019), *The Faculty for the 21st Century: Moving to a Mission-Oriented and Learner-Centered Faculty Model* (Rutgers University Press, 2016), and *How Colleges Change* (2nd ed.; Routledge, 2018).

Susan Elrod serves as the sixth chancellor of Indiana University South Bend. As chancellor, she leads IU South Bend, a regional campus of Indiana University, in fulfilling its mission as the only public comprehensive university serving the communities of Northcentral Indiana. Prior to this position, she has served as a provost, dean, and in various academic leadership positions at public comprehensive universities in the California State University System and the University of Wisconsin system. She also worked for the

Association of American Colleges & Universities in Washington DC as the director of Project Kaleidoscope with a focus on STEM higher education initiatives. She is a nationally recognized leader in STEM higher education on projects centered on leadership of institutional systemic change in higher education as a scholar, leader, project adviser, and consultant. She holds a PhD in genetics from the University of California, Davis and an undergraduate degree in biological sciences from California State University, Chico.

Judith A. Ramaley is president emerita, a member of the board of trustees and Distinguished Professor of Public Service in the Mark O. Hatfield School of Government at Portland State University and former president of both the University of Vermont and Winona State University. She is also a Distinguished Scholar with the Association of American Colleges and Universities (AAC&U). She serves as an adviser for several national projects that focus on equity, student success, science, technology, engineering, and mathematics (STEM) education and the leadership of change. Ramaley has a special interest in civic and community engagement.

CONTRIBUTORS

Matthew Aschenbrener is associate vice chancellor for enrollment and retention at University of Wisconsin-Whitewater.

Ann E. Austin is a university distinguished professor in higher, adult, and lifelong education; associate dean for research in the College of Education; and interim associate provost for faculty and academic staff development at Michigan State University.

Fletcher Beaudoin is director of the Institute for Sustainable Solutions at Portland State University.

Ashleigh M. Brock is assistant to the president at the University of Richmond.

Matthew Carlson is associate dean for undergraduate programs in the College of Liberal Arts and Sciences and professor of sociology at Portland State University.

Joe Cope is a professor of history and associate provost for academic success at the State University of New York (SUNY) Geneseo.

Ronald A. Crutcher is the former president and professor of music at the University of Richmond.

Robert Feissner is a lecturer of biology and director of supplemental instruction at the State University of New York (SUNY) Geneseo.

Todd Ferry is associate director and senior research associate of the Center for Public Interest Design; director of the Architecture Summer Immersion Program; cofounder and Alternative Shelter Initiatives director for the Homelessness Research & Action Collaborative; and Faculty Fellow at the Institute for Sustainable Solutions at Portland State University.

Jacen Greene is cofounder and assistant director of the Homelessness Research & Action Collaborative at Portland State University.

David Hale is executive vice president and chief operating officer at the University of Richmond.

Beverly Henke-Lofquist is a transitional opportunity program counselor and tutor coordinator for access opportunity programs at the State University of New York (SUNY) Geneseo.

Patricia Herrera is an associate professor of theatre and affiliate faculty in the American Studies and Women, Gender, and Sexualities Studies Programs at the University of Richmond.

Maude Hines is an associate professor of English; affiliated faculty in the Black Studies and Women, Gender, and Sexuality Studies programs; and cofounder of the Homelessness Research & Action Collaborative at Portland State University.

Amy L. Howard is the senior administrative office (SAO) for equity and community and associated faculty in American Studies at the University of Richmond.

Glyn Hughes is director of Common Ground and affiliated faculty in sociology and anthropology at the University of Richmond.

Elizabeth A. John is director of First Year Experience at University of Wisconsin–Whitewater.

Alex Johnson is president of Cuyahoga Community College (Tri-C).

Matthew Johnson is a professor of wildlife at Humboldt State University. He also serves as PI on the CSU STEM Collaboratives Grant; co-PI and director for the Department of Education Title III: Hispanic Serving Institutions in STEM Grant; and PI and codirector of the Howard Hughes Medical Institute Inclusive Excellence '17 Award.

Jeffrey Legro is executive vice president and provost and professor of political science at the University of Richmond.

Robert D. Mathieu is the Albert E. Whitford Professor of Astronomy at the University of Wisconsin-Madison and director of the Center for the Integration of Research, Teaching, and Learning (CIRTL).

Karen Miller is provost and chief academic officer at Cuyahoga Community College (Tri-C).

DeLys Ostlund is associate dean for faculty and professor of Spanish in the College of Liberal Arts and Sciences at Portland State University.

Gillian Paku is an associate professor of English literature and director of the Writing Learning Center at the State University of New York (SUNY) Geneseo.

Todd Rosenstiel is dean of the College of Liberal Arts and Sciences and associate professor of biology at Portland State University.

Lisa Smith is a lecturer of mathematics and director of the Math Learning Center at the State University of New York (SUNY) Geneseo.

Amy Sprowles is an assistant professor of biological sciences at Humboldt State University. She is also co-PI for the CSU STEM Collaboratives Grant, co-PI and codirector of the Department of Education Title III: Hispanic Serving Institutions in STEM Grant, and co-PI and director of the Howard Hughes Medical Institute Inclusive Excellence '17 Award.

Greg Townley is an associate professor of psychology and director of research for the Homelessness Research & Action Collaborative at Portland State University.

Marisa Zapata is director of the Homelessness Research & Action Collaborative and associate professor of land use planning in the Toulan School of Urban Studies and Planning at Portland State University.

You Are a Data Person

Strategies for Using Analytics on Campus

Amelia Parnell

The common phrase, "I am not a data person," suggests that some campus professionals may not fully understand their capacity and potential to contribute to data-related activities. This book is intended to:

- provide context for the levels at which professionals are comfortable using data,
- help readers identify the areas where they should strengthen their knowledge,
- offer tangible examples of how professionals can make data contributions at their current and future knowledge level; and
- inspire readers to take the initiative to engage in data projects.

The book includes a set of self-assessment questions and a companion set of action steps and available resources to help readers accept their identity as a data person. The project also includes an annotated list of at least 20 indicators that any higher education professional can examine without sophisticated data analyses.

"As Amelia Parnell states in her opening, it is clear the analytics revolution is here. The timing of this revolution will be critical to higher education's efforts to design programs and student success initiatives that are data-driven and data-informed. Parnell's book is both comprehensive and accessible for faculty and staff who are leading this revolution."—***Kevin Kruger,*** *President/ CEO, NASPA, Student Affairs Administrators in Higher Education*

Neighborhood Democracy

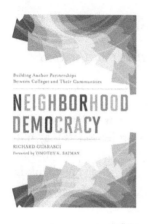

Building Anchor Partnerships Between Colleges and Their Communities

Richard Guarasci

Foreword by Timothy K. Eatman

Published in association with AAC&U

Higher education and America stand at a perilous moment brought about by economic and social inequality, racism, and the fracture of civic cohesion and structures.

From its origins, the mission of American higher education was to promote democratic governance and a free, fair, and orderly society through the education of responsible citizens. Just as its mission has become more urgent, it is being undermined as colleges and universities find themselves trapped in a fiscal crisis that threatens their very institutional viability—a crisis in large part brought about by the very perpetuation of economic and racial inequity, and the consequent erosion of consensus about civic purpose and vision.

This book argues that higher education can and must again take leadership in promoting the participatory processes and instilling the democratic values needed to build a vibrant and fair society. How to do that when, as Guarasci argues, a majority of colleges and universities are floundering under a business model that generates insufficient net revenue while making college unaffordable?

"American democracy and our system of higher education both face perilous times. Drawing on his years of innovation and community engagement as president of Wagner College, Richard Guarasci makes a compelling case that these bedrock institutions can be revitalized through meaningful university neighborhood partnerships. Moving beyond theory to actual practice, *Neighborhood Democracy* is both an important call to action and a helpful guide for solution-seeking institutional leaders everywhere. Well worth reading!"—***Beverly Daniel Tatum,*** *President Emerita, Spelman College*

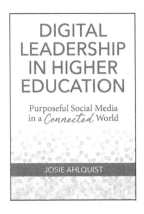

Digital Leadership in Higher Education

Purposeful Social Media in a Connected World

Josie Ahlquist

"If you want to learn both the why and the how behind online leadership in higher education, read this timely book, from cover to cover—from guidance, through development, to putting principles into action, it will be your north star."—***Scott Cline***, *Vice President of Enrollment Management and Auxiliary Services, California College of the Arts*

"I recommend this book for every higher education leader whether you have 100 or 100,000 followers. Reading it not only inspired me to review my own strategies and tactics, it also gave me purposeful questions as a chief marketing officer to put forward to our institution's social media managers."—***Melissa Farmer Richards***, *Vice President for Communications and Marketing, Hamilton College*

"Josie Ahlquist breaks new ground with *Digital Leadership in Higher Education*. The book has a wide range of ideas that meets the reader wherever they are in their digital leadership journey."—***Walter M. Kimbrough***, *President, Dillard University*

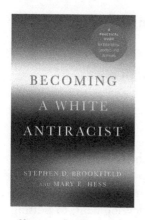

Becoming a White Antiracist

A Practical Guide for Educators, Leaders, and Activists

Stephen D. Brookfield and
Mary E. Hess

"*Becoming a White Antiracist* is a long-essential and timely contribution to antiracist scholarship and practice. This book is the next best thing to Stephen Brookfield's informed and effective facilitation of conversations designed to develop racial literacy in predominantly white spaces. *Becoming a White Antiracist* is an important invitation and resource, especially for people committed to discovering their white racial identity toward becoming an authentic and active agent for inclusive change."—***Nicole Brittingham Furlonge,*** *Professor of Practice and Director, Klingenstein Center, Teachers College, Columbia University*

"Brookfield and Hess offer a range of strategies and methods for liberating white imaginations from the debilitating and life-draining legacies of white supremacy and racism in America. Through storytelling and truth-sharing dialogical methods, they provide readers with roadmaps by which individuals and groups might begin to dismantle structural racism in the United States. The book provides white readers with tools and tactics that can aid them in their efforts to engage systemic racism and dismantle white supremacy."—***Paul O. Myhre,*** *Senior Associate Director, Wabash Center for Teaching and Learning in Theology and Religion*

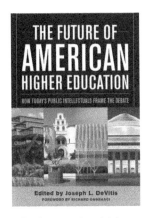

The Future of American Higher Education

How Today's Public Intellectuals Frame the Debate

Edited by Joseph L. DeVitis

Just as our society is polarized, higher education is no less divided as to its mission and purpose, whether it should be preparing students for employment or for engagement as citizens, whether it should be corporatist and profit-driven or promote intellectual curiosity and independent thinking, and whether it should pursue a neoliberal agenda or promote a liberal education. Whose scholarship, culture, and epistemologies should be validated? Should it be a private or a public good? Preserve tenure or erode it? What role should colleges and universities play in addressing economic inequality systemic racism? The answers to these questions are critical for the future of our society as our universities and colleges are the nurseries of the values and philosophies that shape it.

"By focusing on public intellectuals through the lenses of a rich array of scholars in their own right, Joe DeVitis captures the complexity and struggles of modern-day higher education. Are colleges and universities headed down the rabbit's warren as they negotiate larger economic, social, and political goals and their own educational and intellectual purposes? Reasonable minds will disagree about how the academy should balance these interests. *The Future of American Higher Education* is a compelling, lively, and thought-provoking read—and it could not have come at a better time in light of the many existential pressures surrounding higher education."—*Jonathan Brand, President, Cornell College*

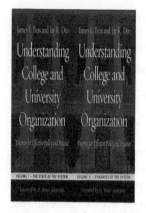

Understanding College and University Organization

Theories for Effective Policy and Practice – 2 Volume Set

James L. Bess and Jay R. Dee

Foreword by D. Bruce Johnstone

This two-volume set is intended to help readers develop powerful new ways of thinking about organizational principles, and apply them to policy-making and management in colleges and universities.

It systematically presents a range of theories that can be applied to many of the difficult management situations that college and university leaders encounter. It provides them with the theoretical background to knowledgeably evaluate the many new ideas that emerge in the current literature, and in workshops and conferences. The purpose is to help leaders develop their own effective management style and approaches, and feel confident that their actions are informed by appropriate theory and knowledge of the latest research in the field.

"Quite simply a tour de force. Not only have the authors written by far the broadest and deepest theoretical analysis of college and university organization I've seen, but they have clearly organized a complex topic, and written it engagingly. This will be seen as a landmark work in the field. It should be required reading for all who claim to understand higher education institutions and the behavior that goes on inside and around them."—***David W. Leslie,*** *Chancellor Professor of Education, The College of William and Mary*

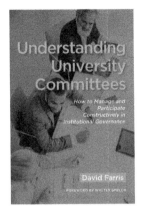

Understanding University Committees

How to Manage and Participate Constructively in Institutional Governance

David A. Farris

Foreword by Walter H. Gmelch

Committees are indispensable to the governance of higher education, yet there is seldom guidance to faculty and administrators on how committees should be conducted or how to maximize committee obligations.

This is the first handbook on how both to manage committees and how to engage effectively as members to achieve departmental or broad institutional goals, and how participation valuably contributes to individual learning and advancement.

"Committees are central to the life and governance of a university. While we may at times dread them, they are quintessential in our culture of shared-governance, critical in the social dynamic of an institution, and effective mechanisms of leadership development and professional advancement. Having worked with David Farris for 7 years at George Mason University, and having witnessed his many contributions through numerous commit-tees, I can't think of a better person to illustrate how committees can serve institutions and its members more effectively."—*Ángel Cabrera, President, Georgia Institute of Technology*

A Guide for Leaders in Higher Education, Second Edition

Concepts, Competencies, and Tools

Brent D. Ruben, Richard De Lisi, and Ralph A. Gigliotti

REVIEWS OF THE FIRST EDITION

"The book provides frameworks and resources that would be highly relevant for new and aspiring department chairs. In fact, this text is ideally designed to serve as a selection for a book discussion group."—*The Department Chair*

"Succeeds in providing accessible and useful resources to individuals across different leadership roles . . . As a midpoint between textbook and reference work, it is successful at both and provides a clear and unbiased background to issues facing current leaders."—*Reflective Teaching*

Leading Academic Change

Vision, Strategy, Transformation

Elaine P. Maimon

Foreword by Carol Geary Schneider

"College students were far more uniform in age, race, and socioeconomic background a few decades ago than they are now, yet colleges and universities have often failed to design programs of study that work for these students. *Leading Academic Change* outlines the steps to take toward change on behalf of the new majority students, the non-white, low-income, working, second language, or adult learners who often find themselves in very unfamiliar territory in college classrooms.

This book is, above all, a call to give all students our very best, both in our classrooms and at our institutions. It is also a well-timed reminder that change is inevitable and that equity can be a means to achieving educational quality."—*Reflective Teaching*

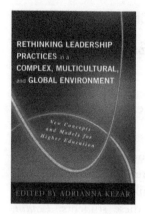

Rethinking Leadership in a Complex, Multicultural, and Global Environment

New Concepts and Models for Higher Education

Edited by Adrianna Kezar

"Adrianna Kezar breaks new ground in this edited volume that focuses much-needed attention on the theory and practice of leadership in higher education. Trenchant analyses by leadership developers and scholars offer key insights on programmatic innovations that are responsive to rapidly evolving organizational environments in American colleges and universities. Their chapters provide readers with a user-friendly text for use in leadership development programs and for advancing the study of leadership in higher education. The exemplars of programs with proven track records as well as recommendations for 'case-in-point' approaches to leadership development provide what Kezar refers to as 'revolutionary' forms of leadership that emphasize empowerment, collaboration, social responsibility, cross-cultural understanding, and cognitive complexity. This book will be of interest to faculty, administrators, and leadership scholars concerned with the context and process of learning leadership in 21st-century institutions."—*Judith Glazer-Raymo, Lecturer, Department of Higher and Postsecondary Education, Teachers College, Columbia University*

PAUL E. LINGENFELTER

"PROOF,"
POLICY, &
PRACTICE

Understanding the Role of Evidence
in Improving Education

Foreword by MICHAEL S. McPHERSON

"Proof," Policy, & Practice

Understanding the Role of Evidence in Improving Education

Paul E. Lingenfelter

Foreword by Michael S. McPherson

"Lingenfelter takes on the longstanding and highly problematic relationship among research, policy, and practice. He unmasks modern-day shibboleths about how performance management and randomized field trials are the new answers. While highly respectful of practitioner wisdom and judgment, he marks out clear limits here too. He argues persuasively that those engaged in the work of education must become active agents of its continuous improvement, and sketches out how policymakers can foster an environment where such systematic gathering and use of evidence is more likely to happen. This is a very wise book!"
—*Anthony S. Bryk, President, Carnegie Foundation for the Advancement of Teaching*

Also available from Stylus

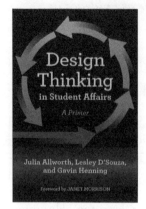

Design Thinking in Student Affairs

A Primer

Julia Allworth, Lesley D›Souza, and Gavin Henning

"*Design Thinking in Student Affairs: A Primer* constitutes such an important and timely contribution to the literature. By focusing equally on the theory, mindset, and practice of design thinking, the book fills a gap by providing a roadmap for theoretically informed practice and culture change. Authored by trusted colleagues with expertise in leadership, innovation, assessment, storytelling, equity, organizational development, change management, and student success in both Canada and the United States—the book makes a compelling case for using design thinking to facilitate human-centered, cocreated, high-impact solutions within and beyond the traditional realm of student affairs.

Given the unprecedented combination of new and exacerbated challenges facing our colleges and universities—decreasing government funding, student mental health and well-being, diversity and inclusion efforts, and affordability chief among them—who among us doesn't need another arrow in their quiver?"—*From the Foreword by **Janet Morrison**, President and Vice Chancellor of Sheridan College, Ontario, Canada*

22883 Quicksilver Drive
Sterling, VA 20166-2102   Subscribe to our email alerts: www.Styluspub.com